Ephesians to Colossians and Philemon

DAILY BIBLE COMMENTARY

A Guide for Reflection and Prayer

Ephesians to Colossians and Philemon

Marcus Maxwell

HENDRICKSON PUBLISHERS

Ephesians to Colossians and Philemon
Daily Bible Commentary
Hendrickson Publishers, Inc.
P. O. Box 3473
Peabody, Massachusetts 01961-3473

ISBN 978-1-59856-194-4

Text © 2002 Marcus Maxwell. Original edition published in English under the title *The People's Bible Commentary: Ephesians to Colossians and Philemon* by the Bible Reading Fellowship, Oxford, England. © The Bible Reading Fellowship 2002.

Hendrickson Publishers' North American edition published by arrangement with the Bible Reading Fellowship.

Printed in the United States of America

First Printing — April 2007

Library of Congress Cataloging-in-Publication Data

Maxwell, Marcus
    Ephesians to Colossians and Philemon / Marcus Maxwell.
      p. cm. — (The daily Bible commentary ; 10)
    ISBN 978-1-59856-194-4 (alk. paper)
    1. Bible. N.T. Ephesians—Commentaries. 2. Bible. N.T. Philippians—Commentaries. 3. Bible. N.T. Colossians—Commentaries. 4. Bible. N.T. Philemon—Commentaries. 5. Bible. N.T. Ephesians—Devotional literature. 6. Bible. N.T. Philippians—Devotional literature. 7. Bible. N.T. Colossians—Devotional literature. 8. Bible. N.T. Philemon—Devotional literature. I. Title.
    BS2650.53.M39 2007
    227'.07—dc22
                    2007004004

Introducing the
Daily Bible Commentary
Series
A Guide for Reflection and Prayer

Congratulations! You are embarking on a voyage of discovery—or rediscovery. You may feel you know the Bible very well; you may never have turned its pages before. You may be looking for a fresh way of approaching daily Bible study; you may be searching for useful insights to share in a study group or from a pulpit.

The Daily Bible Commentary series is designed for all those who want to study the Scriptures in a way that will warm the heart as well as instruct the mind.

- If you have never really studied the Bible before, the series offers a serious yet accessible way in.

- If you want to have both head and heart knowledge of the Bible, the series helps you first understand what the Bible is saying and then reflect on its meaning in your life and in the way you pray.

- If you help to lead a church study group, or are otherwise involved in regular preaching and teaching, you can find invaluable "snapshots" of a Bible passage through the Daily Bible Commentary approach.

- If you are a church worker or pastor, looking to recharge your faith, this series could help you recover the wonder of Scripture.

To help you, the series distills the best of scholarly insights into straightforward language and devotional emphasis. Explanation of background material and discussion of the original Greek and Hebrew will always aim to be brief.

Using a Daily Bible Commentary

The series is designed for use alongside any version of the Bible. You may have your own favorite translation, but you might like to consider trying a different one in order to gain fresh perspectives on familiar passages.

Many Bible translations come in a range of editions, including study and reference editions that have concordances, various kinds of special indexes, maps, and marginal notes. These can all prove helpful in studying the relevant passage.

The Daily Bible Commentaries are designed to be used on a daily basis, with you reading a short passage from the Bible and then learning more about it from the commentary entry. Alternatively, it can be read straight through, or it can be used as a resource book for insight into particular verses of the biblical book.

While it is important to deepen our understanding of a given passage, this series always aims to engage both heart and mind in the study of the Bible. The Scriptures point to our Lord himself and our task is to use them to build our relationship with him. When we read, let us do so prayerfully, slowly, reverently, expecting God to speak to our very being.

CONTENTS

EPHESIANS *to* COLOSSIANS & PHILEMON: INTRODUCTION

A note for plug-and-play readers

I once bought a new component for my computer. The sales assistant assured me it was 'plug-and-play' compatible: 'Just install it and the computer will do the rest.' It didn't. So I took it out, read the instructions, altered a switch, put it back in, and the computer did the rest. The introduction to a book like this is rather like those instructions— but some readers will want to plug in and get on with reading the comments on the Bible. After all, that is why you bought the book.

If you want to plug in straight away, you will at least need a Bible or New Testament alongside this book. Each section deals with a few verses at a time of the letters to the Philippians, the Colossians, Philemon and the Ephesians. Quotations are generally from the New Revised Standard Version, but any version should work just as well. The book is also meant to be worked through from the beginning. While it should be informative for the reader who wants simply to dip into one section, I have tried to avoid too much repetition, so that, for instance, comments on Paul's use of common terms like 'grace' are not covered in full in the comments on each letter, but come in one or another of the four sections, or there may even be complementary thoughts across the various letters.

As we approach the captivity epistles, we will be coming with certain assumptions. If those are understood at the outset, what follows will make more sense. So, if I promise to keep it brief, will you please give it a quick read? It really does help.

The captivity epistles

The letters to the Philippians, Colossians, Ephesians and Philemon are called the captivity epistles because in each of them Paul appears to refer to the fact that they were written while he was imprisoned. This circumstance is about all the letters have in common. Philippians is a response to a gift that Paul has received from the Philippian church, with which he had close ties. In the letter, Paul pleads for unity in the church, but is not seriously worried about any problems at Philippi. He also warns against the influence of certain Jewish

Christians who sought to undermine his ministry with their insistence that Gentile converts should keep the Jewish Law.

Colossians addresses a serious threat from false teaching in a church which Paul had never personally visited, though he knew some of its members and it had been founded under the authority of his mission, probably during his long stay in the neighbouring city of Ephesus. Paul counters the false teaching by stressing the supremacy of Christ. The Colossians need nothing more than the gospel they have received, for Christ is Lord of creation and the redeemer of his people. In him they have all that God has to offer.

Philemon, apparently written at the same time, is a personal letter to a member of the church at Colossae, asking him to receive with love and forgiveness a runaway slave who has since become a Christian. The human relationship of master and slave should become irrelevant in the light of the new relationship of Christian brothers.

Ephesians seems to be closely modelled on Colossians, but instead of countering a specific problem, it seems to be a letter of general encouragement and exhortation, addressed to several churches, or indeed to the universal Church at large. The Church, says the writer, already possesses a share in the new creation that God is bringing about through Christ. It must therefore live in such a way that the new life of Christ becomes real in practice, and can be seen by the rest of the world.

Who wrote them?

'Well, Paul,' we might say; 'that's obvious.' But it actually isn't. In the ancient world, it was quite common for books to be written in the name of well-respected authors, usually by one of their followers. The main reasons were to lend authority to the new work and to update the teaching of the named author for a later period, perhaps addressing issues he had not mentioned in his own writings.

To us, this looks like simple forgery, but the issue is not that straightforward. Concepts such as copyright and intellectual property, which we take for granted, were unheard of. Once a book was published, it was, as we say, in the public domain, and a mark of the respect in which a popular writer was held might be the number of other books which appeared in his name (usually after his death).

Among the letters attributed to Paul in the New Testament, it is widely (though not universally) held that 1 and 2 Timothy and Titus are by a later writer of the Pauline school (that is, in the tradition of teaching established by Paul). Colossians and Ephesians are also held by many to be by later writers. No one has any real doubts about Philemon, and Philippians is universally recognized to be a genuine Pauline letter—though more on that later.

Colossians

Colossians is held to be non-Pauline on three basic grounds—its vocabulary, its style, and its theology of Christ and the Church. It is pointed out that the letter contains a large number of words which do not appear in any of the undisputedly genuine letters of Paul. On the other hand, most of these terms refer to the teaching of the Colossian heretics, and so are probably taken over from them. Paul certainly had the habit of using his opponents' terms, and so probably does the same here. A similar case can be made for the style, which is a bit more elaborate than Paul's normal way of writing, but the difference is most noticeable at points which indicate specific refutations of the false teachers.

The view of Christ that the letter takes is definitely more explicitly exalted than in most of Paul's letters. Christ is seen as the agent of creation, as Lord of the universe, and so on. Yet all these elements are in the undisputed Pauline letters. Philippians 2:6–11 contains a high view of Christ which Colossians can hardly better. In Colossians the status of Christ is to the forefront because the Colossian teachers seem to be denying that Christ offers the only, or a complete, access to God.

Therefore, in this book, we shall assume that Paul was the actual author of Colossians.

Ephesians

Ephesians is a different story. Here, too, there is a difference in style from the undisputed letters, but the difference is much greater. There are many words that do not occur in any of the other Pauline epistles, and the sentences are long and full of subordinate clauses which make them harder to understand. The author of Ephesians piles up words like Lego bricks, giving a spectacular-sounding read, but often obscuring his own meaning.

The main point about Ephesians is that it seems very clearly to be based on Colossians. Although the writer often uses his own words, a comparison of the two letters shows such a close degree of structural similarity that it is almost impossible to avoid the conclusion that one of the two letters depends on the other. The differences in style suggest that it is Ephesians that depends on Colossians. When writing of the work of Christ, the author stresses the resurrection over the crucifixion, while the undoubtedly genuine letters of Paul stress the cross, though in the light of the resurrection. In Ephesians, 'the church' is always the universal Church, while elsewhere in Paul it is usually the local community. Moreover, the letter does not seem to address any particular issue, nor is it occasioned by any mentioned event. Of the obviously genuine letters, only Romans seems to have no obvious cause, though it certainly addresses real issues in the church at Rome.

The historical situation of Ephesians also appears to be later than Paul. For Paul, there was a pressing issue in the relationship of Jewish and Gentile Christians. In Ephesians, this seems to belong to the past, along with the apostles themselves.

Therefore we shall assume that Ephesians is not by Paul, but by a follower of his, writing some time after the apostle's death.

Some readers may find that conclusion disturbing. If Ephesians is not by Paul, is it authoritative? Does it make sense to call a 'false' letter the word of God? Hopefully, the second question has already been answered. God speaks his word at certain times and places, in ways that use the language of those times and places. Thus the Old Testament is (mostly) in Hebrew, and is written in the thought patterns of ancient Israel. The New Testament is in Greek, and takes the literary styles of first-century biography, history and letter writing. One of those styles was the pseudonymous (false name) letter, and is represented by Ephesians (along with 1 and 2 Timothy and Titus, in my opinion, though we won't be referring very much to them).

As to the authority of Ephesians, that comes from its place in the Bible, not from who wrote it. We do not know who wrote a good number of the biblical books, but the Church recognizes them as holy scripture. In the same way, Paul wrote other letters which did not get preserved, because they were not considered to be useful or authoritative for later generations. In short, what matters is that the books are scripture, not whether they were written by Paul or any other writer.

Our approach to the letters' authorship explains the order in which they are taken in this book. We begin with Philippians, which is generally agreed to be by Paul. The view of Jesus that we find there allows us to approach Colossians, seeing its understanding of Christ in the light of Philippians. Philemon comes next, as it was apparently written at the same time as Colossians. Finally, the latest of the letters, Ephesians, can be read in the light of Colossians, which so obviously inspired it.

Where were they written from?

Traditionally, all the captivity epistles were believed to have been written from Rome. Since we take Ephesians to be a later, non-Pauline work, there is no reason to suppose that the writer was actually in gaol: he is simply writing in the *persona* of Paul as he was when Colossians was written. Ephesians seems to be written to churches in Asia Minor, and may well have been produced there.

Philippians and Colossians are both subject to similar questions. Some scholars argue that these cities (especially Colossae, in Asia Minor) are too far from Rome for correspondence to pass as quickly as others seem to assume. As a result, Ephesus and Caesarea have both been suggested as possible places of imprisonment. While it is possible that Paul was gaoled at some point in Ephesus, we have no evidence for this. A Caesarean imprisonment would bring Paul closer to Colossae, but would make him as far from Philippi as Rome is, so at least in the case of Philippians the travel time would be the same, or even greater. While there is no reason to assume that both letters were written from the same place, we will go with the traditional view, that both, along with Philemon, were written from Rome, during the imprisonment mentioned in Acts 28:30–31. Frankly, the place of origin of the letters matters not at all, as far as understanding them goes.

When were they written?

If they were written when we assume, Philippians, Colossians and Philemon can be dated around AD60–61. Early church tradition suggests that Paul was beheaded in Rome. This may have been during the imprisonment that ends Acts, though it is possible that Paul was released, carried on his work for a few more years, and then was martyred in a subsequent visit to Rome.

If Ephesians belongs to a later generation, we may assume that it was written some time after Paul's death. It is impossible to date with any accuracy, but for those who feel happier with numbers, let's say some time after AD80.

Specific problems

Two of the letters have their own particular and famous problems. Philippians has one of construction, and Colossians one of meaning.

Is Philippians an entire letter?

A lot of scholars argue that Philippians is the result of an editor adding together bits of at least two separate letters. Philippians 3:1 seems to consist of the end of a letter, and the beginning of a totally new subject. A similar but less violent change seems to take place between Philippians 4:7 and 4:8. Are these signs that a section has been inserted? If so, it would not matter for the letter's scriptural authority, but it may alter how we understand its meaning. However, there are good reasons for supposing that the letter is as Paul wrote it, and we will look at these more closely in the notes on the relevant verses.

What was the Colossian heresy?

It is clear that in Colossians Paul is arguing against a new teaching which threatens to undermine the Colossian Christians' understanding of the gospel. But what was it? In reading Paul's letters, we are like eavesdroppers who can hear only one half of a conversation. We have to guess what the others were saying.

Guessing what was being said in Colossae is extremely difficult, and answers cover a wide range. One is that the Colossians had merely misunderstood the implications of their first encounter with the gospel, and what Paul is correcting is merely the enthusiasm of new Christians who have got the wrong end of the stick. However, it is hard to guess how Christians who had received Paul's gospel could possibly think it necessary to keep Jewish festivals and particularly to be circumcised (Colossians 2:11, 16).

Another view is that the opponents at Colossae were the local Jews, who were simply putting a good case for orthodox Judaism. However, Paul does not use any of the arguments that we find in Galatians and Romans about Abraham, the nature of the covenant, or the role of the law, and it seems hard to believe that orthodox

Jews would not introduce any of these elements into their teaching. Another view is that the Colossians were being seduced by an early form of gnosticism. The gnostics were members of a large and diverse religious movement which came into full fruition from the second century onwards. Their basic belief was that the soul could achieve union with God only through the correct (and usually secret, available only to the 'chosen') spiritual knowledge (*gnosis* in Greek), which was usually wedded to arcane rituals and practices. There is a strong emphasis in Colossians on knowledge and wisdom, and early gnostic tendencies may well have played a part in the teaching there, but a full-blown gnosticism doesn't seem to be in view. Perhaps the best understanding is that a local religious philosophy had sprung up which included Jewish elements, yet stressed the need for a higher knowledge and a higher spiritual insight than seemed to be provided by Paul's basic Christianity.

Nowadays, we are quite familiar with this approach to religion, and it was common in the Roman world. The aspiring spiritual person picks and mixes bits of various religious traditions to provide a spiritual soup that appeals to the individual's outlook, but fails to belong to any particular definable background. Thus we may encounter people today who believe in reincarnation, God, 'channelling' spirits and the healing power of aromatic oils without any allegiance to any particular religion.

We shall assume that something similar was happening at Colossae. The Colossian teachers peddled a brew which included elements of Jewish ritual and mysticism without any strong moral element of the Jewish Law, taught a 'philosophical' secret wisdom or knowledge, and sought visions of the spiritual realm through fasting and ritual observance, which put them in touch with the spiritual powers that underlay the visible world. Their outlook was essentially other-worldly—a view that Paul insists is neither spiritual nor Christian. Against this heady mixture of ideas, Paul places Jesus Christ as the one and only truly satisfactory answer to human need and human questioning.

Captive of Christ

One theme which all the letters do have in common is that Christ may be served whatever our human circumstances. Writing from prison, Paul asserts that his present situation still allows him to proclaim the gospel, the task to which God has called him. Christians too must see their own place in the world as the opportunity for worship and service, whatever it may be. Thus slaves may be able to use their status as an act of worship and service to God just as much as their masters can. There is no situation in which Christ cannot be served, and no position which cannot be an offering to him.

Further reading

There is a huge amount of literature, of almost every level from simple to abstruse academic, on the letters of Paul. Below are a few that I have found most useful in writing this book. In the book itself, no references are given. This does not mean that all the ideas are mine alone. They have been distilled from work by far better scholars than I. None the less, the opinions given are mine, and so (unhappily) are some of the inevitable mistakes. While I have enjoyed researching for this book, I am aware that far more remains unread than has been read.

Philippians

Markus Bockmuehl, *The Epistle to the Philippians*, Black's New Testament Commentaries, Hendrickson, 1998.

A good, readable commentary with lots of information on the historical and archaeological background, which doesn't require knowledge of Greek, though that would help.

Gordon D. Fee, *Paul's Letter to the Philippians*, The New International Commentary on the New Testament, Eerdmans, 1995.

A thorough commentary on a quite academic level by a leading Pentecostal scholar. Very good, but very heavy.

Gerald F. Hawthorne, *Philippians*, Word Biblical Commentary, Volume 43, Word, 1983.

Another academic tome that explains all the Greek, although you'd still be better off knowing something of the language. All the Word commentaries have fairly plain language 'explanation' sections, but they're rather brief in this one.

Ralph P. Martin, *Philippians*, New Century Bible Commentaries, Marshall, Morgan and Scott, rev. ed. 1980.

Approachable commentary for the general reader, by a scholar who has made Philippians his own.

I. Howard Marshall, *The Epistle to the Philippians*, Epworth Commentaries, Epworth, 1991.

All the Epworth commentaries are aimed at preachers and Bible study leaders, and are approachable, with attempts to look at practical applications of the text. This one is particularly good at that.

Colossians

The two heavier commentaries are:

Peter T. O'Brien, *Colossians, Philemon*, Word Biblical Commentary Volume 44, Word, 1982.

A solid and reliable detailed exegesis.

Eduard Schweizer, *The Letter to the Colossians*, Augsburg, 1982.

A more exciting read. Schweizer argues that Colossians was written by Timothy at Paul's behest.

Ralph P. Martin, *Colossians and Philemon*, New Century Bible Commentaries, Marshall Morgan and Scott, rev. ed. 1978.

Martin crops up all over the place, but usually with good things to say. This is an approachable, more-or-less verse-by-verse exegesis.

Roy Yates, *The Epistle to the Colossians*, Epworth Commentaries, Epworth, 1993.

Another preacher's commentary, more traditionally laid out than Martin's Interpretation volume (see below), and perhaps less inspiring for sermons, but with more meat to it.

Ephesians

Ernest Best, *Ephesians*, The International Critical Commentary, T&T Clark, 1998.

This series aims to be the Rolls Royce of commentaries, and Best's contains everything you could imagine on Ephesians, and lots you couldn't. Frustrating unless you read Greek, though, despite its occasional dry wit. Don't buy it without serious discussions with your bank manager.

Andrew T. Lincoln, *Ephesians*, Word Biblical Commentary, Volume 42, Word, 1990.

To my mind, the best on this letter, but that's probably because I agree with it so much! The explanation sections are a commentary in themselves, and Lincoln is always aware of wider issues in the modern Church.

Rudolf Schnackenburg, *The Epistle to the Ephesians: A Commentary*, T&T Clark, 1991.
A detailed commentary by one of Europe's leading Catholic New Testament scholars. Catholics have always tended to feel more at home in Ephesians than Protestants do, because of its strong stress on the universal Church.

Pheme Perkins, *Ephesians*, Abingdon New Testament Commentaries, Abingdon Press, 1997.
A commentary which looks particularly at the rhetorical construction of the letter, and its links with other ancient literature.

C. Leslie Mitton, *Ephesians*, New Century Bible, Marshall Morgan and Scott, 1976.
Something of a classic—an accessible and thought-provoking commentary.

Larry Kreitzer, *The Epistle to the Ephesians*, Epworth Commentaries, Epworth, 1997.
A preacher's commentary which is not afraid to engage with some of the issues that Ephesians raises but doesn't answer.

Commentaries on several of the captivity epistles

Ralph P. Martin, *Ephesians, Colossians, and Philemon*, Interpretation: A Bible Commentary for Teaching and Preaching, John Knox Press, 1991.
Readable, paragraph-at-a-time commentary for preachers.

Bonnie Thurston, *Reading Colossians, Ephesians and 2 Thessalonians: A Literary and Theological Commentary*, Crossroad, 1995.
Exactly what it says. Very readable and informative.

ACKNOWLEDGMENTS

I would like to thank the St John's, Heaton Mersey, Bible study group, who have worked through the captivity epistles with me, and provided many insights and questions. I would like to dedicate this book to them.

Thanks too, to my colleague, the Reverend Jenni Williams, for reading key parts of it. Unfortunately, I can't honestly blame any of its inevitable mistakes on her.

I am also grateful to the late Shelagh Brown for asking me to produce this book. Her sudden death in 1997 was a great loss. I am grateful too, to her successor Naomi Starkey, for her patience, and for understanding the pressures of parish life.

Finally, thanks to my family, Sarah, James, Laurence and Polly, for tolerating my eremitic existence whilst writing.

1   PHILIPPIANS 1:1

DEAR FRIENDS...

Suppose someone hands you a piece of paper. You see at a glance that it is a letter. Why? Because by reading hardly a word, you can see the format: address of sender (perhaps a printed letterhead), maybe your address, and certainly the giveaway word, 'Dear...'. Letters written in the first-century Roman empire also had a set formula for greeting and ending. It would go something like this: 'Marcus Rufinus to his dear friend Sergius Paulus, greetings.' Then might follow a prayer— something like 'I think of you often, and pray to Apollo for your health.'

Paul uses the typical Greek or Roman form when he writes, but in his hands it becomes much more than a formula. The prayer in particular becomes a heartfelt statement of faith, and often sets the tone of the letter that is to follow. The exception is his letter to the Galatians, which launches straight into his readers' latest doctrinal problems—a sure indicator of how upset Paul was. Philippians is as far in tone from that hurt and angry letter as it is possible to get. It is shot through with references to love and joy, and has repeated affirmations of Paul's deep affection for his Philippian friends.

In recent years, scholars have studied ancient letters and the books that were written to instruct in the art of rhetoric—the craft of speaking. This also applied to a great extent to writing, which was regarded then as being an extension of speech, since everyone always read aloud anyway. It is worth remembering that Paul, like many writers, dictated his letters, and they were delivered by public reading at church services. Attempts have been made to analyse Philippians according to the literary types of the ancient world. These have been only partially successful—Paul was not writing to impress an audience of literary critics. Perhaps the closest formal parallel to Philippians is the so-called 'letter of friendship'.

Although Philippians is a friendly letter, Paul still writes as an apostle, claiming a special ministry and authority from Jesus Christ. This comes across strongly in the warnings against false teachers in chapter 3. Perhaps it is best to say that Paul is writing to friends but in the awareness of his responsibility and concern for their growth in faith and the knowledge of God. The letter comes from Paul and

Timothy together, both servants (literally 'slaves') of Jesus Christ. Paul has no need to introduce himself explicitly as an apostle, for there is no question of his role in the church being doubted at Philippi. Instead, he includes Timothy, whom he will soon be sending as his envoy. By doing so he reminds his readers that Timothy is a closely trusted friend and helper who should be seen as sharing Paul's work and, to some extent, his authority.

Philippi

The letter is addressed to the saints in Philippi. Philippi was a medium-sized city in north-east Macedonia which had originally been founded by Greek colonists in the fourth century BC and named in honour of Philip of Macedon, father of Alexander the Great. In 42BC it was the site of a major battle, where Octavian (later the emperor Augustus) and Mark Antony defeated Cassius and Brutus, the killers of Julius Caesar. Later, Antony and Octavian fought for supremacy (wars were as confusing then as now). Mark Antony was defeated at the battle of Actium in 31BC. Augustus later refounded Philippi as a Roman colony, named Colonia Iulia Augusta Philippiensis in honour of the Julian family. With him as its patron, the city's population was increased by the addition of retired veterans of the legions and Italian farmers who were displaced for supporting the wrong side in the civil war. As a colony, the city was governed by the laws of Rome rather than of Macedonia, and was answerable directly to Rome. In effect, it would have been seen as a bit of Rome separated only by distance from the capital.

While there is evidence of pagan worship, both of Roman and Macedonian gods, there is no sign that Judaism flourished in the city, which would explain why Paul's first contact with Jewish believers was at an informal place of prayer outside the city (Acts 16:13).

As we will see, Philippi's status as a colony colours Paul's imagery as he writes to the church there. It is not mentioned in the address, though, for Paul is not concerned with status and citizenship, other than the status that derives from a relationship with God.

A PRAYER

Lord, help us also to see our value in terms of your love,
and not of our worldly status.

SAINTS & SERVANTS

Paul writes to the saints, together with the bishops and deacons. The first part is easy enough to understand. 'Saints' is Paul's general term for Christians. We are used to thinking of saints as specific Christians who in one way or another have been widely (and in some sections of the Church, formally) recognized as examples of holiness; indeed, the word means 'holy ones'.

For Paul, though, 'holy ones' refers to all Christians. Holiness primarily means 'set apart for God'. The saints are those who, by responding to God's call, have been set apart in several ways. They are now part of God's people, different from others in that they are aware of God's love for them, and his gracious offer of salvation. They are set apart by recognizing a different ultimate authority: they are now citizens of heaven, obeying its laws rather than those of merely human institutions. In short, they are holy because they belong in a special way to God: they are his children, adopted through faith in Christ. They are 'in Christ Jesus'.

This is Paul's favourite description of Christians, and the term carries a range of meanings. It can mean those who are joined in one body in Christ, those who have become bound to him and his new life through baptism; it can mean those who have put their trust in him and more besides. It stresses what, for Paul, is the obvious and overriding fact of Christianity—that it is centred on Jesus Christ. It is Christ who makes Christians what they are, he who has died for the sins of the world, he who is its source and goal.

Overseers and helpers

As well as the general greeting to the saints, Paul specifically addresses bishops (the Greek word *episkopoi* literally means 'overseers'), and deacons. Although 'deacons' (which means 'servants' or 'helpers') are mentioned in other places by Paul, this is the only use of the word 'bishops' in the letters that are universally agreed to be by Paul. Naturally, debate rages about the meaning of these titles and the function of their bearers.

It is unlikely that Paul meant anything like bishops in the modern sense. For one thing, as the later office of bishop developed, there came to be only one bishop for a given area. In Philippi there was certainly more than one. That is really all that we know about church government in Philippi. It's a fair guess that there were church leaders known as overseers, who were helped by deacons with a specific calling to serve the church. It seems likely that other churches had a similar office, since the 'elders' (*presbyteroi*) whom Paul meets in Acts 20:17 are also described as *episkopoi* in verse 28. Presumably the bishops/elders had roles of leadership, administration and general oversight within the church.

Even less is clear about the deacons. In Romans 16:1 Paul introduces the 'deacon' Phoebe, which suggests that her church in Cenchreae (near Corinth) gave that title to certain ministers, and that the title would have been recognized by the Roman Christians. We may guess that deacons took on roles of a practical, serving nature, such as Phoebe's trip to Rome with Paul's letter, but it remains a guess.

It is just as unlikely that every church had the same pattern of ministry. In the Corinthian church, prophets seem to have played an important role, while the list of ministries in Ephesians mentions apostles, prophets, evangelists, pastors and teachers—but neither bishops nor deacons.

What we can say is that the church was developing recognized patterns of ministry. Some of these functions (such as prophets) would be based on the discernment by the church of the spiritual gifts of individuals. Other people might have taken a lead because they were wealthy enough to have houses with sufficient space to host church meetings, such as Philemon, whom Paul greets in Philemon 2.

The vague but diverse picture of church organization that the New Testament gives us should make us aware that the Church, like any other human institution, needs structures. At the same time, it should make us wary of claiming too much for the way in which our own particular church or denomination does things.

A PRAYER

*Lord, may the holiness you give us by our calling show in the way
we live and work and worship, so that we who are saints in fact
may become saints in practice.*

3

GRACE & PEACE, THANKSGIVING & JOY

Paul's initial greeting ends with a benediction in which he wishes his friends grace and peace (v. 2). This is not an empty phrase, but a joining of two important terms. The typical salutation of a letter in Paul's day would be *chairete* (literally 'rejoice', but in this setting, 'greetings'). Paul replaces it with *charis*, 'grace'.

Grace is a free and undeserved act of giving. In Christian terms, grace is God's giving of himself in love. He gives salvation to sinners, love to his enemies, the Holy Spirit to his people. God's grace is the distinctive hallmark of the gospel. It is the statement that God reaches out to us before we turn to him. What *follows* from this is peace, a point that many English translations miss: Paul writes 'grace to you; and peace' (as in the NRSV), rather than 'grace and peace to you'.

Peace is the state of mind that flows from knowing God. Paul is undoubtedly thinking in terms of the Hebrew *shalom*, a word that carries connotations of wholeness and well-being as well as the absence of trouble and strife. Peace is not so much about quiet and calm as about knowing that under all the troubles and cares of life lies the certainty of God's love and the hope of eternal life.

Paul's prayer report

Paul turns the brief optional prayer into a lengthy account of his prayers for the church at Philippi. Prayer is not a matter of mere form for Christians. It is what binds us to God, enables us to share in his work and draws us close to one another. So Paul wants his readers to know that he does pray for them, not occasionally, but all the time—that is, each time he prays.

Even more strikingly, his prayers are primarily prayers of thanksgiving (v. 3). The churches that Paul founded were not only his offering to God (see 2 Corinthians 11:2) but God's gift to him. The greatest gift that God gives (apart from salvation itself) is other people. It is through human beings that God does most of his work in the world: his love reaches us through their love and support, his words reach us through their speech. In our relationships with others we learn to love, to forgive and to receive. Paul knows that well, and his thanksgivings are always for people rather than things. Here Paul stresses that he prays for *all* the Philippian Christians. He is worried to some extent about church unity in Philippi, and so paves the way for his later comments on that subject.

It is worth noting that Paul prays to 'my God' (v. 3). This doesn't, of course, mean that Paul thought of God as his personal possession. It means that, for him, his relationship with God was intensely personal. God was a part of Paul's life, his constant companion, helper and Lord, not merely a God 'out there somewhere'.

Paul has reason to give thanks because of the sharing, or participation, of the Philippians in the gospel (v. 5). No doubt Paul has in mind the gift that has been sent to him with Epaphroditus, but his thought goes beyond this. The Philippians have not only helped him financially, but have been sharers in the task of preaching the gospel. They are not passive in their support but active in the task of evangelism. Nor was this a passing fad, the embarrassing enthusiasm of new converts. They have been constant in their desire to spread the word about Jesus, from the moment they first heard it until the time of Paul's imprisonment.

This is a good reason for Paul's thanksgiving to be joyful, but it is not the full basis of his joy. (Joy is another theme that will crop up throughout the letter.) Like peace, joy is based primarily on the Christian's relationship with God. As such, it is largely independent of worldly circumstances: Paul can pray joyfully in prison! Such joy is based on the assurance that God can turn defeat into victory, and death into life. It is less an emotion than a state of mind, and as such can be cultivated, and even commanded (as in 3:1).

A PRAYER

Father, give me such confidence in your love and power that I too
may find joy in the midst of distress.

4 PHILIPPIANS 1:6–8

The GOSPEL *on* TRIAL

The confidence in God that gives rise to joy also assures Paul that the Philippians will continue to grow in faith and good works until they are fitted for heaven (v. 6). This work of transformation into the image of Christ (2 Corinthians 3:18) is the work of God, the Holy Spirit, and so is certain in its results. The Spirit is not mentioned explicitly, to be sure, but the process is precisely the effect that Paul elsewhere attributes to the Spirit's work (for example, Galatians 5:22–25). At the same time, it is a work with which Christians co-operate, through prayer and obedience. Its final completion comes with the 'day of Jesus Christ'; that is, the day of judgment, of Christ's return, when God's victory will transform the present creation and make all things new.

Paul has taken the term from the Old Testament, where 'the Day of the Lord' denotes just such a victory of God (Joel 2:11; Amos 5:18; Zephaniah 1:14). That Paul can so easily substitute Jesus Christ for God is a clear indication of the high view of Christ that he held. While Paul never explicitly equates Jesus with God (except possibly in Romans 9:5), it is clear that he thinks of the two in the same way. This attempt to identify God and Christ with each other and at the same time keep them separate was later to be worked out as the doctrine of the Trinity—that God is three persons in one divine being.

Partnership in the gospel

Paul has this attitude ('think' in verse 7 denotes what we might call a 'mindset') firstly because of his own deep affection for the Philippians, and secondly because of the way in which they share in the work of God. (The Greek of verse 7 can also be taken to mean that it is they who hold Paul in their hearts, as in NRSV, but the passage is really about his feelings, not theirs.) Their sharing or, better, 'partnership' in the grace of God (which is almost certainly a reference to the sharing of the gospel) has shown itself in their continual support through prayer, practical gifts and a concern that has stayed loyal even during Paul's imprisonment. That support is an important part of the spread of the gospel, which is, by virtue of Paul's captivity, on trial.

He speaks of the Philippians' partnership in defence and confirmation of the gospel. These are legal terms, suggesting that Paul's impending trial before Caesar is on his mind. The outcome of that trial, though, is really of little importance. What matters is what people will think of the message of Jesus Christ.

Obviously, the gospel message is likely to be mentioned at the trial, but Paul is probably thinking more widely than that. His imprisonment raises all sorts of questions. Will his trust in the gospel be sufficient to keep his hopes up? Does it bring a way of life that can cope with adversity? If Christians can be gaoled or even executed, does God really care for them? There were Christians then, as now, who believed that comfort and prosperity were signs of God's blessing. That the great apostle Paul was in prison would call for a re-evaluation of the gospel. There were pagans who would become aware of the Christian message as never before. Would they see something attractive and praiseworthy? In all these concerns, the partnership and support of the Philippians was a sign of the power of God's grace to draw people to himself, and to hold them through thick and thin.

Feelings

Paul genuinely longs to see them all again, and calls on God as witness to his sincerity (v. 8). Even so, his love for the Philippians is not merely affection for people he naturally likes, nor does it wholly spring from their obvious support of him.

Paul longs for them with, literally, 'the bowels of Christ' (v. 8). The 'bowels' were seen as the seat of emotion in the ancient world, where we would tend to say 'heart' (though we still have 'gut feelings'). Paul's love for the Philippians grows out of his love for Christ, and out of Jesus' command to love as he has loved.

Christian love does not start with feelings. It is an act of will, of deciding to cultivate the attitude that desires the best for others, and this is what makes it possible to command love. No one can be commanded to fall in love, but everyone can be told to have a certain attitude. Yet once that mindset is cultivated, feelings follow in its wake. To love fully is to care, and caring can grow out of the decision to love.

A PRAYER

Lord help me to act for others' good, and so come to love
as you love us.

29

5

LOVE & KNOWLEDGE

Paul has told the Philippians that he gives thanks for them, that he holds them dear and values their share in the work of spreading the gospel. His concern doesn't end there; he also prays for them. His first prayer is that their love (of which he is one recipient) may continue to grow—indeed, to overflow (v. 9). In this, he wants them to mirror God, the source of all love, and whose own love overflows in the great acts of creation and salvation.

This love, contrary to the way we tend to think, is neither blind nor undiscriminating. Paul wants the Philippians' love to overflow in knowledge. The word he uses (*epignosis*) is one that he tends to use for the full knowledge of God. Such a love is not content to sit and admire the one who is loved, but wants to know him fully, to understand and explore his riches. So, it is first and foremost a love for God, out of which springs love for each other in the church and for those outside.

We are often tempted to make a distinction between love (which belongs to the emotions) and knowledge (which is intellectual). Paul sees no such separation. Love drives the need to understand, and to understand is to discover love. To be sure, there can be knowledge without love, and that is useless (1 Corinthians 13:2), but love without knowledge lacks direction and purpose. True love wants to know the beloved, to explore his interests, to know his mind, to become interested in what interests him.

Someone once pointed out that there are lots more Christians in the United Kingdom than there are anglers (the country's most popular sport). Yet a look at any magazine rack will show dozens of angling magazines, and not one of Christian interest. It makes one wonder about people's thirst for the knowledge of God.

The knowledge of God should go hand in hand with insight into his will. It is only as we get to know someone well that we are able to understand their opinion and taste. It is similar with God. As we get to know him, we grow in understanding of his purpose for our lives. Elsewhere, Paul sees this discernment of God's will as growing from a mind that develops ever greater sympathy with God's outlook, and the Spirit's guidance (Romans 12:1–2).

Forward movement

The purpose of such knowledge and insight is to prepare the Christian for the final encounter with Christ (vv. 10–11). When the day of judgment arrives, and God's kingdom is fully established, will it be a day of rejoicing or sorrow for his followers? Of course, in the long run, it must be joy, for it is the day of the final victory of God. Yet there is an element of judgment. Whether the dawning of God's day will be glorious enlightenment or searing heat (compare 1 Corinthians 3:13) will depend on how ready we are for it. This life is lived in preparation for that meeting. It is as the Christian learns to live in conformity with God's will that he or she is prepared for the life of heaven.

Paul's continual stress on the coming day of Christ (v. 10) may well be because his own thoughts are tending heavenwards in the light of his coming trial, but it is a strong and constant theme throughout the New Testament. It could (and does) lead some to argue that Christianity is too concerned with the life to come to be of much use in the here-and-now. There are two answers to this. The first is to remember that Christians should not have to justify their faith in non-Christian terms, as though knowing God were only useful if it could make us healthy, wealthy and wise. It is worth knowing him for his own sake, and the awareness of his loving presence.

The second answer is that looking forward to the coming of Christ is a motivation for how we live here and now. Paul envisages the Philippians being able to present Christ with a 'harvest of righteousness' (v. 11), that is, a record of having lived according to his will in thought and deed. It is no paradox that this comes about through Christ himself. It is as the Christian seeks to live in accordance with God's will that the Spirit works in his or her life to bring about a transformation into the image of Christ himself. Christian living is a process of co-operation between the believer and the Spirit of God— a co-operation that is enabled and enhanced by prayer, and gives glory by its very existence to God himself. It also draws attention to the work of God and enables others to meet him and offer their praise in turn.

A PRAYER

Father, work in me through your Spirit, to inspire a love for you,
a desire to know you and do your will, which will draw others
to the light of your love.

6   PHILIPPIANS 1:12–14

WORKING *for* GOOD

When he wrote his letter to the Roman church, Paul told his readers that 'all things work together for good for those who love God' (Romans 8:28). Now, imprisoned in Rome, he declares that the good that has come out of his own difficult situation is the spread of the gospel to areas which no one would previously have imagined (v. 12). For one thing, the élite imperial guard, the Praetorians, cannot help but know that Paul is imprisoned for the Christian cause. They would know this because Paul was under what we would call 'house arrest' rather than in a prison cell, and his freedom would be limited by being chained to one of his guards. Those detailed to guard Paul would spread the news of the man who was awaiting trial by the emperor for the sake of a new variant of the Jewish faith. Paul is sure that that news has spread widely in the upper circles of Rome.

Paul is not merely putting a brave face on a bad situation. He has dedicated his life to the spread of the gospel. If his arrest can bring about further progress, that is cause for celebration. It is also a reminder that God's idea of what is for the best is often very different from ours.

Pre-evangelism

It may seem a bit over the top to regard such gossip as spreading the gospel, and indeed Paul goes on to speak of more direct forms of evangelism. However, the effect of rumour should not be underestimated. One of the biggest hurdles faced in the task of telling the gospel message is the first one, of attracting enough interest to make people want to know more. It is when word begins to go round that something interesting or odd is happening that curiosity is piqued, and explanations of the interesting oddity are readily listened to. In the context of modern churches, evangelism becomes much easier once the standard preconceptions about Christianity are undermined by word that something different is being done by the local church. In Paul's day, the rumour that someone was awaiting trial before Caesar would have done a lot to clear the way for the explanation of what the good news about Jesus entailed.

Willing explainers were apparently readily found. An even more encouraging effect of Paul's situation had been the renewed dedication to evangelism that sprang up among the Roman church. Paul's steadfast loyalty to Jesus has apparently overcome any fears his imprisonment may have sparked, and has inspired the local Christians to proclaim the gospel with extra boldness (v. 14). Paul's obvious rejoicing at the renewed evangelistic activity of his Roman brothers and sisters gains an added dimension when we remember that this was taking place in the early 60s AD. Nero's madness was reaching a peak, and suspicion of Christians was probably on the increase. In a few years' time, Christians would become the official scapegoats for the great fire of Rome, and would be mercilessly persecuted.

The Roman Christians' new zeal springs from a desire to have the degree of faith and love for God that Paul shows. Examples such as Paul's are encouraging because they demonstrate that such faith and service are in fact possible. The few who show such devotion become beacons to the rest of us.

Brothers and sisters

The Roman Christians who are fired with new zeal are Paul's 'brothers and sisters'. (The NRSV rightly translates the Greek *adelphoi*, 'brothers', in this way; Greek, like recent English, used the masculine gender inclusively of both male and female, a practice which is falling out of use in modern English. In fact, brother, *adelphos*, and sister, *adelphe*, are much more closely related words than their English counterparts.) In the ancient world, initiates in various religions, philosophical groups and societies also saw each other as belonging in some sense to the same family. Nowadays, similar language is used in groups like the Freemasons and (until recently) trade unions.

Christians claim to belong to one family because they are adopted children of God, their Father. Faith in Jesus brings entry into a fellowship of believers who are united in service to God and whose relations with each other are also based on Christ. For Paul, the notion of being fellow children of God is no mere turn of phrase. It must govern the behaviour and thinking of those who belong to the Church.

A PRAYER

Father, help me to look on those who join together to worship you as my sisters and brothers, and let that be the deciding factor in how I behave towards them.

7

COMPETITIVE GOSPELLING

After the joyful news of increased evangelism in Rome come two surprises. The first is the news that some of those who are working hard for the spread of the gospel are doing it from spiteful motives. The second is that Paul is so tolerant of them.

The best basis for telling the good news of Jesus is love, and for some, that love is indeed the motive. Paul probably means in the first place love for Paul himself (v. 16). Because he is being used by God in so public and dangerous a way, he has become someone to be emulated. He could also be thinking of the love of others which wants them also to know Christ, and of the love for God that drives willing Christian service. There is no real need to distinguish between these various directions of love. Love tends to overspill, and where it is directed to one, it is more easily shared with others.

The motive of love contrasts with that of the second group of evangelists (v. 17). Their spreading of the gospel is described as insincere. This need not mean that they do not sincerely believe in Christ, or that they do not care about the spread of the gospel. No doubt they are committed deeply to both. However, instead of rejoicing that God is continuing to use Paul, they probably see his imprisonment as a comedown and are happy to contrast their own apparent success with his seeming failure. They look to their activities as something which will increase their own standing and be a put-down for Paul—the 'envy and rivalry' of verse 15.

So who were these rival Christians? Theories abound, simply because in all honesty we have to say that we do not know. One plausible suggestion is that they are (some of) the Jewish Christians in Rome. We know from Paul's earlier letter to the Roman church that there was probably tension between Gentile and Jewish Christians in Rome. Paul's main topic in his letter to them was the need for both Jews and Gentiles to know Christ, and a secondary topic was the need for tolerance of fellow Christians. It could well be that Paul's letter did not wholly resolve the issue, and that some remained resentful of him.

Tolerance

Whether or not this theory is true, Paul's response to them is surprisingly mild. He can be extremely strong in his reaction to his opponents (see 3:2 later in the present letter, for instance), but here he shows remarkable tolerance. The best reason seems to be simply that, whatever their motives, they were proclaiming the gospel to non-Christians. Paul's strong language is always reserved for those who interfere with his own converts. The Jewish Christians who caused so much trouble for the Galatian church, and against whom Paul will shortly warn the Philippians, were, in Paul's eyes, casting doubt on the sufficiency of faith in Christ for salvation. The limits of Paul's tolerance seem to lie at the point where he perceives a threat to the gospel and to the faith of his converts.

Elsewhere, he argues strongly that those who differ on points of doctrine should accept each other as brothers and sisters in Christ (1 Corinthians 7:18; Romans 14:4–6). Paul's response, then, while no doubt tinged with sadness, is to rejoice that the gospel is being proclaimed 'in every way' (v. 18).

That 'every way' is an important lesson. It is easy for Christians to fall into the trap of assuming that their own particular tradition, outlook or theology is the one and only true way of being Christian. It's a view that dogs both large denominations and small sects. The ideal, of course, is to hope, pray and work for mutual acceptance among differing Christians. Even where that is not possible, or seems only a distant goal, we must remember that these different Christians are different brothers and sisters. Paul makes this clear in verse 15: 'Some,' he says, 'proclaim Christ from envy.' Some what? The noun has to be supplied from the context, and the context is provided in the previous verse: 'most of the brothers and sisters'. These jealous rivals, considered by Paul to be misguided, no doubt, are still his brothers and sisters.

As fellow Christians, even though they may dislike or despise Paul, they are being used by God. As long as they proclaim the gospel, Paul will rejoice. And in similar circumstances of difference and mutual suspicion, we can do no less.

A PRAYER

Father, help me to see those who differ from me, those with whom I may even quarrel or whom I may dislike, as my brothers and sisters, your children, and to rejoice in their faith and service.

8

The BIG PICTURE

Verses 15–18a stand as a brief digression in the midst of Paul's theme of rejoicing while imprisoned. The digression about the motives for evangelism in Rome has served an important purpose. There is some degree of division or conflict in the Philippian church. Paul will deal with this later, but he paves the way by showing his own attitude to Christians who oppose him. If he, in prison, can rejoice even over his detractors, the Philippians can surely deal charitably in their disagreements.

Paul can take such a line because he has his eye on a much bigger picture than the portrait of himself. His calling and commission is to preach the gospel to the Gentiles, and opposition can be tolerated if it leads to the furtherance of the primary goal.

This is not an approach that commends itself to the modern Western way of thinking. We live in an age of individualism, with a shopping-trolley attitude to spirituality. We will make our way round churches and religions looking for what seems to fit our needs, and moving on when it does not. We find it difficult to see ourselves as part of a larger plan or working to a goal that is not on our own initial agenda. Yet to belong to Christ is to be part of a larger vision and to be caught up into the purposes of God. It is to be given a task which is not merely of self-fulfilment (though it should bring that) but which aims to contribute to the establishing of God's kingdom. Paul's vision is a challenge that we need to hear as clearly as ever the Philippians did.

Still rejoicing

Paul now returns to the theme of rejoicing, and develops it. He is certain that his present situation will work out well. It is clear that, on the whole, Paul reckons that his approaching trial will result in his release (1:25). As a result, it is easy to assume that this is what he means in verse 19, but that is far from clear. 'I know that… this will turn out for my deliverance' looks at first glance like a confident expectation of acquittal. But acquittal by whom? And what does 'deliverance' mean? The Greek word is *soteria*—salvation or healing, or maybe vindication or wholeness. For Paul, *soteria* is generally something that lies in the end times, the day of the Lord, and refers to the final salvation that comes with God's acquittal and the healing of resurrection.

Moreover, Paul's phrase is a direct quotation from the Septuagint, the Greek translation of the Hebrew scriptures which was current in Paul's day. It is the Septuagint version of Job 13:16: 'even this will turn out for my deliverance'. Here Job is stating his certainty that his present undeserved suffering will end in his vindication by God. Paul *knows* that this will be the case, whereas he is uncertain whether his trial before Nero will end in life or death (v. 20). So Paul is certain that whether he lives or dies, he will stand before God as one who is innocent, and more than that, as one whose testimony will have done credit to the gospel as he proclaims it boldly.

He is certain of this because the Philippians are praying for him, and God will answer their prayers by supplying the Holy Spirit in fresh measure for the occasion. God gives the Spirit constantly, in response to prayer and to the demands of the situations faced by his people. Once again we see the idea of co-operation with God. By prayer, his people become sharers in God's work—and he works as they are prepared to share in the work.

Bold speech

Paul's certainty that he will speak boldly (v. 20), and will not make a poor and shameful presentation of the gospel, is based not on his confidence in his skill as a preacher but on the ability of God to see the job through. Paul is not a mere puppet in the process, though. It is in Paul's own person (literally, 'body') that God will act to exalt Christ. He is able to work only in so far as Paul is willing to let him work and to be the agent through whom the Spirit will speak.

It is significant that Paul prefers to use 'body' as the term for self (see also Romans 12:1). He knows that serving God is a matter of action, of deeds and words, and of relationships with others—all of which are about our public, physical life, not about some sort of interior 'spirituality' which is divorced from everyday living.

A PRAYER

Lord, give me grace to give myself to you, so that in what I do and say I may be a vehicle for your Spirit, your words, your love.

Seize *the* Day!

Paul expects God to use him to exalt, or glorify, Jesus by his bold testimony, now, in the present situation. For Paul, the apparently insignificant word 'now' is often loaded with meaning. It is the moment of opportunity, in which God can be served. Writing to the Corinthians, and quoting an Old Testament reference to God's help in the past, he writes, 'Now is the time of salvation!' (2 Corinthians 6:2). It is not enough to hope that opportunity will come in the future, nor is it enough to hark back to past times. The question is always, how can God be served here and now? What is the opportunity that he provides today?

There is an urgency about the gospel that will not wait for tomorrow. When Jesus was faced with a healing that could have waited until the Sabbath was over, and so avoided conflict and the appearance of breaking God's Law, he none the less acted straight away (Mark 3:1–5). Who knows what tomorrow will bring? Now is the time to act; now is the time to receive God's grace. Those who wait until a more opportune time may well miss it altogether.

Paul can be confident of God's grace for the present moment because he has experienced it time and again. God has always acted to honour the call he has given to proclaim the gospel. Of course, none of this means that Paul did not plan, or that we should not. It is simply a reminder that when opportunities come for proclamation, for works of love and compassion, they are opportunities to be seized before they are gone for ever.

The Greeks had a word for the opportune moment—*kairos*. Although the word does not appear in this passage, it is significant that it is the most common New Testament word for 'time'. Once I saw an ancient carving of Kairos. He was a young man with a long forelock and no hair on the back of his head. The idea was that he could be grabbed by his hair as he approached, but once he had passed, there was nothing to get hold of.

Life and death

Seizing the moment can be dangerous in human terms. Paul is sure that he will not disgrace the gospel. He will speak boldly and make a stand for Christ. And it may be the death of him. It won't matter, though. If he lives, he will have made his testimony and will continue to serve God. If he dies, then he will demonstrate that the gospel gives hope even in the face of death, and that love for Christ is something to die for, if need be. Living or dying, he will be for Christ an effective witness (Greek *martys*, which gives us 'martyr').

The reason Paul can be so sanguine about his possible demise is straightforward: his life is centred on Christ (v. 21). To live is Christ. Life is lived in the knowledge of the love of God embodied in Jesus Christ. Jesus is Paul's constant companion, the one he loves and serves, worships and strives to know more fully. To die is gain. Gain of what? Of Christ. In death, Paul will enter eternal life and be present with Christ himself. The vision that here is cloudy and uncertain will there become polished and bright (1 Corinthians 13:12).

Viewed in that light, death is far from unappealing. To continue in this life will give Paul more opportunities for his task, and no doubt will bear fruit in terms of new converts and new churches. Given a choice, though, he is not sure which he would prefer. After all, Christ has been his life and his goal for many years. Now, that goal is in sight. In fact, in purely personal terms, death is what he would choose.

NRSV tones down Paul's actual word, 'choose' (v. 22), in favour of a vaguer sense of 'prefer', but there is no need to do so. In reality Paul has no choice: the decision will be up to the emperor, and Paul is unlikely to have contemplated suicide in the noble Roman manner. On the other hand, his using the definite language of choice presents the force of his dilemma: 'If I really had to choose, I'd not know which way to go.'

Most of Paul's readers, then and now, would be hard pressed to agree with him. Death may well lead to eternal life, but this world is the one that is more real in our experience. The thought of leaving it fills us with trepidation and fear, both of the unknown and for those we leave behind. Once again, Paul sets us an example. He lives this life to the full, but does so in the context of a faith in which Christ becomes ever more discernible, and the wonders of this world point to the glory of the next.

A PRAYER

Lord Jesus, give me a vision that sees you at work in this life, and draws me in your good time to the next.

10 PHILIPPIANS 1:23-24

ONE PURPOSE, ONE GOAL

Paul's indecision over whether he would prefer death with its gateway to the presence of Christ, or life with its continuing opportunity to serve God, raises a question to which there is no simple answer. If he saw the resurrection as lying in the future with the return of Christ (for example, see 1 Corinthians 15:22–23; 1 Thessalonians 4:16), in what sense is death before that event a 'going to be with Christ'? Just how Paul envisaged the 'afterlife' between death and resurrection is unclear. He uses the image of sleep to refer to death (1 Corinthians 11:30; 15:51–52) and many interpreters think that he saw a period of unconsciousness between death and resurrection. However, in Philippians Paul clearly assumes an immediate awareness of the presence of his Lord, and in 2 Corinthians 5:4 and 8 he seems to envisage a bodiless ('unclothed') existence which is less preferable to the resurrection body but still preferable to life on earth, separated from the direct awareness of Christ. It seems likely, then, that Paul saw a period of consciousness which was less than full resurrection, but was still life in the presence of Christ.

In the end, such issues are secondary to the main reality of Paul's existence, that of knowing and serving Christ. As long as he was doing God's will and living his life for Christ, as long as his final destination was the presence of Christ, all other questions were of little importance. This attitude sets the pattern for the Christian understanding of life after death. We have the hope of resurrection, the promise of eternal life, but the details are not clearly spelt out. We do not offer a blueprint for eternity; instead we offer a relationship with the living Christ. We commit ourselves to his care, and trust that whatever life and death may hold, they are in his hands and he is central to what things may come.

It is this centrality of Christ that governs Paul's life. It may seem repetitive to stress the point again, but it cannot really be stressed enough. One of the marks of the post-modern world in which we live is the fragmentation of values and meaning. There is no core to many people's existence, no over-arching principle that binds all together and gives coherence to the whole. Many would deny that such a principle is possible. Even among Christians, faith is threatening to become merely one aspect of life, not integrated with other parts. The pursuit of career, happiness, family, religion, hobbies or whatever become varied bits of a hectic and fragmented life.

For Paul and, I dare to suggest, for all Christians, there remains a single goal, a single binding reality, which is found in Christ. It is he who can bring unity to the fragmentation of life, whether in the first or 21st century. In the light of Christ, work and rest, family and friendships find their place and are enhanced and given meaning. It must always be a subsidiary meaning, though, for they become pointless and trivialized if Christ is not the primary goal and the summation of all hopes and desires.

Desire and necessity

Paul's soliloquy on life and death, the question of which he would choose, is tipped by one consideration—the need of the Philippians (and no doubt his other churches) for his continuing ministry. He feels that he still has much to offer them, and so in the end would choose life in this world.

Paul presents this choice as a conflict between his *desire* (v. 23) to be with Christ and the *necessity* (v. 24) of ministry to the Philippians. He undoubtedly gains personal satisfaction from his work, so he could well speak of his (lesser) desire to remain, but that is not the main issue. He knows that there is work to be done, and is prepared to postpone his greater desire in the interests of others.

There is no need to doubt that this was a real motive, and the main one at that. All the same, telling the Philippians about it serves a purpose. They are in danger of division, and there are definite problems between individuals and probably between the groups they represent. Paul's own example of sacrificial service is a reminder of the Christian love they should be showing. That love looks first of all to the needs of others, and is prepared to give way rather than force its own will. When Paul comes explicitly to deal with the Philippian problems, he will be doing so from an advantageous position: he not only preaches mutual love, but practises it.

A PRAYER

Father, in your Son, you have shown us that service is
the essence of love. Give me the humility to serve, and in serving
to discover the depths of love.

GROWING *in* FAITH

Paul is certain that the Philippians still need his ministry, and so declares that he knows his trial will result in acquittal. In fact, he can know no such thing, in absolute terms, and verse 25 is worded rather less strongly than verse 19, where he expresses his certainty of salvation. None the less, his inclination is to expect that he will see them once again in person. He looks forward, when he does meet them, to working once again with all of them. The slight stress on 'all' is probably another subtle hint about their disagreements. Paul is taking no sides, but reminds the church that they all share a common faith and task.

Paul's help is necessary to the Philippians because they still need to progress in their faith—or perhaps in *the* faith, the Christian religion. Christianity was not, in Paul's view, a collection of tenets and doctrines which could be more perfectly understood merely by study, although for a man as steeped in the scriptures and as imaginative in his theology as he was, study undoubtedly would be important. For Paul, the understanding of the meaning of Christ, of the actions of God in history and in the world today, was part and parcel of a continual walk of faith in Christ. Today we separate theology and spirituality in a way that would have been alien to Paul and to most of his successors in the early Church. To understand is to be inspired to pray and worship; to encounter Christ and experience the life of the Spirit is to be driven to deeper understanding.

Spirit-led lives

Paul has chosen to use the same terms—of progress and joy—with which he characterized the spread of the gospel in Rome. Just as the gospel itself progresses from person to person, and brings joy to Paul and to those who receive it, so individual Christians are called to progress in their understanding and practice of the faith that the gospel brings, and in the joy that springs from it. Paul is frequently at pains to remind his churches that being a Christian is a process rather than a finished state. The ultimate goal is the final 'day of the Lord' but leading up to that is the continual movement into a deeper knowledge of God, a richer experience of his love and a closer following of his teaching. Although Paul does not mention the Holy Spirit explicitly here, it must never be forgotten that progress in the faith is part of the ongoing work of God's Holy Spirit in the life of the Christian. In all aspects of the Christian life, the Spirit is the guide, enabler and supporter of those who attempt to walk with Christ.

The Philippians certainly had room for progress. Although Paul does not see any serious problems at Philippi, there is still opposition to the gospel from the church's neighbours and there is conflict within the Christian community. Both of these difficulties have to be faced with the resources that the Spirit gives, and one of those resources is the guidance and teaching that Paul himself, as an experienced Christian and apostle, will be able to share with his converts.

Bragging?

So Paul is fairly sure that he will be able to return to them. Was he right? Did he get released, and return to further evangelism and teaching for a few more years? The answer is uncertain. The tradition of the early Church is that Paul eventually died a martyr's death in Rome. Whether that happened shortly after the writing of Philippians or later on, Paul would not have been disappointed at his fate. His life was always Christ's, to be used as would best further the progress of the gospel.

Should he return, though, he looks forward to sharing in the Philippians' 'boasting' in Christ (v. 26). 'Boasting' here means to have something as a source of encouragement and support. Paul is sure that God will continue to work in the life of the Philippian church, and so give them a source of pride and hope.

In this, he strikes a remarkable contrast with the sources of pride (wealth, honour, achievement) which would normally have been sought after in the ancient world. For that matter, it is a contrast with modern ideas, too. For the Christian, the basis of value, of self-worth, is found in the love of God shown in Christ. Beside that, worldly achievements pale into insignificance, and even the least significant person in the world's eyes has a value beyond price.

A PRAYER

Father, let me boast about what you have done for me,
and not what I do for myself.

12 PHILIPPIANS 1:27–28a

CITIZENS of HEAVEN

As we noted previously, Philippi was a Roman colony, and its inhabitants were proud of their status as Roman citizens, answerable to Roman law. Paul almost certainly has this image in mind as he asks the Philippian Christians to live up to the gospel. The Greek word he uses in verse 27 for 'live your life' is *politeuesthai*. It has the meaning of living as citizens (it is related to the word for 'city', *polis*), though it also more generally means 'way of life'. The message of Christ forms their identity, as nationality and citizenship form the identity of pagan Philippians. In contrast to those whose lives are patterned on Rome, the Christians must be those whose living follows the template of the gospel of God's redeeming love.

In no way is Paul suggesting that Christians possess some innate worthiness which fits them for the kingdom of heaven. Instead, as always, he is asserting that because they have been made citizens of heaven by the grace of God, they must now live up to what they have been given. Elsewhere he uses the language of joining (Romans 6:4), calling (1 Corinthians 1:26–27) or adoption (Galatians 4:6), but the point is the same. Christians are called to live up to what they already have.

Living in this way is a mark of the work of the Spirit, and a sign of spiritual growth. In addition, the best witness to Christ is the visible effect of his presence in the life of his Church. So both for their own sakes, as growing Christians, and for the spread of the gospel, Paul wants to find the Philippians standing firm in their faith, and showing unity in their fellowship.

Firstly, he stresses the need for a unity that they were lacking. The divisions in the church do not seem to be severe, or over issues that Paul feels it necessary to address in detail. As a result, we do not really know what they were. All the same, at this stage of the letter Paul signals the need for the Philippians to work side by side, suggesting a pattern for Christian unity that could well speak to us today. The very fact that he does not single out the issues which cause disunity suggests that the cure is found in concentrating on a common goal. All are agreed that they share the task of proclaiming the gospel that gives rise to faith in God. Then they should concentrate on that task, accepting their unity as sharers in the Spirit of God. The phrase 'one spirit' could mean the human spirit, as in a shared purpose, but given Paul's normal emphasis on the Spirit of God, the latter is more likely. Their common calling, their common experience of the Holy Spirit, and their common task should take precedence over wrangles and disputes. In this at least, they should be as one.

Opposition

Such unity is a witness, and a tool in the Christians' struggle for the advancement of the gospel. It is a struggle against a real opposition, which has brought them suffering. Indeed, it may bring death, which would explain why Paul has stressed his own inner struggle about living and dying. He wants the Philippians to realize that whatever the world may throw at them, their relationship with Christ is what really counts.

Who were the opponents who persecuted the church at Philippi? One common answer is Judaizing Christians, against whom Paul will warn in chapter 3, but this is unlikely. There was little Jewish presence in Philippi, and it is unlikely that Jews or Jewish Christians would have been a powerful enough influence to intimidate Paul's converts. More likely are the official authorities and state religion of Rome. As a colony, worship of the Roman gods (including the colony's new founder, the 'divine Augustus') was a major factor in Philippi's self-identity and good standing with Rome. Those who had given their allegiance to a lord other than the emperor, and who proclaimed a saviour other than Caesar, would have been seen as subversive and possibly even rebellious.

Such charges, if brought, could carry extreme penalties. Even if imprisonment and execution were not in sight, social ostracism, loss of jobs or trade and public disapproval would have been an intimidating prospect.

Against such opposition the Philippians must present a united front and a common faith.

A PRAYER

Father, give your support and courage to all who suffer for their faith in you, whether by mere disapproval and mockery or by threats to their lives, families or livelihood.

13 PHILIPPIANS 1:28b–30

JUDGMENT & SALVATION

The steadfast unity that Paul calls for in the face of opposition will be seen as a demonstration of the truth of the gospel—and the consequences of human response to its message. For the Philippians, it will signal their salvation, their ultimate destination to be with God, and acquittal by the one judge who truly matters. For their opponents, it will be a sign of their ultimate destruction (v. 28). Paul may well have in mind the possibility that steadfast faithfulness to Christ will be a compelling emotional argument to the persecutors. In the great persecutions which were to come a couple of centuries after Paul, the courage of the Christians became the Church's greatest asset in winning converts. It was that observable fact which enabled the Christian writer Tertullian to pen the much-quoted comment that 'the blood of the martyrs is the seed of the church'.

Many modern readers find the stark contrast between salvation and destruction rather uncomfortable. Yet the two are opposite sides of the same coin. If God's kingdom is to triumph, and all that is good and wonderful is to be preserved, then that which is evil, which opposes the kingdom, must necessarily pass away. That this may include those who wilfully oppose the gospel and reject God is a statement of the degree of freedom that God gives to his creatures. One thing that can be stated with certainty, though, is that nothing will be lost that can possibly be saved.

The context of opposition leads Paul to speak in verse 30 of the struggle (a military or athletic image) that he and the Philippians share (and which is another indication that their troubles stemmed from Roman authorities, as did Paul's). The struggle, though, takes the positive form of proclaiming the gospel of salvation rather than a negative one of attacking their opponents.

Suffering for Christ

Why is Paul so sure that the Philippians will be able to find unity and steadfastness in the face of opposition? Quite simply because its source is in God (v. 28b). Of course, it has a human component, as all Christian discipleship has, but once they have set themselves in the right direction, God will give them the necessary fortitude and courage.

The startling reason for this is that suffering is a part of following Christ. The salvation that comes through faith in Christ is God's free, undeserved gift. So is the suffering that it entails.

As Paul will go on to show in the next chapter, the pattern of death and resurrection that is found in Christ is the pattern also for Christ's followers. The way to eternal life lies through the cross. As citizens of God's kingdom in a fallen world, Christ's people are strangers in a strange land. The values they are called to hold challenge the values of the world. That of which they boast is at variance with the world's sources of pride. Conflict is surely inevitable.

Moreover, the suffering of Christians on behalf of Christ (that is, in his service) is in some sense a sharing in the sufferings of Christ himself. For Paul, his own suffering was a part of the total of Christ's suffering (Colossians 1:24; 2 Corinthians 4:10), to be accepted joyfully as part of the road to the kingdom of God. Those who are baptized into Christ are joined with him in his death and his resurrection (Romans 6:3–5). That is no merely symbolic language. Just as union with Christ brings the certainty of resurrection, so it brings to the faithful disciple at least the likelihood of sharing the reality of suffering for the cause of the gospel.

For many Christians in the world today, this is no mystery. Persecution is a living reality for a large part of the Church, and the list of modern-day martyrs is grimly impressive. For many in the Western world, though, it seems an unreal notion. For European and North American Christians, life often seems cosy, our status socially acceptable. Part of this is due to the long Christian history of those parts of the world, but part may be due to a complacency about the gospel which ignores its radical challenge to our world's values. One may wonder whether a gospel that draws no fire truly offers an audible call to repentance and salvation.

However that may be, the Philippians had seen the suffering aspect of discipleship in Paul, both in his first visit to their city (Acts 16: 11–40) and in his present situation (v. 30).

A PRAYER

Lord, we find it hard to face the prospect of suffering for you.
Give us such a vision of your love and your kingdom that it is
truly seen to be worth any price.

GOD, *the* SOURCE *of* UNITY

Being a Christian is not simply a rather grim call to suffer with and for Christ. It brings its own encouragement, consolation, love and fellowship, which add up to a fulfilling and exciting life. So Paul now returns to his main theme of unity with a frankly emotional appeal to his readers: see what life in Christ brings, and live up to it!

Many commentators spend a lot of time discussing the precise meaning of the words Paul uses in verse 1, but this can make us miss his point. Paul is almost certainly much less concerned with the precise meaning of encouragement and so forth than with providing an emotional impact. All the same, his words are chosen to heighten that impact and to make the Philippians feel that unity is desirable not only on the intellectual level, but in their hearts as well.

So 'if there is any encouragement...', he begins. 'If' here has the sense of 'since', or perhaps of a rhetorical question: 'Is there?' Of course there is! 'Encouragement' here means something like 'strengthen' or, as in the original meaning of the English word, to 'give courage and support'. To be in Christ, united with him by faith and the experience of his Spirit, is to have a source of strength and hope to undergird the life of discipleship. It is also to know his love, both as a resource to share with others and as something directed at the believer. Christians know their worth, not because they are good or deserving, but because they are loved by God. In the face of life's ups and downs and, indeed, persecutions, to know that one is loved by God is a consolation indeed.

Christians also share in God's Spirit. Here, as in 1:27, 'spirit' could mean the human spirit, so that the phrase would read 'any spirit of fellowship or communion'. In the context, however, it seems more likely that Paul intends a reference to the Holy Spirit, since this is one of the factors that he hopes will lead to a spirit of unity. Once again, we see that unity arises not only out of doctrinal agreement, but out of common experience. Once it is recognized that those with whom one disagrees in the church are also people who are indwelt, guided and gifted by the Spirit, it is hard to deny them recognition as fellow pilgrims on the way of discipleship.

Trinitarian language

The first three terms—encouragement, consolation and sharing, each with a qualifying statement of its source—carry an interesting echo of 2 Corinthians 13:13, known to many Christians as 'the grace': 'the grace of our Lord Jesus Christ, the love of God, and the fellowship of the Holy Spirit'. Some commentators see in Philippians 2:1 a deliberately trinitarian formula: 'encouragement in Christ, consolation of (God's) love and fellowship in the Spirit'. This is probably pushing the evidence too far. Our verse has a fourth element in the closely linked 'compassion and sympathy', and God the Father is not explicitly mentioned.

On the other hand, the first three qualities are all qualified in trinitarian terms, while the next pair stand alone, and perhaps signify a move in Paul's thought from the Philippians' relationship to God (the first three items) to their attitude of compassion and sympathy for Paul. It is probably fair to say that while Paul is not deliberately using a trinitarian formula, his way of thinking tends automatically to fall into that mode: the mention of a couple of the persons of the Trinity will elicit a reference to the third. This is not to say that Paul had a developed doctrine of the Trinity as it is found in later Christian teaching, but that it was already natural for him to think in a way that bound together God, Jesus Christ and the Holy Spirit as inseparable elements in Christian faith and experience. Romans 8:9–11 is a good example of this, where the Spirit is variously spoken of as the Spirit of God, of Christ and as the indwelling Christ himself. It is also worth remembering that the later attempts to express the Trinity in satisfying philosophical terms were in fact attempts to put into careful words what had long been an experience of Christian life, touched by the love of God, sharing in the life of the Son of God, and empowered by the Spirit of God. All our experience of God is ultimately trinitarian.

A PRAYER

Father, may I too know your love, the strengthening presence of your Son, and be bound in one fellowship with all who are touched by your Spirit.

15   PHILIPPIANS 2:2–4

COMPLETE JOY

Verse 1 ends with the similar terms 'compassion and sympathy', which are variously translated in English Bibles, but are to do with feeling for another. Probably they describe how the Philippians feel about Paul. After all, their concern for him has resulted in their sending of Epaphroditus with a gift to support him in his imprisonment. The thrust of Paul's rhetoric so far, then, is something like this: since you have in God—Father, Son and Holy Spirit—a source of love, encouragement and fellowship, and since you feel such compassion or affection for me, bring my joy to completion!

Of course Paul already rejoices in his love for the Philippians, in their concern for him, and in their work for the gospel. Yet his joy can be even greater: all they have to do is to show him that they are united, having the same outlook, a shared love and a common way of thinking. Paul twice uses words that mean 'to be of one mind', driving home the fact that he is aware of the disagreements among the Philippians, and their remedy—get together and agree! The term Paul uses does not mean specifically intellectual agreement. He is not trying to get the Philippians to sign up to some sort of doctrinal statement of faith which will stifle thought and debate. It is rather about outlook, or mindset—a sharing of aims and goals, a common purpose. To know that they are united in this way will fulfil his joy. He will be content that all is well with them.

Unpopular virtue

How can they get to this point, though? The answer lies in having respect for one another and, more than that, in humility. Put aside your own ambitions, says Paul, and look to the needs, the hopes, the aspirations of others (vv. 3–4). Do you want to win the argument? Do you want to be seen to be right? Do you want to be respected and valued, to have others look up to you? Is it your burning ambition to set the agenda for the church's future direction? Forget it. Instead, seek to support others, do what is best for them and put yourself in the background. In short, put aside selfishness and devote yourself to others' good.

This essential quality of humble love is as hard to attain as it is unpopular. We all want to be recognized and given praise for what we do. It is much easier to be virtuous when we are seen to be virtuous, to be loving when we are loved. To set out to regard others more highly than ourselves is a painful and thankless task.

Yet, though it can be so, in the Church it should not be. It is easy for an individual reader of an English translation to read these verses (and many like them) as a personal instruction. This is true as far as it goes. But it is a personal instruction to each member of the Church as a whole. Unlike modern English, New Testament Greek has both a singular and a plural second person ('thou' and 'you' in older English). Here, as in almost all instances in Paul's letters, the 'you' is plural. These are instructions to *all* the Philippians.

In short, each member is meant to put others first, to recognize each other's needs and interests. There will be recognition of achievements, and an ear given to ideas, because each wants to hear what others are saying and to offer encouragement and support. Moreover, such recognition and support will be truly deserved, not the self-praise that stems from a less-than-realistic assessment of their own abilities.

Verses 1–4 are all one sentence in the Greek, though they can't be translated that way. The effect to Paul's first listeners would have been a piling up of emotive terms designed to sway their hearts rather than their heads. There's nothing wrong in itself with an emotional appeal, and it would probably have been needed, because humility of this sort was a specifically Christian virtue in Paul's day. In the ancient Greco-Roman world, lowliness was something to be despised and avoided; it was a virtue only in slaves. There is also a reasonable argument. To the followers of the crucified Christ, the very nature of God's love is found in humility. It should be the hallmark of true discipleship, the stamp of those who are marked as belonging to him. That is what Paul will now go on to explain.

A PRAYER

Father, help me to love—to put others first.

16 PHILIPPIANS 2:5-11

COSMIC STORY

After his heartfelt plea for unity in the Philippian church, Paul turns to the simple basis for his call. Unfortunately, in the Greek, verse 5 has no verb, and so its exact meaning is debatable. The most obvious one is, 'Have the same outlook as Jesus had'. Some scholars, though, point out that in the verses following, about the incarnation and exaltation of Christ, there is little that can easily be imitated by Christians. In that case, so the argument goes, Paul must be saying something like, 'Have the outlook that is fitting for those who have new life in Christ'. The first view, in other words, takes Jesus as an example to be followed; the second takes the new life he gives as the starting point for Christian behaviour.

There can be no argument that the Christian life is based on God's grace, and that Christian behaviour flows from that. All the same, it seems more likely that Paul is here presenting an example to be followed, since that is exactly what his argument so far would seem to lead up to. In verse 5 Paul is offering the attitude that lies behind the story of Jesus as the pattern on which Christians should base their lives. This pattern, says Paul, is what underlies all reality, and by which God will ultimately judge his creation. It is a story of cosmic proportions; it is *the* story, of which all others are either pale reflections or perversions.

The Christ-hymn?

Verses 6–11 can make a fair bid to be the one New Testament passage on which more has been written by modern biblical scholars than any other. One recent list of books and articles on the passage listed over 600 titles!

The importance of the passage lies in what it says about Jesus and his relationship to God. Another issue that has exercised scholars is the origin of the passage. It has a poetic feel to it and, with some slight alterations, can be made to fit a poetic sort of form. Many therefore argue that Paul is quoting an early Christian hymn. In fact, this view is so widely held that the passage is often referred to simply as 'the Philippians Christ-hymn'.

There is a problem with this approach, however. For one thing, while it is possible that Paul is quoting a hymn, it is one that he must have altered a bit. As it stands, the passage does not fit neatly into poetic lines, so various scholars seek to identify words or phrases that Paul must have added. However, there is no agreement on exactly which bits Paul has altered. A second point is that Paul is most unlikely to have quoted something he disagreed with, so if it is an early hymn, it is an early hymn that says what Paul would have said anyway. The upshot is that whatever its source, it is basically a passage that expresses at least part of what Paul would himself have said about Christ. As a result, we may as well assume that the passage is Paul's own work. After all, we know that Paul was perfectly capable of producing poetic-sounding passages of his own (for example, 1 Corinthians 13) and there is no reason to suppose that he could not have done so here.

Adam and Christ?

Finally, one line of interpretation taken by some commentators is that in these verses Paul is deliberately modelling Christ's story on the story of Adam. Where Adam strove for equality with God, and fell, Christ makes no such attempt, but follows the way of obedience and so is lifted up. There is no doubt that Paul does make that comparison elsewhere (Romans 5:12–21; 1 Corinthians 15:45), and it is likely that the story of the fall (Genesis 3) underlies his treatment of human sinfulness in Romans 1:18–32. However, in the present passage (or in Philippians as a whole) there is no clear mention of Adam, which would be expected at some point if that is what Paul had in mind. The mirror-image similarity of Philippians 2:6–11 to the Adam story seems to me to be simply the result of stating what the earliest Christians believed about Jesus, his incarnation, Passion and glorification. Here, Paul is not so interested in fitting Jesus to the story of Adam as in having Jesus' followers fit their lives to his story.

A PRAYER

Father, in the midst of the many interpretations of scripture, keep me always ready to hear your story and make it mine.

The NATURE *of* GOD

Much of the discussion that modern scholars have over this passage is caused by the fact that Paul is discussing the very nature and thought of God. This means that the words he uses can only at best be seen as metaphors, images which do not relate directly to a reality that we cannot see. As a result, much debate centres on shades of meaning. On the whole, the basic thrust of the passage seems fairly clear.

Verse 6 contains two parallel phrases:

> *who, existing in the form of God*
> *did not consider equality with God something to be exploited*

'In the form of God' and 'equality with God' are terms which explain each other (a similar construction is found in 2:7, where 'form of a slave' is qualified by 'human likeness'). To be in the form of God is to be equal to God. Within this general statement, there are puzzles. The first is the meaning of 'form'. The Greek word, *morphe*, occurs only twice in the New Testament, and is rare in the Greek Old Testament, the Septuagint. It almost certainly does not mean 'image' as in the image of God in human beings (Genesis 1:26), but rather refers both to something's outward, visible appearance and its essential nature. Paul, of course, did not believe that God was literally visible. What he is essentially saying is that Christ existed before his appearance on earth, and that if it were possible to see him, the vision would be the vision of God.

Traditionally, this verse has been seen as a clear statement both of the pre-existence of Christ and of his divinity. There is no need to doubt the rightness of this view. It is strengthened, in fact, when we look at the word I have translated as 'existing', which brings out the full force of the Greek. Paul is quite definite that the one who appeared as Jesus of Nazareth previously existed in a state of equality with God. To put it in more modern terms, Jesus shows us the human face of God.

If this is so, we might ask (as some have!) why Paul nowhere makes the simple statement, 'Jesus Christ is God.' Paul stops short of identifying Jesus completely with the God of the Jews because he is trying to do justice to two elements—the role of Jesus as Son of God and Jesus' equality with God. These he has to hold together under the umbrella of monotheism, his Jewish conviction that there is one true God. It needs to be remembered that monotheism is the statement that there is only one God; it is not a statement about what God is like in his innermost being. In fact, in their speculation about God's Word and Wisdom (see comments on Colossians 1:15, p. 117), some Jewish writers came close to suggesting that God's own being was far from a simple monolithic unity. By asserting Jesus' equality with God and distinction from God, Paul already has in place most of the vital elements for the doctrine of the Trinity, as it would come to be expounded by later theologians.

Grasping God?

Another word that causes much debate is that translated here (and in NRSV) as 'something to be exploited', *harpagmos*. It's another rare word, with a basic meaning of 'something (to be) grasped'. Basically, this could mean that Christ did not consider divinity to consist of the action of grasping, but rather of giving; or that he did not consider it to be something to be held on to; or that he did not see it as something to be aimed for (assuming that he didn't have it already). The third view tends to go with the Adamic interpretation of the passage, where Christ's pre-existence is sometimes denied. However, this view does not hold water if what we have discussed above about the meaning of *morphe* is correct. The first view is much more likely, but raises the question of what one who is God could possibly grasp after. So the most probable meaning is the second, that Christ did not consider his divinity to be something to be held on to selfishly for his own ends.

This fits well with the point that Paul is making to the Philippians. They should not act out of selfishness or self-aggrandisement but, like Jesus himself, should put aside their status and self-interest for the good of others (2:4–5).

The picture of God that this paints is staggering. The eternal creator of all things sees his power and glory simply as a means to the help and salvation of his creatures.

A PRAYER

Lord, make me also, in my small way, a helper of others.

SELF-OFFERING GOD

So, instead of standing on his pride, the divine Christ emptied himself (v. 7a). The basic thrust of the statement is clear. But what exactly does it mean? Early in the 20th century, it was often argued that the incarnation consisted of somehow laying aside divinity, an emptying of divine power and glory. This is not indicated by Paul's words. Some English translations tend to support the view by beginning 2:6 with 'although', which is not in the Greek, and which would suggest that Christ's divinity was an obstacle to his taking the form of a slave. Almost the reverse is true: it was the nature of Christ's divinity that he *should* take the form of a slave. This is the radical rethinking of the nature of God that the coming of Jesus entails. At his very heart, God is defined not by power and glory but by self-sacrificing love.

With that idea in view, it is more likely that Paul is speaking the language of sacrifice. Christ emptied himself in the sense of pouring himself out, an image Paul will use of his own possible death in 2:17.

Fully God and fully human

The first stage of Christ's emptying of himself is expressed in two parallel phrases:

> he took the form of a slave
> having become in likeness of human beings

As in 2:6, these phrases illustrate each other. The 'form of a slave' means much the same as the 'form of God'—the outward appearance and the inner essence. That is, Christ became a genuine human being. (Paul's use of the plural 'human beings' is a deliberate statement that Christ shares our common humanity.) At the same time, Paul gives no indication that Christ somehow became less than divine, which explains the use of 'likeness'. Yes, Christ was human (hence NRSV is correct to translate 'having become' as 'being born'), but with a certain difference: he was also divine. Paul uses a similar phrase in Romans 8:3 where he describes Christ as being 'in the likeness of sinful flesh'—sharing the human condition, but with one vital difference, in that he did not give way to sin.

Paul's use of such language shows a concern like that of his description of Christ's divinity. There he wants to ascribe equality to, but not complete identity with, God; here he wants to stress humanity, but not at the cost of denying divinity.

Slave of God

Christ, then, became human. He who shared God's form descended to the level of a slave (v. 7b). In the Greco-Roman world, one could not get much lower than the level of a slave. A slave was property; in legal terms, and sometimes in experience, a slave was a living tool, a thing rather than a person. Paul's prime concern is simply to stress the huge change in status that the incarnation brought about. There is no need to ask to whom Christ became a slave, as some have done in the past, and to suppose that he became a slave to the devil or to the powers of the universe. Paul simply cannot find a lower status to illustrate the degree of the divine humility.

Having said that, there may be other ideas associated with his choice of image. Crucifixion was a typical punishment of rebellious slaves, and so the mention of death on the cross follows naturally from this. Christ not only became the lowest of the low, but suffered the most humiliating and terrible fate for a slave. There may also be echoes here of the suffering servant of Isaiah 53, who is counted with the outcasts and dies for the sins of others.

Incarnate offering

The most intriguing point is that the sacrificial self-emptying of Christ takes in not only his death but also his incarnation. Some Christians speak as though all that matters is Christ's death, while others stress the presence of the incarnate God in the world at the expense of his death and resurrection. Paul holds both together. The total act of self-giving that brings redemption is the incarnation, death and resurrection. Jesus' life, teaching, ministry and Passion are all part of the one great act of redemption in which the divine love reaches out to the world.

A PRAYER

Reach out to me, Lord, in the message of your life and death,
that I may know your risen life.

19 PHILIPPIANS 2:7c-8

HUMBLE GOD

The next part of verse 7 seems to be adding a third description of Jesus to the two already mentioned, but there is actually a subtle progression of thought here. Having established that Christ shares human nature, he focuses on Jesus the individual: 'and being found in appearance as a human being' draws attention to the specific acts of this specific human. Taken on its own, 'appearance' might be thought to suggest that Jesus only *appeared* human, while *being* something else. (NRSV has 'form' again, but this is a third Greek word, *schema*, which suggests outward and visible appearance or shape—that is, what anyone could quite plainly see.) However, Paul has already made it clear that Jesus was truly human, even though his humanity was not all that could be said about him. The point is that Jesus the man voluntarily humbled himself, just as the pre-existing divine being emptied himself.

The final step in the process of divine self-offering is Christ's obedience to God. As a man, he accepted God's will entirely, even though it led to death. It is impossible to offer any greater obedience than that. Jesus was prepared to do God's will, whatever that may lead to. And it was no glorious, heroic death, of the sort that might feature in edifying tales or be regarded as honourable in the view of those times, but the death of a slave or traitor, the ignominious torture of crucifixion. Romans regarded crucifixion as an abhorrent punishment, fit only for the basest of people and crimes. Jews too regarded it with horror, for to be hung up on a tree was a sign of God's curse (Deuteronomy 21:23).

For Christians, bearing the curse of sin was, of course, the essence of Jesus' death, a sign not of his rejection by God but of his complete trust and obedience. Paul is not, however, concerned here to explain the meaning of the cross. He does that elsewhere, and the Philippians were well aware of the significance of their Lord's death. Here, the point is about humility and obedience, virtues which the Philippians are called to put into action in imitation of Jesus.

It is hard for us, after two thousand years of Christian tradition, to imagine the revolutionary change in the concept of God that Christianity brought. For Paul to be able to speak of one who is equal to God as emptying himself and humbling himself was a new departure. God's love was not a new idea, and nor were his power and glory. His humility, shown in Christ, certainly was. Yet it follows from the person of Jesus himself. If Jesus truly shows us the nature of God, then God is self-sacrificing and humble, willing to give all for the sake of those he loves. This view of God lies behind Paul's own conviction that his imprisonment is not a failure but part of the working of God. If the gospel has its roots, and its victory, in the cross, its messengers cannot see defeat in their own suffering or apparent setbacks.

Obedient slave

By now it should be clear that for Paul there was no contradiction between Christ's divinity and his obedience to God, of the 'If Jesus was God, who was he praying to?' kind. His careful refusal simply to identify Jesus with God solves that problem. In later theological language, the second person of the Trinity is obedient to the first, even while sharing in the same divine nature. That obedience is probably also another reason for Paul's use of 'slave' as a good description of the incarnate Christ, for the obvious example of complete obedience in Paul's world was that of the slave.

For that matter, 'slave' is a good term for the human condition, from Paul's point of view. It is his favoured term for himself as a servant of Christ, given wholly and completely to the service of God. Moreover, it is the characteristic of human beings. For Paul, true freedom consists not in going one's own way, which is the essence of sin, but in finding one's true place as a servant and child of God. The choice that faces human beings is not whether to be a slave but whether to be a slave of sin or of God, to be ruled by one's own desires and passions or to be ruled by the love of the creator (see Romans 7:21–25).

In this sense, Jesus shows the nature of true humanity: one who found his rightful place in obedience to God and in giving himself up to that service found eternal glory.

A PRAYER

Lord, help me to decide for you, and give myself freely to the one who made me for himself.

Super-High God

Paul's poetic telling of the story of Christ has hit rock bottom. Pouring himself out in self-giving love, Christ has taken the form of a slave and suffered a slave's ignominious death. He has voluntarily sunk as low as can be. It cannot end there, though. The story of Jesus is not a tragedy but a rescue mission, and his loving sacrifice brings its vindication. If God is just, there must be a payback for innocent suffering, a balancing of the books that affirms God's loving purposes. So the one who freely gave now receives, being raised up again. Paul's word is literally 'hyper-exalted'—God has vindicated Jesus, and then more (if more is possible!). The single word, often translated 'highly exalted', takes in the resurrection, ascension and present reign of Christ.

This is the story of Jesus set against its cosmic background. The humble life of the peasant prophet was only the earthly and visible manifestation of the humility of God. His resurrection, staggering though it was, was only the visible part of the glory to which he returned.

It is easy to see how the story of Christ's humility is a fitting example for the Philippians, in need of humility themselves. Commentators often assume that the second part of the story is less fitting, but just as it is necessary for Jesus to be vindicated, it is necessary to balance the call to discipleship. Jesus indeed called his disciples to lose their lives, but only that they might gain eternal life (Matthew 16:25). The way of the cross is not an end in itself, and suffering and self-denial are not absolute virtues, but necessary stages on the way to resurrection. If Paul calls his readers to humility and service, to denial of self and affirmation of others, it is because this is the way to the presence of God, to being more than conquerors and to sharing Christ's risen life.

The divine name

As a result of his incarnation and death, Jesus has been given the name above every name. Names were important in the ancient world. It was felt that a name carried something of the actual person in it, and names could bestow character. Hence names were chosen carefully, either paying homage to great figures of the past (Jesus is the New Testament Greek translation of Joshua) or carrying special meanings (for example, Theophilus means 'lover of God'). So the name that God has now given to Jesus is a measure of who he is and what he has done. However, what that name is is not immediately apparent. Some would say that the greatest name is now simply 'Jesus', for Jesus is far above anyone else. This is possible, but not all that likely, since Jesus was hardly a name bestowed after the resurrection. More likely is the notion that the name is finally explained in 2:11, when Jesus the Christ is confessed as 'Lord'. 'Lord', of course, is a title rather than a name, except in one special case. It was the normal way of saying the name that was too holy to speak aloud, the sacred name of God, YHWH. That, after all, is surely the one name that is truly above all names. This is also given weight by 2:10–11, verses which are modelled on Isaiah 45:23, a statement about God himself.

This raises its own questions. If Christ was already equal to God, how could he be *given* the name of God? Is it possible that he could be promoted from the highest conceivable position? The simplest explanation is that Paul is using exaggerated language to stress the return of Christ to his former glory. I think, though, that there is more to it than that. All it takes to be a king is an accident of birth. All it takes to be a prime minister or a president is a certain amount of ambition and a lot of financial backing. But to do the job well is another matter. To be just and merciful, courageous and honest, wise and loyal, to do what is right rather than what is expedient, takes qualities which are rare indeed.

In his self-emptying love, shown to the world in Jesus Christ, God has shown that he is not only God in fact, but a God who is worthy of worship and service. He calls us to be his children and his lovers, not because he made us, not because he has the power to bend us to his will, but because he has shown that he is worthy of our discipleship. Another New Testament writer put it in the following words, our prayer for today.

PRAYER

*You are worthy… because you were sacrificed and
with your blood you bought people for God of every race,
language, people and nation.*

Revelation 5:9–10

LORD *of* GLORY

These two verses are consciously modelled on Isaiah 45:23: 'By myself I have sworn, from my mouth has gone forth in righteousness a word that shall not return: "To me every knee shall bow, every tongue shall swear."'

In Isaiah, this verse is part of a passage which makes two important affirmations—that there is only one true God, the God of Israel, and that he will bring salvation to his people, triumphing over Israel's enemies and their false gods. That Paul applies it so clearly to Jesus is a final confirmation that he thought of Christ as sharing equal status with God.

It is also a statement that in Christ, God has brought his promise of salvation to fruition. Christ is the one in whom God triumphs. The incarnation, death and exaltation of Christ together make up the fulfilment of the hopes and desire of Israel. God has come to his people to set them free—and not only Israel, but the whole world, for every knee will bow, in all creation, 'in the heavens and on the earth and in the depths'.

Paul's phrase sums up the whole biblical picture of the universe, which was constructed like a high-rise building. At ground level was the world we know, and above it the various tiers of heaven (often seen as consisting of seven storeys, each with its appropriate planets, stars, and orders of angels). Below was the realm of the dead, Sheol or Hades. It is impossible to say whether Paul actually thought of the world in such terms; almost certainly he was aware of other views (the mathematician Eratosthenes had calculated the circumference of the spherical earth in the fifth century BC). Paul's point is the inclusiveness of Christ's rule, the scope of his salvation. Both angelic powers and human beings, alive and dead, will one day acknowledge the rule of Christ. The word Paul uses for that acknowledgment can mean either a glad confession of faith and thanks, or a reluctant recognition by those who have opposed Christ. In the end, Christ will rule, and judge, irrespective of the opinions of human beings.

All this is to the glory of God the Father. The work of Christ is to bring God's kingdom, his rule, to bear over all his creation. Salvation is not an act of Christ apart from God the Father. It is all the work of the one God, and as the incarnate Christ was obedient to the Father, so his mission draws the world back to its creator God. Human beings were created to give glory to God, and they find their true selves in a relationship with him, a relationship made possible by the outpouring of the incarnate Lord.

Lord of all

The confession 'Jesus Christ is Lord' will one day be the cry of all creatures, but until then it is the distinctive creed of the Church, a mark of the Holy Spirit's inspiration and guidance (1 Corinthians 12:3; Matthew 16:16–17). Christians live with one eye on the future, experiencing now, in the work of the Holy Spirit, something of the coming kingdom, and called to live here and now as citizens of that coming rule.

Declaring Jesus to be Lord is therefore not just an abstract theological statement. Like all good theology, it has implications for daily living. To proclaim Christ as Lord is to say that he is the one who sets the agenda for his followers. In 2:6–11 Paul has been demonstrating that agenda, set by Christ's own precedent. If Christ spent himself for others, then so should they. If he found glory through the way of the cross, then that is the path to glory for his followers.

In a world where the emperor claimed the title of Lord and demanded the honour due to a god, allegiance to another Lord than Caesar could be the way of the cross indeed. To recognize the kingdom of God as one's true homeland is to stand apart from the systems of the world and to judge them in the light of God's rule. This clash between the claims of earthly power and those of Christ as Lord would come to be the origin of much martyrdom in the early Church—and it still is.

One has only to think of some of the 20th century's most famous martyrs—Martin Luther King, Oscar Romero, Janani Luwum—to see that while being a Christian is in many places a safe thing to be, acting as though he truly is Lord is far from safe. 'Jesus Christ is Lord' is a call to shake off complacency and acceptance of the world's ways, and to live as though the welfare of others, the rights and hopes of others, truly do matter.

A PRAYER

Lord, let me say 'Lord', and mean it.

FOLLOWERS *of the* LORD

Paul now returns to the practical consequences of following Jesus, at least as far as the Philippians are concerned. What he has to say follows on from what he has written about the incarnation: 'therefore…' or 'so, then… work out your own salvation' (v. 12). This verse has been used to bolster the idea that salvation depends on human effort, but a look at its overall context shows this to be a non-argument. It is God who is at work in the Philippians, as in all believers. They, though, have their own role to play. The key to understanding these verses is Paul's idea, which we have already met, of a kind of co-operation between God and his people, a working together of the human spirit and Holy Spirit.

Christians are indeed given salvation by God's grace, but a salvation that has no effect on human life is no salvation at all. It must be put into effect. Christians are called to become what they are—to make real in their lives the status that God has graciously given. Indeed, for Paul, salvation is both a present process and a future goal. In Greek, the present tense (used here in 'work out') means a continuous action; so it means, 'Continue to put into effect your own salvation'. The 'your own' is plural; it is as a Christian community that the Philippians together put into practice the consequences of their salvation.

The big difference between what Paul has in mind and normal human efforts to 'be good' is that their outworking of their salvation is not done by the Philippians alone. God is at work in them, through his indwelling Spirit, strengthening and directing. He is the senior partner in the co-operative. He provides the gift of salvation and both the ability to carry out their calling and the strength of purpose, the inspiration, for the task. It is, of course, possible for anyone to will to do good. Many succeed to a greater or lesser degree, but anyone who has tried to keep a New Year's resolution will know that there is more to doing what is right than merely wanting to. Part of the Spirit's role is to enable his people, to give the gifts and strengths necessary for the task.

While Paul was able to be with them, he himself was a helper and director, but now that he is separated both by distance and imprisonment, it is up to them to carry on themselves; hence they are to work out their *own* salvation, without help from the apostle. Paul is sure that they will manage this. He knows from his time with them that they are obedient to God (not to Paul, as NRSV has it in verse 12: the context really demands that we see a reference back to Christ's own obedience, to be imitated by the Philippians). Now they will surely carry on as they started, as long as they do so in the right attitude.

Working in the sight of God

The right attitude is with 'fear and trembling'. This biblical phrase is often used for encounters with God, and suggests that the Philippians must work and live as though they were standing before the presence of God, in all his awesome majesty—which, of course, they are. The problem is that it is all too easy to act as though God were not present.

There are moments when the presence of God is an inescapable experience. It may come in times of worship or contemplation, of quietness or stress. In such instants, there is no problem in desiring to live up to his love, his wonder and joy. For most of the time, though, it is easy to act as though he is not watching or does not matter. The problems at Philippi (and anywhere else) would soon disappear if all concerned could seriously ask, 'What do I suppose God thinks of this?'

God's pleasure

The obedient outworking of the salvation that God has given is for God's good pleasure—that is, because he wills it. At first, this may sound as though God is being capricious and might just as well have decided to do something else, but that is far from the truth. God wills the salvation of, and good works by, his creatures because that is his nature. What pleases him is the good of his creatures, because God is himself good and self-giving.

A PRAYER

Lord, help me to remember that even when I forget you,
you never forget me.

23 PHILIPPIANS 2:14–16

SALVATION *in* PRACTICE

So what precisely does it mean for the Philippians to work out their salvation? Firstly, as Paul has been stressing all along, it demands their working together in unity. Verses 14–16 are virtually composed out of quotations from or references to the Old Testament. Whether this is deliberate, and Paul wants his readers to conjure up images from the scriptures, or whether it is simply a product of the way his mind was working at the time, is hard to say. Probably it is the latter, since the Gentiles of Philippi might not have been expected to pick up all the allusions, and the passages from which they come do not exactly fit the situation at Philippi, even though the words Paul uses do. Either way, consciously or unconsciously, Paul is affirming the place of the Philippians in the history of God's people. What could be said in the scriptures about Israel can now be said of the Christian Church. The warnings and teachings of Israel's scriptures are now also for those who follow Jesus, whether Jew or Gentile.

Murmuring, or grumbling, and arguing were a common feature of Israel during its time in the wilderness with Moses (see, for example, Numbers 14:2–3). The Israelites grumbled against God and Moses. Perhaps dissatisfaction in the Philippian church expressed itself as complaints against the church's leaders. That certainly happens today! The Philippians may not have been explicitly grumbling at God, but Paul's call to obedience needs the additional reminder that obedience should be given gladly, not grudgingly. That there was arguing at Philippi is certain. Once again, unity is the watchword. It is necessary both for the Philippians' growth to spiritual maturity and for their task of proclaiming the gospel.

Spiritual maturity is here expressed as being blameless and pure children of God, people without blemish (v. 15). In the Bible, animals that were offered to God had to be spotless—the very best. In the same way, Christians are called to offer themselves to God as a 'living sacrifice' (Romans 12:1). That they can do so only in the light of their status in Christ, who has borne the burden of their sins, goes without saying.

Shining out

The Philippians' blameless purity (or, to be realistic, as near as they can get to it) is a vital part of their work of evangelism. If the Church, empowered by the Spirit of God, cannot offer a brighter and more attractive alternative to the world, then its mission is handicapped from the first. The 'crooked and perverse generation' is another quotation, from Deuteronomy 32:5, where it refers to the faithlessness of the wandering Israelites. Paul uses it to refer to the pagan society in which the Philippians must live out their Christian discipleship. It is a world that owes its allegiance to other gods—to Caesar, to the idols of paganism, to social climbing and financial success. By their very example, the Philippians are to offer an alternative based on love and consideration for the poor and disadvantaged, on service and self-sacrifice.

That contrast will enable them to shine out like stars in darkness. Daniel 12:3 has a similar phrase, but it refers to the saints after resurrection. But then, the Philippians have the Holy Spirit, who brings into the present something of the world to come. Their life together should mirror God's coming kingdom and hold out to the world a hope of something better, to be found in Christ and his people.

In verse 16, 'holding out' can also mean 'holding on to' (as in NRSV) but the context of evangelism seems to demand the former reading. Perhaps Paul means it in both senses. Those who hold fast to the gospel will be those who also proclaim it. Words must be backed up by lifestyle, but lifestyle must also be explained in words.

At its best, the Church has always offered an alternative to the world around it, either in its worship and prayer or in the kind of community it offers to its members, or in the help it gives to those around it. At its worst, it has been so thoroughly absorbed into its surrounding culture that it has merely become an arm of that culture. It is worth asking where it stands today in our own society, and where, therefore, its witness lies.

If the Philippians hold fast to and offer the gospel, if they are united in faith and service, then Paul will be able to stand before Christ on the day of judgment and take pride in his work (v. 16). There is little more that he could ask—and nor could we.

A PRAYER

Lord, help me to work for unity in the church, and to be a part of its witness to the world.

SERVICE & JOY

Paul ends his long plea for unity at Philippi by returning to his under-lying themes of suffering and joy. In explicitly sacrificial language, Paul sees himself as being poured out like a libation (a drink-offering) over the sacrifice that the Philippians offer to God (v. 17). The image is drawn from the Old Testament, and refers to the poured-out wine that accompanied some sacrifices in the temple. In the light of what he has written about Christ's emptying of himself, and the possibility of his own death, it is hard to imagine that Paul is not writing of his own possible martyrdom. The image goes further than that, though. Even if, as he hopes and expects, he will be released, his life is still an offering, spent in the service of God. The race he runs (v. 16) and the labour he offers go together with the offering of his converts as his glad gift to God. Whether he lives or dies, he is Christ's, and so he rejoices, even in the midst of the suffering that his service can bring.

Paul's rejoicing is increased by the knowledge that he shares with the Philippians in their sacrifice, so he presents the apparently awk-ward phrase, 'I rejoice, and rejoice with all of you' (v. 17). That is, he rejoices personally—if he alone followed Christ, it would be cause for rejoicing—but even more, he rejoices in the company of his fellow Christians.

Similarly, the Philippians are called to remember that they are united in faith and service with Paul, and likewise to rejoice doubly—for their own service and faith, and for their partnership with him (v. 18).

Paul's emissary

Now Paul begins an update on his plans. Timothy will soon be coming to them, as soon as Paul's immediate future is more clear (v. 19). Of all Paul's helpers, Timothy is the most reliable, the most like Paul in his commitment to the gospel. He is an experienced mis-sionary himself, and well known to the Philippians, who will no doubt welcome him and provide him with more news to bring back to Paul. His relationship with Paul is close—like a son (v. 22). In the ancient world, this was (hopefully!) a relationship of love and respect, but also one of learning and apprenticeship. Sons were generally expected to learn the trade of their fathers and to carry on the family business.

Timothy is therefore someone like Paul in his concern for the Philippians and his desire to serve Christ. This stands in stark contrast to 'everyone else', who are seeking their own interests (v. 21) and forgetting their primary loyalty to Christ. This is probably not as sweeping a statement as it sounds. It cannot mean all Christians in Rome, since Paul has already commended the diligent work of the church there (1:14). Presumably it refers to Paul's circle of companions and helpers, or at least such of them as have, for one reason or another, remained in Rome.

We are not told what the problem was, either. It could be that as Paul's imprisonment dragged on, some of his supporters began to look for other areas of work, or began to fear for themselves, that they might be suspected by association with Paul. Or it could be that they saw his imprisonment as a sign of divine disfavour. Imprisonment was seen in Roman society as a shameful and humiliating experience, and it could well have been more than some would wish to be associated with. Whatever the reason, Timothy has stood firm, both out of personal loyalty and through faith in Christ. In this, he is modelling the very pattern of Christ-like service that Paul has commended to the Philippians. Presumably, Timothy's own interests do not lie in keeping company with a prisoner and sharing his apparent disgrace. But the call to put others first, and to offer oneself in loving service, keeps him by Paul's side and offers yet more opportunities to serve Christ—in this case by being Paul's link with his distant friends.

Verses 19–24 begin and end with hope and trust in the Lord. Christ is the one who is the final arbiter of human plans, but at the same time the one who guarantees the outcome of plans made in faith. So, as always, Paul's intention to send Timothy, like his eventual release from prison, are dependent on the will of their Lord. At the same time he is one to be trusted, and, whatever the outcome, it will be as always the outworking of God's gracious love and compassion.

A PRAYER

Lord, may I be given grace to stick with you and your people when the going gets difficult.

25 PHILIPPIANS 2:25–28

ENVOY

Before Timothy arrives, the present letter will be delivered, almost certainly by Epaphroditus, a member of the Philippian church. He had been sent bearing the Philippians' gift to Paul, and perhaps also to stay with Paul and offer support and help in his work from prison.

All we know of Epaphroditus comes from Philippians, here and at 4:18. His name, from the Greek goddess Aphrodite, suggests that he was a pagan convert, and Paul's comments show that the apostle thought highly of him. He is Paul's 'brother', a term for fellow Christians, which here may suggest a closer degree of familiarity and friendship. He is a co-worker, Paul's term for those who actively share in his task of evangelism. He may have worked with Paul during his time in Philippi, and it is quite likely that he has earned the title again during his time in Rome. Moreover, he is a 'fellow soldier', someone who has faced adversity in the cause of the gospel.

Paul's use of military metaphors is distasteful to some modern Christians, who consider images of violence to sit uneasily with the gospel of love and forgiveness. Paul's use of the image is quite deliberate. There are times when the Christian mission faces opposition, either by violence, social attitude or personal rejection. It can be a struggle, and calls for discipline and action. The action, however, is not physical violence, but prayer, fortitude and perseverance.

Epaphroditus has also been considered trustworthy by the Philippian church, in that it sent him as its envoy. Epaphroditus has been sent to minister to Paul, either by merely bringing the gift or, more likely, by staying on as a helper. All this he has presumably done satisfactorily, though in the course of his stay he became ill and indeed came close to death.

God, however, had mercy and Epaphroditus recovered (v. 27). There is no conflict between seeing his recovery as an act of mercy and saying that to die and go to be with Christ is gain. As in Paul's case, to remain on earth is an opportunity for further service, and will avoid premature pain for those who would grieve his loss. Not least among the grievers would be Paul himself, who has been spared 'grief upon grief'. The second, additional grief would be at the loss of his 'brother'. It is tempting to suppose that Christians should feel no grief at the death of someone they love; after all, the loved one has gone to be with Christ, and so is better off. This, though, fails to understand the immense sense of loss such a parting brings. Grief is the response not to another's death as such, but to the separation that death brings. It is a measure of love and respect. Those who are not mourned are not loved and not missed. Thus grief, far from being a measure of faith's lack, is a measure of love, which, after all, is more important even than faith (1 Corinthians 13:13).

Paul's already existing grief is also about loss—the loss of those companions who have left him, whose faith has fallen short or whose love has proved inadequate to their task. It is about those whose proclamation of the gospel is spiteful and done out of malice towards him. Paul may indeed have learnt to be satisfied with whatever he has (4:11, 13), but that does not mean that he is immune to normal human feelings. Betrayal or abandonment by his friends hurt deeply.

News of Epaphroditus' illness has travelled back to Philippi and caused worry, so Paul is now sending him back home so that the Philippians, and Paul himself, may be spared further worry. There is no hint that Paul was in any way dissatisfied by his help.

Travels

The present passage is often cited as evidence that the letter to the Philippians must have been written from Ephesus or Caesarea. Epaphroditus has travelled to Rome, and fallen ill, so someone has carried a letter back (there was no official postal service for non-governmental letters, so they had to be carried by helpful travellers). Then the Philippians must have sent some message expressing concern at their messenger's illness. In all, it is said, this is a lot of travelling for the long distance between Philippi and Rome. However, Philippi was on a major trade route, and journeys from there to Rome would be frequent, taking about 40 days. The whole process could have taken only a few months. If anything, the exchange of correspondence between Paul and the Philippians is evidence that travel in the Roman empire was more frequent and efficient than we tend to imagine.

A PRAYER

Father, help me to keep in touch, and be prayerful for, those distant friends whom I see rarely and am tempted to forget.

HONOURED SERVICE

When Epaphroditus returns, the Philippians should welcome him joyfully. Paul is not suggesting that their inclination is to do anything else, but he is leading up to reasons for joy which they may not have thought of. The first is that people like Epaphroditus deserve such a welcome. They should be honoured for the sacrifice they are willing to make in the Lord's service (v. 29). While Paul would be the first to agree that the only commendation that really counts is God's, he knows full well the value of human encouragement. Those who work hard and give their best, whether for God or anyone else, deserve recognition, and will do all the more for the encouragement they receive. Moreover, the church ought to pay credit where it is due.

Epaphroditus has represented his fellow Christians in Philippi. Far from Paul, they could do little to help him, apart from sending their gift. Their messenger has worked on their behalf, and to recognize his effort is to affirm their own care both for Paul and for the gospel of Christ. Indeed, his effort has nearly cost him his life (v. 30). He has not (as far as we know) been threatened with persecution, but his illness, contracted in the course of his Christian service, was no less a brush with the ultimate offering than would be a threatened martyrdom.

Conundrum

Then comes one of the most difficult verses of the letter (3:1). It isn't all that important theologically or spiritually, but in terms of simple understanding, it raises major problems. 'Finally,' says Paul, and then launches off into an apparently unrelated topic. What is going on?

It is pretty clear that Paul intends to draw to a close here, but a close of what? Many scholars suggest that he is about to close the letter, and argue that 4:4 originally followed on from 3:1 (or 3:1a) and that 3:2—4:3 are (part of) a separate letter which has been inserted at this point by a later editor, who combined parts of at least two Philippian letters in a way he thought would be useful to the wider church. Those who take this view tend to point to a similar, if less pronounced, disparity between 4:9, which looks like a final benediction, and 4:10, which begins an apparently belated thanks for the gift first mentioned in chapter 1.

As a result, a common scheme identifies three original letters, probably sent in the following order:

- 4:10–20: an initial thanks for the gift.

- 1:1—3:1 (perhaps with 4:4–9, 21–23): an appeal for unity and joy, with the return of Epaphroditus.

- 3:2—4:3: a later warning about false teaching.

The big problem with this sort of scheme (apart from the fact that there is no agreement about the details) is why anyone should disperse the parts of the letters so carefully within the whole (and why in that particular order) and yet leave such obvious joins. Therefore, interesting and ingenious though such suggestions are, it seems better to assume that the letter exists now in the same form in which Paul wrote it, and to look for reasons for the apparent breaks within it.

For our purposes, it makes sense to assume that Paul's 'finally' in 3:1 brings the opening section to a close, and reiterates his call for joy. Rejoice, for, in summary, joy is at the heart of Christian life and service.

The second part of the verse is also difficult. What 'same things' is Paul writing again? Two possible interpretations seem likely. It could mean that Paul is repeating his stress on joy. Joy is a safeguard to the Philippians because it is the response to God's saving and protecting strength—a common theme in the Old Testament. Or it could be that he is about to deal with a topic that they have heard from him many times (warnings about false versions of the gospel) but, for whatever reason, he feels it necessary to repeat the warnings in what follows.

Either way, the verse draws the section on joy and unity to a close, and begins a new topic.

A PRAYER

Father, help me to value those who give their time and talents
for the work of the church, and to praise you for them
without envy or suspicion.

27

RECONVERTERS

With startling abruptness, Paul now turns to a new topic, and one which he addresses vigorously. Why? There is no suggestion either that the Philippians had asked for advice on the matter or that Paul had heard there was any particular concern about it at Philippi. On the other hand, such a sudden change is quite plausible. We need to remember that Paul's letters, like most in his time, were dictated to a scribe. A sudden change of thought, or flash of inspiration or concern, can easily cause the letter to change tack. Again, there is no reason to assume that his letters were all dictated in one session. He could have returned to a topic after a break of hours or days, depending on his circumstances and the availability of a scribe. It is therefore easy to imagine Paul breaking off after 3:1, which concludes his first section, and returning later with a new manifestation of an old problem fresh in his mind from a recent conversation or train of thought.

'Beware of the dogs, the evil workers, the mutilators of the flesh!' he cries, and our new section is under way. He is railing against the activities of those Jewish Christians who had so often dogged his steps with a revisionist gospel. For Paul, seized by the overwhelming experience of Christ, membership of God's people, or salvation, depended fully and completely on putting one's faith in Christ. There were others, proudly aware of their Jewish heritage (but in fact no less so than Paul himself), who claimed with a convincing logic that Jewishness was a necessary qualification for salvation. After all, Jesus was a Jew. The Messiah had been promised to the Jews, who were God's chosen people, marked out by the rite of circumcision and called to obedience to the all-encompassing way of life of the *Torah*. Surely, then, since Christ is the fulfilment of the promises to the Jewish people, a response to the gospel must entail taking on board all the demands of Jewishness. So the argument ran, and it seems to have convinced quite a few Gentiles.

Paul is half in agreement. Jews who are Christians should by no means try to be anything else (1 Corinthians 7:18). However, in Christ, the Law had found its fulfilment: Christ was the living embodiment of all that the Law required, and faith in him was equivalent and more to keeping the *Torah*. Moreover, there were practical consequences. For men, conversion to Judaism was both painful and dangerous, in an age before hygiene and antibiotics. The idea of putting such an unnecessary barrier between converts and their salvation was probably a real point of Paul's objection to his fellow missionaries' demands.

Even more, it was an attack on his efficacy as an apostle. To have his new converts visited by a second group of Christians who confusingly explained that Paul's own gospel was deficient was both insulting and damaging to the spread of the faith.

The mutilators

All these considerations must be borne in mind in order to understand the violence of Paul's antipathy: they are dogs!

In the Israel of the Old Testament, and indeed in much of the ancient Mediterranean region, dogs were seen as scavengers, eaters of dead bodies and other unclean things. As creatures that could not differentiate between clean and unclean, and as unclean beasts themselves, they became in Jewish parlance a metaphor for the Gentiles, who also had no idea of God's laws of cleanliness (compare Mark 7:27–28). Paul's use of the term turns the tables on his opponents. In their zeal to bring Gentile converts under the Law, they themselves fail to recognize that God has made the Gentiles righteous in Christ and has already declared them clean. By raising obstacles to salvation, those who believe themselves to be carrying out the works of God's righteousness end up working evil. The cruellest pun, though, is 'mutilators': by trying to enforce circumcision (*peritome*) they merely put their trust in an outward and physical sign, much like the pagan priests who slashed their flesh in religious ecstasy. They mistake the outward for the inward, and so enforce mere mutilation (*katatome*).

In short, by enforcing redundant regulations, they cast doubt on the sufficiency of Christ's gift of salvation, and come to be that which they themselves most abhor—people who deny the works of God, Gentiles in all but name.

A PRAYER

Father, help me to put my trust fully in you, and let the signs of my faith be the changes you make in my life.

FLESH & SPIRIT

The most obvious demand of Judaism was circumcision. It marked membership of God's covenant people and, as such, became the central bone of contention between Paul and his opponents. In contrast to their assertion that belonging is defined by physical marks, Paul insists that the 'true circumcision' (a term which here means the people of God) are those who serve God by the Spirit and boast in Christ.

The Greek of verse 3 is better rendered, 'You... who serve by the Spirit' rather than NRSV's '...worship in the Spirit'. Those who are the true people of God (whether originally circumcised as Jews or not) are those whose service is enabled by the gift of the Spirit, whose coming depends on Christ. The Spirit is the one who fulfils the call for a circumcision of the heart, the true inner self, rather than merely the outward flesh (Deuteronomy 30:6; Jeremiah 4:4).

Moreover, the true circumcision, the true people of God, are now those who boast—who put their trust—in Christ rather than in outward signs. To rely on anything else is to demote the work of Jesus and to say that it is incomplete.

Putting faith in outward signs is putting confidence in 'the flesh'. The obvious contrast is between the physical sign of circumcision and the spiritual experience of the Spirit's enabling. Paul, though, uses 'flesh' in another and more subtle sense. For him it refers to unaided human nature and ability. The flesh is that part of humanity which is weak and prone to failure, selfish and self-serving. To put confidence in the flesh is to shift faith from what Christ has done, and what the Spirit equips the Christian to do, on to what one is able to do for oneself.

Paul the super-Jew

Paul knows this from his own experience, for the ironic fact is that he himself could claim to be much more successful in keeping God's *Torah* than those who now try to force it on his converts (v. 4). Paul is of the Jewish race (perhaps in contrast to some of his opponents, who may have been Gentile converts), circumcised in infancy on the correct day after birth and a member of the one tribe that remained loyal to Judah and the house of David. He was brought up in a Hebrew-speaking family (which is what 'a Hebrew of Hebrews' means in verse 5). Although most Jews outside of Palestine spoke and read the scriptures in Greek, some stuck with Hebrew, which seems to have remained a living everyday language until the second century AD, though most Palestinian Jews would have spoken mainly Aramaic. Paul, then, was born and brought up in the most strictly orthodox tradition (v. 5).

In adulthood, he went even further, becoming a Pharisee. Pharisees, for all the bad press they get in the Gospels, had an admirable agenda. Convinced that all of life should be lived to the glory of God, they tried to keep the same level of commitment and ritual purity in everyday life as was demanded of all Jews when they entered the temple to offer sacrifice. This, coupled with their conservative and nationalistic approach to scripture and tradition, made them widely respected and probably much more influential than their numbers would suggest (about 6,000 according to the Jewish historian, Josephus, who wrote towards the end of the first century).

I remember a well-known evangelist who threatened to withdraw from a parish mission unless the vicar stopped preaching that accepting Christ was also about giving up smoking, drinking and dancing (this was a long time ago!). These things may or may not be incompatible with serving Christ, but they are not things that detract in any way from salvation or the completeness of what Jesus has done.

Those who feel a need to point to the outward signs of belonging, be they circumcision and kosher food or confirmation and communion, are in danger of belittling the true signs of membership—faith in Christ, and the work of the Spirit. This is not to say that other things are not important. Christians who do not take part in the eucharist or declare their allegiance to Christ publicly are missing out. But they are not any less members of God's covenant people.

A PRAYER

Father, keep my eyes focused on what you offer in Christ
and my heart open to your Spirit's guidance.

29 PHILIPPIANS 3:6–9

BLAMELESS PHARISEE

Paul's old religious credentials were fiercely put into practice. 'Zeal' was seen as a commendable virtue—the active desire to put faith into action and to maintain the purity of the faith. One of the great heroes of zeal was Phinehas (Numbers 25:6–11), who killed an Israelite man and his Midianite wife for marrying outside of the covenant people. Phinehas was commended and became a prominent priest. Paul's own zeal took a similar turn, and so he persecuted the Church. There is a subtle dig at his opponents here: thinking that they are calling Gentile converts to true faith, they are in fact persecuting it by undermining the sufficiency of Christ's work.

When Paul became a Christian, he remained as zealous for his Lord as ever, but his understanding of zeal changed. Once, he had been prepared to make others suffer for their faith. Now he is content to do the suffering with Christ, and leave conflict to the verbal arena. This is a lesson the Church has often failed to learn: the spirit of Phinehas sadly lives on.

Even more virtuous in his opponents' terms was his keeping of *Torah*. It was blameless. This may be hard to imagine, and seems at first to conflict with other passages, such as Romans 7:7–11, where Paul recounts the impossibility of keeping the Law's demands. However, here in Philippians Paul is considering the matter more narrowly. The Law does not enable a true and full righteousness in the sense of being in a blameless relationship with God, for it cannot do away with the problem of sin. But in terms of simply keeping its rules (which at one time may have been Paul's chief concern), it is little different from keeping the Highway Code. Paul could say with all honesty that he kept the commandments and the ritual purities of Pharisaism. As it turned out, none of this was enough.

Smelly stuff!

Paul met Jesus on the Damascus road. He was turned around, or converted. From that new viewpoint, he came to see his former righteousness as nothing. Paul is not making a contrast between Christian religion (good) and Jewish religion (bad). The *Torah* he so assiduously kept was God's Law, and a good thing, but it was a means to an end (Galatians 3:24). Paul found that end in Christ (v. 9). The righteousness, the standing before God, that he so prided himself on turned out to be merely his own achievement—good as far as it went, obedient to God no doubt, but not all that was available. It was based on the same assumption as Christianity, that of God's grace to the undeserving, but it formed the foundation for an edifice of law-keeping which became a scramble to provide assurance of belonging to God, and in the end was simply placing confidence in the flesh (3:4). According to Psalm 106:31, the actions of Phinehas were counted to him as righteousness. Paul's own law-keeping, and that of the opponents he combats here, had the same sort of goal— to give self-confidence and assurance of his status in the covenant people. In Christ, Paul found a new standing with God, whose assurance was based firmly on the work of Jesus and enabled by the living presence of God, the Holy Spirit (v. 9). Compared with all that, his old attempts to stand before God were rubbish and worse (v. 8). The word *skybala*, variously translated as rubbish, garbage, dung and so on, means 'smelly refuse'. Think of the unidentifiable stuff that gathers at the bottom of the dustbin and is probably the remains of last Sunday's lunch!

More politely, it is all loss (vv. 7–8) in Paul's spiritual ledger. The gain side is all Christ. It is Christ's act of salvation, outlined in 2:6–11, that has set Paul in a right relationship with God (v. 9). This is a gain of such tremendous value that Paul has been content to lose everything he once prided himself on. This means primarily the religious endeavour that he is discussing directly, but it is worth con-sidering some of the other things his new Christian life lost him. His status as a Pharisee, respected for his deep religion; his career in Jerusalem; friends and colleagues, possibly family, have all been thrown into the debit column, and still do not make a nett loss. Knowing Christ out-weighs all this and more. To know Christ and be placed in a righteous standing with God requires only one thing—faith. Verse 9 stresses that role of faith. Faith enables Paul to be 'found in Christ' and faith counts for righteousness before God.

A PRAYER

Lord, keep me aware of the temptation to base my standing with you on my observances, and not on your grace.

KNOWING CHRIST

Paul's great gain, compared to which all other achievements and measures of religious status are nothing, is knowing Christ (3:8). Knowledge (*gnosis*) was something of a religious buzz word at the time. There were many systems of esoteric teaching, both religious and philosophical, which claimed to give privileged knowledge of ultimate truth. Christianized versions of this 'gnostic' outlook would, in the next couple of centuries, pose one of the greatest threats to orthodox Christianity, and many of their practitioners would quote Paul in their own support. In fact, it is likely that some of Paul's own converts had been influenced by gnostic ideas, demanding spiritual 'wisdom' which would place them in a religious élite (see 1 Corinthians 2). Here in verse 10, Paul's knowledge of Christ has nothing to do with secret doctrines, or even public ones. The tradition that lies behind his use of the idea of knowledge is a very different one, drawn from the Old Testament and later Jewish tradition.

There, it refers to the close relationship between God and his people, marked by mutual obligation and love. Just as Paul's relationship with God leads him to refer to 'his' God (1:3), so it calls him to an ever-deepening awareness of Christ. For Paul, Christ was not a concept, or a distant figure, but someone to be known through prayer and reflection, someone to be spoken to, and someone who replied (2 Corinthians 12:8–9). The 'personal relationship with Jesus' so beloved of evangelical preachers would not have been a mystifying term for Paul.

In 3:9 Paul could speak of his existing knowledge of Christ, which far outweighs anything he previously had, but it is not yet complete, nor, therefore, fully satisfying. There is more to be had, a deeper love to be shared, and that is something to be pursued with might and main. Later Christian mystics would come to speak of the pursuit of Christ's love in frankly sexual terms, striving for an analogy that expressed the depth of their relationship. Paul stops short of that, yet it is hard to avoid the impression that he is describing something deeply personal and passionate. It is worth noting that although he frequently refers to himself as the slave/servant of Christ, 3:8 is the only reference in this personal passage to 'my Lord'.

The path to true love

To know Christ is, as Paul has laid out in 2:6–11, to have the mind of Christ and to be set on the path to resurrection. It involves an encounter with the power of God over death itself, the power that raised Jesus from the dead (v. 10). The phrase 'the power of his resurrection' could mean the power that flows from Jesus' resurrection, which is his as risen Lord. This is unlikely, though, since for Paul the resurrection is always an act of God's power—something that works on Jesus rather than flowing from him. That the resurrection is the work of God reminds us that salvation is from start to finish the work of God—Father, Son and Holy Spirit—and not, as some simplistic explanations come close to saying, a work of Jesus against the wrath of his vengeful Father.

The power of the resurrection is not a future promise but a present reality, the empowering by God's Spirit which makes Christian life possible. It is a necessary empowering, because knowing Christ is also intimately tied up with sharing in his sufferings. This is a point that Paul has already made (1:29), but it needs to be reiterated, both to encourage the Philippians in their own troubles and to stress once again that Paul's present situation is an integral part of his path of discipleship.

This is a path that Paul gladly walks (indeed, runs) to reach the final resurrection. The 'somehow' of verse 11 does not indicate uncertainty about resurrection so much as willingness to walk towards it through whatever circumstances may be necessary. One necessary element is 'being conformed to his death' (v. 10). Paul no doubt has in mind the possibility of dying for Christ, as Christ died for him, but the thought is wider than that. 'Being conformed' is a present participle in Greek, with the connotation of continuous action. Paul, like all Christians, must put to death his old self (see Colossians 3:5, and comments on pp. 146–147) in order to live the life of the Spirit. To live to Christ is to die to self.

A PRAYER

Lord, give me grace to live for you, and to put behind me
all that hinders my walking your path.

31 PHILIPPIANS 3:12–14

RUNNING *the* RACE

At one time, Paul may have thought that he had all he needed for spiritual completeness (3:6) but now he knows that that is far from true. He knows Christ and seeks to serve him, but there is still more to be known, more service to be carried out, and the resurrection life to be reached. It may seem obvious to modern readers that Paul was far from perfect, and indeed that all Christians still have a long way to go. Paul could not be sure that his readers would take it that way. At Corinth, he had found that some of his converts considered themselves already to be full partakers of the resurrection, and to have achieved a sort of spiritual perfection (1 Corinthians 4:8). So both the danger of misunderstanding, as well as personal humility and honesty, make him stress that he still has far to go.

Therefore, he presses on (v. 12) and strains towards the goal (v. 13) like an athlete striving for the finishing line. For Paul, there is no contradiction between this language of strenuous effort and his gospel of salvation as God's free gift. Some of his converts, as well as some of his opponents, seem to have assumed that the idea of being saved by faith led to a *laissez faire* attitude in which one's efforts were pointless at best, and at worst anything could go. Nothing could be further from the truth. For one thing, there is the possibility that God's gift might be rejected. Paul, in another use of sporting analogy, considers the possibility that he might be disqualified from the race (1 Corinthians 9:27). After all, a gift that is never used might as well never have been given.

Some Christians find this a very disturbing notion. After all, if salvation in the end does depend on our running the race, how does justification by faith differ from salvation by works? If 'once saved, always saved' is not a valid Christian motto, how can we be sure of our salvation? Posing the question this way fails to understand the nature of salvation. It is not about a legal status, much less a legal fiction which somehow counts sinners as being good when they are really bad. It is about relationship with God. Faith accepts the knowledge of Christ (as Paul puts it here) and begins a walk of friendship and obedience to God. As long as the relationship continues, salvation is assured, and it is God's free gift. Once the relationship is broken off, and fails any longer to have an effect on the believer's life, the relationship becomes at best questionable.

Being good

Hence, Paul pushes on towards the completeness of heaven. He does so not in a spirit of fear, but in love and a desire for a deeper knowledge and an all-consuming relationship with Christ. The fixed point in his life is the awareness that he has been seized by Christ (v. 12) and so wants to make real in his own life the new status he has been given by God and which will be brought to completion on the day of the Lord.

This is the nub of Christian living. Most non-Christians today (and sadly, some Christians) seem to think that the main idea about Christianity is that if you are good enough, one day God will let you into heaven. It is in fact the reverse. Having been granted heaven, we respond by attempting (with the Holy Spirit's help) to be worthy of it. After all, it is our goal and our eternal residence.

Paul, like all Christians, has been called 'heavenward' (v. 14). The Greek is more accurately rendered as 'upward call of God' but the meaning is clear. God's call encompasses all of life, as a call to discipleship and service, but its ultimate destination is heaven.

It is unfashionable to put too much emphasis on heaven. We live in an age and a society which as a whole has nothing to look forward to beyond death. Living in an affluent present, we deny the one certainty of life and hide it from sight as much as possible. Professionals deal with death—medical staff, funeral directors, clergy. Christians are tempted to join in the mass delusion that death either does not exist or does not matter. So we try to justify our faith in terms of the here and now: it makes life better, gives us purpose and strength, and so on. All this is true, but our faith has purpose and direction because ultimately it looks beyond death itself to the life of eternity.

Few people could live life more fiercely and purposefully than Paul. Yet he did so because he knew that, in the end, his life was a preparation for eternity.

A PRAYER

Lord Jesus, you have taken hold of me and made me yours.
May I make you mine in thought and deed.

SHARED OUTLOOK

Paul has told his own story and now calls on the Philippians to apply it themselves, in much the same way as he asked them to apply the story of Jesus. In each case, the point is to have a certain mindset, a way of looking at life. In the Greek, verse 15 begins with 'therefore'—'Because of what I have recounted,' says Paul, 'let us think this way.' Presumably he expects his friends to learn from the whole story. As Paul was willing to cast aside the religious advantages that he once saw in Judaism, so the Philippians are to put away anything they may value more than Christ, or which may hinder them from following their Lord wholeheartedly. Paul has discovered the cross to be the pattern for Christian living, and his Philippian friends must join with him in accepting a share of suffering for Christ's sake as part of the path to knowing Christ fully. Like him, they need to grow in their knowledge of the risen Lord, as they move towards the full knowledge that the life of heaven will bring.

Together, Paul and the Philippian Christians must press on towards the life of heaven. Paul is not issuing mere instructions, but an invitation to share with him in the journey of exploration into the knowledge of Christ. It is a journey with dangers and difficulties, like any exploration, but it is a shared journey. The Church travels together, sharing experiences and offering mutual support. This is the thrust of verse 15's call to those who are 'mature', a term that Paul seems to apply to all the Philippians as well as to himself. There is certainly no suggestion that the Philippian church could be divided into some for whom Paul's advice applies, being mature, and others who are somehow unready for it. Moreover, by aligning himself with all the Philippians, Paul once again stresses the need for (and here the presumption of) unity.

Christian maturity

'Mature' translates the same word which, in its verb form in 3:12, the NRSV paraphrases as 'reaching the goal', and which more literally means 'complete' or 'perfect'. Paul has not reached perfection, but he and his friends have reached a degree of completeness in their approach to the faith. True perfection lies in the heavenly goal, but here and now it is possible to possess a well-rounded integrity which, in another meaning of the Greek word (*teleios*), can be described as maturity.

Mature Christians are those who 'hold fast to what they have attained' (v. 16), though precisely what they have attained is a matter of some debate. In Romans 12:3 Paul exhorts his readers not to have too high an opinion of themselves, but to have a careful sense of their own faith, as God has given it to them. If this is the sort of idea behind Paul's words here in verse 16, he is saying that a mature Christian is one who knows how far and well he or she has progressed in the race of faith, and is determined not to slide back but to maintain and improve their walk with God. That Paul speaks here of the Christian's own attainment, and in Romans of God's gift, is no contradiction, for as we have already seen, the Christian journey is one in which God's grace and human effort go hand in hand.

Tolerant friendship

In the midst of his appeal for a shared outlook, Paul drops in a sort of throwaway line which seems rather out of place to those more used to his argumentative style. If anyone happens to disagree with him, fair enough, but God will hopefully show them so, should they need to change their minds (v. 15b). At least, that seems to be the gist of what he means.

As with his earlier attitude to those who preach the gospel out of rivalry (1:18; see comments on pp. 34–35), Paul is presumably not envisaging any disagreement on fundamental issues, but on matters which are open to varied interpretation. His real point is to stress the friendship in which he writes and the underlying unity that he assumes is present between himself and the Philippians, and, by implication, among them. In effect, he is calling for them to imitate him in another area: 'If I, your founding apostle, can write as a tolerant friend, surely you can behave the same way among yourselves!' So he paves the way for his explicit call for unity in 4:2. First, though, he will make one more digresssion about differences that really do matter.

A PRAYER

Father, teach me to know where I am in my walk with you, and to press on to know you more fully, as you meet me in Jesus Christ.

33   PHILIPPIANS 3:17–19

GOOD EXAMPLES

Paul's own example is not the only one that is worth watching and emulating. Others live a similar life in Christ, and they too are a worthy example for their fellow Christians. In our individualistic age, it seems presumptuous to suggest that one person's experience and lifestyle should be more worthy of following than another's. We are used to the idea that everyone finds their own way of living out their faith, and that all experiences are equally valid (whatever that popular term may mean). Paul, though, has been arguing all along that the prime example for Christians is Christ himself. If others can be seen to fit into Christ's pattern, then they too should be copied, for ultimately the only true human existence is that which is formed after Christ, the blueprint of the new humanity that God is bringing into being.

For that matter, while we may flatter ourselves that we make up our own minds and find our own path, in reality we are influenced by many things, not least the lives and outlook of those around us. Paul is well aware of that fact, and in giving himself and his fellow workers (note the 'us' in v. 17) as examples, he recognizes that there are those who most certainly should not be followed.

Bad examples

Verses 18–19 are a conundrum. Who are these poor examples of Christianity? One view is that they are, once again, the Judaizing Christians who want Paul's converts to take on board a full-blown Judaism. By putting their faith in the observance of *Torah*, they deny the all-embracing sufficiency of the cross, and by their zealous observance of dietary restrictions, they end up paying more attention to what goes into their stomachs than what comes out of their lives (v. 19). They are so set on material manifestations of faith that they forget the heavenly goal to which that faith points.

On the other hand, Paul has already dealt with the Judaizers in verses 2–11, and it seems strange that he should return to the topic. Moreover, he never identifies the Jewish Law with idolatry, so perhaps another sort of Christian is in view. It is clear that these 'enemies of the cross' (v. 18) are indeed Christians, or at least have been, for their lifestyle, denoted by 'walk' (NRSV 'live'), causes Paul real grief, as opposition from pagans does not. It is therefore likely that he has in mind Christians who have forgotten the call to holy living and indulge their appetites for food and sex (indicated by 'shame' in v. 19). There was a group of such believers in Corinth, who, believing themselves to be spiritually perfect and accepting half of Paul's teaching that they were put right with God through faith alone, came to the conclusion that their earthly behaviour was of no consequence. Since what matters is one's spiritual life, they argued, the physical could be indulged with impunity. If one is hungry, one eats; if one is lustful, one seeks out sex, from whatever source (1 Corinthians 6:12–20). As a result, their lifestyle became, in effect, idolatrous. The main topic that ruled their lives was actually their appetites, and Christianity was merely a means of rationalizing away what they might otherwise see as wrong.

For Paul, this was a disastrous attitude. Faith indeed puts us right with God, but faith that does not affect our lifestyle and our way of thinking is, as he has argued all through Philippians, a pointless exercise. Indeed, it is hard to say how such faith exists at all. True faith is the outworking of a relationship with God, not a magic formula to wash away conscience or responsibility.

To sum up, the pattern for Christian living is the self-sacrificing pattern of Christ himself. Some Christians, such as Paul and his helpers, are themselves models of the lifestyle and mindset that he wants the Philippians to have. But they must not take that on trust. They must observe (v. 17) and discern by comparison with the ultimate example of Jesus, before following any earthly teacher. Throughout history, and all too often in our own age, that discernment has been missing. Political leaders, from Stalin to Pol Pot, and gurus of cults which have resorted to mass murder and mass suicide all bear witness to the dangers of misplaced faith. One might, with little exaggeration, say that we have little choice but to pattern our lives on something. We have great choice in what that something is, and the best example that has been found is Jesus Christ.

A PRAYER

Lord, may I be an example worthy for others to follow,
because I follow yours.

34 PHILIPPIANS 3:20–21

OUTPOST *of* EMPIRE

In contrast with those whose faith is concerned only with the appetites of this world, true Christians know that their homeland lies elsewhere. When the author of 1 Peter wrote his letter to the churches of Asia Minor, he addressed them as the *diaspora* or 'dispersion', a term for Jews living outside of Judea. Christians, he was saying, are those who live in a strange land, looking always to the homeland of heaven for which they are destined. Paul uses a similar idea in verse 20, where he reminds the Philippians that their citizenship is in heaven. The word translated 'citizenship', or more often by the rare (in modern usage) 'common-wealth', is *politeuma*, and it doesn't actually mean quite the same thing as citizenship, although it includes that idea. It means something like the rule, or government, which makes us what we are, even though that rule is not close at hand. In that sense, it would be well understood by the citizens of the Roman colony of Iulia Augusta Philippensis. Though situated in Macedon, it was ruled by the laws of Rome; its citizens were Roman citizens, officially belonging to an Italian tribe, and were exempt from many imperial taxes. The laws of distant Italy made Philippi what it was. Christians are made what they are by the rule of heaven; they are part of the kingdom of God, and answerable first and foremost to him.

It is important to recognize that Paul does not make the mistake of confusing the Church with the kingdom of God. The rule that governs Christians is that of heaven, not of the Church, though at times the Church has forgotten that fact and claimed an authority it does not possess. Nor does Paul suggest that the Church is actually a present manifestation of the life of heaven. That is its goal and its governing idea, but as a colony of heaven the Church also partakes of the region where it exists. Just as the Roman citizens of Philippi shared Greek culture and ideas as well as Roman ones, so the Church is marked by its existence in a fallen world and it will always share the failings of a sinful world.

The most startling and subversive element of Paul's analogy is simply the relocation of ultimate loyalty from the earthly emperor to the heavenly king. It is Christ who is the Saviour of the Church (v. 20) and it is to him that the Church looks for its rule and its self-definition. In a world where 'saviour' was a title of the absolute ruler of Rome, that claim would be bound to bring trouble. It is likely that it had already caused problems for the Philippians. In years to come, it would be the touchstone by which Christians were tested, and which would lead many to martyrdom. The claims of Christ outweigh all earthly loyalties.

If the Church must beware of claiming heavenly perfection for itself, it must also be careful not to identify too fully with any systems of the present world. Today, there are all too many instances of political and social views being adopted wholesale by Christians, from the 'Christian democracy' of Europe to the 'religious right' of the USA. No matter how dear any cause or principle may be, it should always be subjected to the rule of Christ, in comparison with which all things in this world are imperfect and temporary.

Coming king

The day of the Lord to which Christians look, and which is their goal and their purpose, is the coming to reign of the one who now rules in heaven, Jesus Christ. That coming marks the point at which his rule is made final and complete, by the transformation of his people into his own likeness. The power which is his by right and by deed (2:11) will bring about his final triumph. In other words, it is at the resurrection that Christians can expect finally to become the people they are destined to be. Those who become bogged down in merely earthly endeavours, whatever spiritual excuses they may make for them, are ultimately on the path that leads nowhere (3:19).

Verse 21 gives a rare glimpse of Paul's understanding of resurrection: it is a transformation of that which already exists. Paul is never concerned with the precise mechanism of resurrection, but here (and see 1 Corinthians 15:51–52) we see that his basic supposition is the changing of the present body in some way. Paul envisages some sort of real continuity between the present and the resurrection body, but where that continuity is to be found remains uncertain. The point Paul is making is the contrast between those who are foolishly satisfied with whatever they have in this life and those who live in expectancy of something better.

A PRAYER

Lord, let me live my life as one fired by the hope of salvation and trying to reflect here the light of what is to come.

35   PHILIPPIANS 4:1–3a

BELOVED FRIENDS

Paul rounds off his long exhortation to his Philippian friends with a final appeal to stand firm against the pressures that may threaten their faith. They are to seek to have the same outlook as Christ, patterning their lives on him and on Paul and his fellow workers. They should look to each other's needs and keep their eyes fixed on the goal of heaven, in whose light they are to live in the here and now.

Verse 1 is marked by no less than four expressions of affection. The Philippian Christians are Paul's brothers and sisters in Christ, but moreover, they are his joy and crown; that is, they are both a delight to him now and they will be his vindication at the last judgment. Like the crown of the winner in an athletic event, the existence of his churches is proof that he has carried out the task entrusted to him by his Lord (see also 1 Thessalonians 2:19 and, for a similar thought, 2 Corinthians 3:1–3). Their close support and deep love for him makes him in turn long for their presence.

There is no doubt that Paul's sincere expression of affection paves the way for a delicate issue, as he addresses by name two people who are falling short of having the mind of Christ.

Open quarrel

We know almost nothing about Euodia and Syntyche. They are among Paul's 'co-workers' and are described (v. 3) as fellow fighters, a gladiatorial term, which continues the athletic imagery that Paul has used to good effect so far. Together with Clement (of whom we know nothing more than is mentioned here), they have done good work for the spread of the gospel, and there is no doubt about the depth and sincerity of their faith and the certainty of their salvation: their names are in the book of life. The whole team of Paul's Philippian fellow workers is known to the church, and therefore need not be named, but the real commendation comes from God. Named or not, those who serve God faithfully are never forgotten by him.

Euodia and Syntyche are probably among the leadership of the church, and they have fallen out for some reason. It has been suggested that each was the leader of a rival faction, but nothing Paul has written so far suggests that the church was seriously divided. It may be that each is representative of a particular point of view which has the potential to divide the church, or it may simply be a personal quarrel that has gone public. This seems the most likely explanation. The two women, both friends of Paul, are an obvious example of the disunity that he has been warning against. So they should share the same mind (v. 2) in the Lord; that is, they should seek to be the sort of example of the common outlook based on Christ which Paul says that he and his co-workers (normally) are (3:17).

Mediator

As Christ himself is the go-between between humanity and God, both in his nature as incarnate God and in his work as redeemer, so Christians are called to proclaim that offer of reconciliation and to put it into practice as peacemakers. So Paul calls on one of his fellow workers to help to reconcile Euodia and Syntyche (v. 3a). We know nothing at all about this 'true yoke-fellow', but that has not prevented speculation. Some have suggested that it is Clement, or Luke, who may have travelled to Philippi from Rome. Others have suggested that 'yoke-fellow' (*syzygos*) is the man's name (so the NEB and the NRSV footnote) and others that it is Paul's wife, since the term was sometimes used in Jewish literature to describe a spouse. This last suggestion is most unlikely, since Paul was, at least a few years earlier when he wrote 1 Corinthians, unmarried (1 Corinthians 7:8).

The identity doesn't matter, though. What is important is the reminder that differences within the Christian community can be helped by sensitive and loving intervention. It is worth saying that disagreement and even heated debate are in themselves no sin; what is a problem is the hardening of disagreement into enmity.

Was Paul's appeal successful? We don't know, but if it was accepted, the Philippians would see a living example not only of disunity, but of the uniting mind of Christ.

A PRAYER

Father, may I have the sensitivity and the courage
to be an agent of reconciliation.

CONTINUAL REJOICING

Paul's fellow workers (and by implication all the Philippians) are named in the 'book of life'. That is, they are known to God, and belong to him, enrolled on his membership list. This image, drawn from the Old Testament (Exodus 32:32–33; Psalm 69:28), seems to have been popular in the primitive church (it occurs seven times in Revelation—see Revelation 3:5; 13:8 and so on). Salvation is assured, not because the Philippians, or Paul, have worked hard in the cause of the gospel, but because God has marked them as his own.

Therefore, rejoice (v. 4)! Rejoice always, and then rejoice again! Paul's double call to joy is not a bland 'keep on smiling'; it is a reminder that in the Lord, in that deep-seated relationship with Christ which is the bedrock of Christian living, there is a certainty of love and hope that will not allow despair or disillusionment. No matter what comes in this life (like Paul's doubts over his earthly fate), ultimate reality is the eternal life found in Jesus Christ, whose presence is close at hand. With this assertion, Paul begins a passage (vv. 4–6) that acts as a bridge between the body of the letter and his concluding comments.

Commentators debate the precise meaning of 'The Lord is near' in verse 5. Does it mean that he is about to return in judgment and glory? Does it mean he is always at hand to strengthen and guide? Really, it doesn't matter. He is indeed close at hand, and since that is so, his nearness in time is always assured. He is close enough to break into the world with his transforming power, whether in the lives of individuals or to bring final salvation to the world as a whole. The one who is near is the one who is coming, whose day of salvation is assured, and in the light of that day Christians live their lives. So at the close of the letter, Paul returns to the assurance of salvation for which our lives here and now are a preparation (see 1:6, 10).

Lives that are lived in the knowledge of God's salvation, in the awareness of the presence of Christ, will carry the mark of that knowledge: they will show the imprint of the mind of Christ. So, says Paul in verse 5, let your gentleness be apparent to all. Rather than the quarrelsomeness which has marred the Philippian church, there must be a calm even-handedness which betokens the respect that Christians must have for one another and for those beyond their community. Joy displays itself in an attitude to others of tolerance and understanding. All these ideas are present in the word (*epieikes*) that Paul uses here.

Such a gentleness is the antithesis of worry—and it springs from a prayerful reliance on God, which faces life secure in the knowledge that he is in charge.

Prayer life

So, says Paul, instead of worry, concentrate on prayer (v. 6). Let God know what troubles you and what your needs are. Paul is surely here reflecting Jesus' own teaching on anxiety (Matthew 6:25–34). Those who trust God need not fear.

Considering Paul's own situation, it is hardly likely that he is simplistically suggesting that every material need or want will be met by prayer. A better way of looking at it is to see prayer as handing our own concerns over to God, to do with as he will, in the certain faith that whatever he does with them will ultimately be for the best. On the other hand, prayer should not be over-mysticized. A lot of modern teaching on prayer suggests that the deepest, most satisfying prayer is that which moves 'beyond' mere supplication into the realms of meditation and contemplation of God. This may well be true, but there is something comforting about the simple fact that for Paul, as indeed for Jesus, asking for things is a major, perhaps even the main, part of prayer.

God is to be approached as a loving parent, eager to hear what we want but always tempering his reply with what he knows to be best. If asking for things is the easiest and most simple form of prayer, it is also the one that stresses God's accessibility. He is always there for us, always willing to listen and to respond.

For that very reason, prayer always contains an element of thanksgiving—thanksgiving for what we receive in answer to prayer, and also for the relationship in which the Christian now stands with God because of Jesus' incarnation, death and resurrection.

A PRAYER

Father, let our requests be great, to match the abundance of your love.

PEACE *of Mind*

The end result of prayer is peace (v. 7). The main thought here is surely of peace of mind. The believer who has handed his or her fears and worries over to God, trusting him to make the best of them, will then be at peace. Following the teaching of Jesus (Matthew 6:25–34), Paul sees anxiety as a bad thing (compare 1 Corinthians 7:32). It prevents wholehearted service to God and denotes a lack of trust in him.

Paul and Jesus were not the only ones of their day to see anxiety as harmful. Stoic teachers also aimed to promote inner peace and tranquillity, through the idea that fate was unalterable and should be accepted come what may. For Christians, however, peace is found in knowing that come what may, God is in charge, and works for the good of his loved ones (Romans 8:28).

Peace is much more than inner calm. For Paul, writing as a Jew, it carries the overtones of the Hebrew word *shalom*, which means not only tranquillity and the absence of conflict, but also healing, wholeness and well-being. The peace that God brings is a whole-person peace, a part of the remaking of human nature, indeed of all creation, which is the goal of salvation (Romans 8:19–23). Those who trust God are freed from anxiety and begin to find a personal wholeness which is the first instalment of God's new creation.

This explains why such peace will keep ('stand guard over', or 'keep watch over') their hearts and minds (or 'thoughts') in Christ Jesus. The peace that Jesus brings is the foundation of the Christian's attitude to others, both within and outside the Church.

Whatever is good

The mention of thoughts leads Paul to flesh out the sort of thing he has in mind. In verse 8 he continues with a list of six virtues: whatever represents these is the stuff of Christian thought. The most notable thing about Paul's choice of words is that none of them would be out of place in a piece of pagan advice on right living. These are universally recognized virtues, and there is nothing specifically Christian about them.

At first this may seem a strange contrast with Paul's previous assertions that the mind of Christ and the outlook of the world are opposed to each other (see, for instance, 1:27–30; 3:19–20). The difference, however, is not in the desire to pursue what is good, but in the understanding of what 'good' precisely means. This leads to two conclusions.

Firstly, that Paul can use such terms at all suggests that there is a considerable overlap between Christian and non-Christian understandings of virtue. Christianity does not speak a language that is totally foreign to the world. Truthfulness, justice and purity mean much the same to everyone. This, after all, is what ought to be expected if God is the creator of the world. Christians believe the world to be fallen and in need of salvation, but to suggest that there is nothing good in it at all is to deny God any part in his creation. So in Christ we see God coming into the world in terms that already make sense to the world, and the Christian gospel speaks in terms that the world already values.

Secondly, in verse 9 Paul once again holds up his own example. If everyone can agree that commendable behaviour is good, what exactly is commendable from a Christian position? Precisely the kind of thing that has been seen in Paul and his helpers (3:17).

To put it another way, the gospel says, do you seek what is true, honourable, just and so on? Then look at Jesus Christ, and see truth, honour and justice made flesh. Do you want to know what is right? Then look at what God presents as the definitive example of righteousness.

Practice makes perfect

Once again, we see that Paul does not regard Christian living as something that happens automatically. It has to be learnt and put into practice. Therefore, he exhorts the Philippians to set their minds on desirable things—to practise the mind of Christ—or, as we have seen earlier, to co-operate with the Holy Spirit in bringing the mind of Christ into being in their lives.

A PRAYER

*Father, help me to keep in mind and to put into practice the things
I know to be true and desirable.*

Prayer
Peaceful Thoughts
Practice

95

THOUGHTS *of* VIRTUE

As Paul dictated his list of ways in which the Christian should think, his choice of virtues was probably not significant, save in one way. He does *not* mention in so many words the classic trio of 'goodness, truth and beauty', perhaps because that was so well-known as a goal of pagan ethics that Paul avoids it in order to distance himself from a purely pagan way of thinking.

The first virtue is 'whatever is true' (*alethe*), which can mean simply 'upright and honest', or even 'real' as opposed to 'false'. In those senses, it will refer to how a Christian should behave, and to the call to hold fast to the truth of the gospel. However, it has other implications which we sometimes miss.

People of all persuasions tend to feel threatened when their assumptions are challenged, and this can be particularly true of religious beliefs. So there are many Christians who, for instance, reject the findings of science about the age of the universe, the processes of evolution and so on, because these findings threaten the way they look at the Bible and their concept of God. Others in the Western world try to deny the decline in numbers attending church or believing in God, because it suggests that people are able to live without faith and makes Christians feel outnumbered and sidelined. Yet if we are called to hold to what is true, then this must also include unpalatable truths.

Christians need not fear truth. A faith that faces facts is more robust and appealing than one which expects its followers to suspend all critical faculties. After all, churchgoing will continue to decline until someone asks why and begins to look for a new way to proclaim the gospel in today's terms. Pretending it isn't happening hardly does justice to God or to the needs of our neighbours.

'Honourable' (*semna*) means what is morally good—and is defined for Christians by the whole body of Christian teaching. 'Just' (*dikaia*) is one of a group of related words that Paul usually reserves for talking about the believer's relationship to God, and is usually translated as 'righteous'. Here, though, it has its more secular meaning of 'just and fair'. Those who are in a right relationship with their creator and saviour will value all right relationships, including those in law and society. Thus, being justified (the same word-group) by faith in Christ should lead naturally to a demand for justice in the world.

'Pure' (*hagna*) probably refers to acting out of pure and unmixed motives (at least as far as is possible!).

Things of beauty

'Whatever is pleasing' or 'lovely' (*prosphile*) is a term that is not found in other lists of virtues from Paul's time. It points not so much to moral qualities as aesthetic ones—what is attractive and beautiful. There is a strand in Christianity that has been suspicious of beauty, feeling that it leads either to idolatry or vanity. But to give glory to God for the beauty of his creation and to give free rein to human creativity in his praise has more commonly, and rightly, been seen as a proper response to his love and abundance. What is pleasing goes together with 'whatever is commendable' (*euphema*), which tends to mean what is fair-sounding, perhaps of speech (it gives us the term 'euphemism', which means making something sound better than it might). Together, these terms stress that there is not only a quality of uprightness and justice in Christian thinking, but also a search for what is beautiful and uplifting.

Paul draws his list to a close with a summary: in short, concentrate on things of 'excellence' (*arete*) and which are 'worthy of praise' (*epainos*). The former word originally meant courage and warlike virtues, but in Paul's time had come simply to mean whatever was most valuable in a person. The two words are thus virtually synonyms. Those with the mind of Christ will be thinking on the best and most desirable things.

It doesn't end with thought, though. These things must fuel Christian actions, so Paul ends with a logical consequence (v. 9). As you are meant to think, so act, in the way you have seen me acting. Let the mind of Christ govern your life and works.

A PRAYER

Lord, let me set my mind on what is good and wonderful,
that I may do good and wonderful things for you.

GRUDGING THANKS?

Paul finally turns to the subject of the Philippians' gift to him, and modern readers might well mutter, 'About time!' Paul is in fact treading a narrow line between friendship and obligation—one which, if he is not careful, could threaten his role as an apostle and missionary.

In Paul's day, those who were powerful or wealthy would give favour to their protégés, who in turn would have an obligation of service or deference to their patron. This system of patronage extended into the political, financial, commercial and social world. By accepting a gift, Paul could be seen as becoming indebted to the Philippians, who would then be in the position of patronage over him. As one who saw his apostolic calling as allowing the patronage of Christ alone, this could threaten Paul's view of his apostolic authority and put a check on his ability to act only as he perceived the Holy Spirit to be leading him.

The Philippians almost certainly did not intend their gift to be taken that way, nor did Paul suppose that to be their motive. It did raise the question, however, of the proper response. Since gratitude was the sign of being under patronage, a different approach was called for. Paul was not the only one to see the difficulty. Other letters from the same period seem to show that help given between friends was not responded to in the same effusively grateful way as the help of a patron.

On the other hand, Paul certainly needs to respond, and he does so as an equal partner in a shared enterprise. He rejoices over their gift (v. 10) but 'in the Lord'. It is Christ, then, who gets the praise for the Philippians' helpfulness. This helpfulness has just now come back into full flower. Their concern for him has not been dead, but merely lacking in an opportunity to show itself. Whatever the reason, they have now seized the opportunity to help him once again.

Paul rejoices in the Lord because it is the shared relationship with Jesus that defines the nature of their help. They are not extending patronage to a prospective protégé, nor are they offering charity to a mendicant. They are doing their part in the shared enterprise of spreading the gospel. As fellow Christians and fellow workers, they do their fair share of missionary work by supporting Paul.

This is a point that a good many churches today could do well to remember. We give to the church, to missionary organizations and other charities not because it shows how good we are, or because it is a sort of necessary evil of church life and finances, but because it is a part of the shared work of the church's mission.

Deep faith

In verses 11–13 Paul goes on to explain that it is this aspect of their gift which is most important. He himself knows how to cope with both need and plenty. This is not because he has developed the iron-willed self-sufficiency of a good Stoic (the philosophers who have given their name to that very attitude) but because he has come to know and trust Jesus Christ, who gives him the ability to cope with whatever circumstances life presents.

'I can do all things through him who strengthens me,' writes Paul (v. 13). This is often quoted out of its context. Paul does not mean that he can leap tall buildings in a single mighty bound, or even produce miracles to order. He means that Jesus has given him the faith to trust, and thus to cope, in extremes. He could face death, privation and hardship because he had learnt through experience that Jesus would see him through. That kind of trust was the result of a long period of faith, prayer and service. It was something Paul had learnt (v. 11), often at considerable cost (see 2 Corinthians 1:8–11).

We are sometimes misled into thinking that faith exists in a sort of vacuum, self-sustaining and there to be called upon when needed. Nothing could be further from the truth. It is something that is learnt through experience, strengthened through use, and honed through prayer. It is the ability, quite simply, to trust God. Trust only exists when it is put to use, and to expect to face life's great challenges with a faith that has rarely seen the light of day is foolish. Just as Paul's faith grew through experience, so must ours.

A PRAYER

*Lord, help me to trust you in small things, so that in
great difficulties I may still keep sight of you.*

The GOSPEL plc

Once he has made it clear that there is no question of mistaking their help for patronage, Paul acknowledges the personal kindness that lies behind the Philippians' gift.

We do not know what made Paul allow the Philippians such a privileged role in his ministry, but they were the only church from which he would receive financial help (v. 15; contrast his attitude in 1 Corinthians 9). They had supported him in the past and continued to do so. Indeed, once he left Philippi, he had only travelled as far as Thessalonica before they helped him out. This recollection is in itself an acknowledgment of the special place they played in Paul's work and, indeed, in his heart.

In verse 17, Paul makes it clear that he is not seeking for gifts; that is, he is not placing himself under an obligation of clientship. In fact, he is looking for them to make a profit. Throughout this passage, Paul uses the language of a business partnership. He and the Philippians are in the business of proclaiming the gospel. If they expend money, they receive in return a share in the privilege of serving God, and are blessed by him.

This sort of language can make modern Christians uneasy on two counts. Firstly, we are tempted to think of financial matters as somehow 'unspiritual'. Some feel that we should be above money, focusing on things of the spirit. However, the world in which we live is the world in which we serve God, and our discipleship extends to every part of it—including our cash. The degree of pain that may cause is often a better indicator of our spiritual state than the number of prayers we pray!

On the other hand, there are Christians who would claim that the amount of money given to a Christian leader is proportional to the amount of blessing (usually in terms of more wealth, health and success) that the believer will receive from God. Where Paul departs from the company of some modern fund-raisers is that he specifically does not ask for money. He asks for a partnership in mission. That may come through the Philippians' prayers, their support of their own envoy, Epaphroditus, or their love for Paul.

They are an active part of mission. In this case, sharing the task has taken the form of a financial gift, and one which Paul would sorely have needed. The welfare of Roman prisoners was a matter for their friends and family rather than the state, and Paul, deserted by many supporters (2:21), would have been in straitened circumstances.

Practical worship

So the Philippian gift is timely, and Paul is once more adequately provided for (v. 18). That gift, though, is first and foremost a gift to God—an act of worship, in fact. Paul uses the language of sacrifice, the offering of incense in a temple as a symbol of prayer and self-offering.

We tend to distinguish sharply between worship and practical service. The one we do in church, the other in the world. Paul sees no such distinction. Deeds are as much acts of praise and thanksgiving, of self-offering, as hymns and liturgy.

So, God will also respond with his part of the bargain: he will meet the needs of the Philippians as they have met Paul's (v. 19). The thought here is probably primarily about their spiritual needs, as in verse 17. They are storing up treasure in heaven. It need not be confined to that, however. God can use other Christian churches to meet the needs of the Philippians, just as he has used them to make up Paul's shortfall.

The partnership between Paul and the Philippians is a three-way arrangement. As they share together in the work of the gospel, they are in fact junior partners with God. He is the owner of the business, and they work both for and with him.

Paul once again (1:3) writes of 'my' God. It is even clearer here than at the beginning of the letter that God is also the Philippians' God, but for Paul the relationship is intensely and deeply personal. Whatever God is to others (and Paul strives to ensure that God is everything to everyone) he is Paul's God, to be loved and served with all his being. This God has riches and glory beyond imagining, and they are entered into through faith in Christ.

A PRAYER

Lord, may I be your partner in the gospel business, and have a share in the riches of your kingdom.

FAREWELL—FOR NOW

Since the Philippians' gift is an act of worship, it is natural that Paul ends with a doxology. Talk about worship, and particularly about God himself, leads to actual worship, however brief.

Doxologies such as that in verse 20 are common in Jewish and Christian literature, and enshrine a truth—that Christianity, and its parent faith, are about worship above all else. Christians spend a great deal of time worrying and arguing about right doctrine—correct teaching. This can give the misleading impression that doctrine is the most important thing in our faith. In fact, arguments about doctrine are essentially arguments about worship. Our understanding of God colours the way we pray, the way we praise and give thanks, as well as the way we act. But at the end of the day, it is in our prayer, praise and thanksgiving that God is met.

Signature

Paul's brief final greeting was probably written in his own hand, as was common in letters of the time (see Galatians 6:11). Firstly, he commands the readers to greet all the Christian community (every saint, v. 20). Paul's letter is for everyone, even those who are not present at the meeting when it is read out, and his love and prayers are for the whole community as well. Moreover, they are for each one of the congregation. Paul's term addresses individuals rather than the group as a whole. If there were serious differences between members of the church, Paul is reminding them that he is not taking sides, but cares for each. If there are some who feel on the sideline, or less important, he wants them to know that his greeting is for them also.

In this, Paul shows an unerring instinct for good theology, good pastoral practice and good psychology. Churches that find ways of including all their members in significant events (in this case an apostolic letter) will both keep their members and see them grow in faith. Those who focus attention and responsibility on a small key group will find it much harder to hang on to fringe members or encourage greater commitment.

Secondly, Paul passes on the greetings of the Christians who are with him in Rome (v. 21). Although he is the prime mover in the mission to the Gentiles, he has throughout the letter stressed his need for partnership with others. The Philippians are not merely supporting him, but joining in a combined effort with other members of the mission, and so engendering fellowship with a wider group of believers. Indeed, their role in Paul's mission is a part of the work of the whole Church. Their partnership with Paul is merely their particular manifestation of the outworking of Jesus' command to spread the good news (see Matthew 28:20). So, thirdly, Paul includes greetings from all the Christians he is in contact with (v. 22).

Paul gives particular attention to the Christians who are members of 'Caesar's household'. This term was used for the civil service, and could include very highly placed officials or quite lowly ones. Many of them were slaves, but their power and influence could be considerable. The gospel has penetrated even into the corridors of power. There is nowhere where it is not being heard. Even though Paul is in prison, the work goes on, and imprisonment itself becomes the tool of evangelism (1:12).

Paul ends with a benediction identical to that in Philemon 25 and similar to Galatians 6:18. In each case, Paul wishes for the grace of Christ to be with his readers' spirit. In mentioning 'spirit' rather than simply saying 'you', he draws attention to the fact that grace operates through their relationship with God. While Paul does not divide human beings into body and soul and spirit in any technical way, he uses these terms to stress different aspects of human nature. 'Spirit' is usually used when he wants to speak of humans in their capacity to know and serve God. So, he wishes them a deeper knowledge of God.

But why is 'spirit' singular? Perhaps the best explanation is that Paul, though he knows the value of individuals, knows too that a church is a single entity, the body of Christ in that place. It will have its own particular character, its own particular gifts. As such it is called to relate to God, to work for God, to worship God, with one mind—the mind of Christ.

A PRAYER

Lord, bind together my church into one community, one body, and one spirit, that it may serve you wholeheartedly.

GREETINGS

Like Philippians, the letter to the Colossians begins with a greeting from its senders, and is again from Paul and Timothy. There is one immediate difference, though. Paul here describes himself as 'an apostle of Christ Jesus by the will of God'. Writing to the Philippians, Paul was effectively among friends, and could describe himself alongside Timothy as Christ's slave.

Colossae, however, was a city Paul had never visited, though he knew some of the Christians there (see 4:12, 15). He had been asked to address a problem at Colossae, and so must establish his credentials. Firstly he is an apostle. The word simply means 'one who is sent', an envoy or messenger. Already, though, it was becoming a technical term for one sent directly by Jesus and, moreover, one who had been a witness of the risen Christ (1 Corinthians 9:1). Secondly, as an apostle, Paul is chosen by God. Paul understood his calling in the light of the Old Testament prophets, particularly Isaiah and Jeremiah. Like Jeremiah, he had the sense of being chosen against his will, and of having been left with no other option but to proclaim the gospel, though without any sense of Jeremiah's reluctance.

Paul, then, writes with the authority of one sent to speak the word of God. At the same time, he is never a loose cannon. He works with supporters and helpers in the overall context of the Church's mission. So the letter comes also from Timothy, here described simply as a fellow Christian, a 'brother'.

Holy people

Like Philippians, the letter is addressed to the saints, the holy people, of Colossae, who are 'in Christ' (see comments on Philippians 1:1, p. 24).

Paul writes to the 'faithful brothers and sisters at Colossae'. This does not mean that Paul is addressing only the orthodox or trustworthy members of the church. He is writing to all the Colossian Christians, both those who are in error in their understanding of their faith and those whose grasp is more sure. Ultimately, important though understanding and doctrine are, the Colossians, together with all Christians, are saints not because of their understanding or even their faithfulness but because they are 'in Christ Jesus'.

Colossae

These saints are members of the church in Colossae. At one time, Colossae had been a rich and vigorous city, but in Paul's day it was in decline. There was probably a Jewish community in Colossae, as in most cities of Asia Minor. The brand of Judaism that flourished in the region was remarkably liberal by Palestinian standards, and may well have taken on some elements of paganism. There is evidence that the influence was in both directions, as inscriptions from pagan cults in the region seem to indicate Jewish influence as well. In fact, the region was a melting-pot of religious ideas. The mysteries of Isis, an Egyptian goddess, were celebrated, and she was identified with the local mother goddess. It is likely that the cult of Mithras (from Persia) was followed, along with traditional Greek, Roman and Phrygian deities. All borrowed ideas from each other, though Judaism and Christianity, with their traditional suspicion of idolatry, probably did so to a lesser extent.

To the church in this place, Paul sends greetings in the grace and peace of God. These are no empty words. For Paul, they lie at the heart of the gospel. God has shown grace—undeserved favour—and called all people to respond to his gift of salvation by putting their faith in Jesus Christ. Such faith brings peace, for the long-standing breach between God and his creatures has been healed; the war between humanity and God is over. This leads to the personal experience of peace, an inner calm and sense of wholeness based on the certainty of salvation (see comments on Philippians 4:7, p. 94).

A PRAYER

Lord, you have called us to be saints in Christ. May we be immersed in him, that he may colour all that we say and do.

FAITH, HOPE & LOVE

As usual, Paul begins with a prayer report. Although he had never visited the church, there is no reason to suppose that Paul is merely being polite. The Colossians were part of his overall mission, probably an offshoot from his evangelism in Ephesus, at which time, according to Acts 19:10, the gospel spread throughout the province. So Paul's concern for them would be natural, and he would be expected to keep abreast of developments there as much as possible.

Paul's prayers are addressed to 'God the Father of our Lord Jesus Christ'. To modern Christians, the familiarity of this formula almost robs it of meaning. In Paul's day it would have been startling to Jews and pagans alike. God was addressed as 'Father' in Jewish prayers, as were various pagan gods such as Zeus and Jupiter. The difference is that for Christians, God's fatherhood is not based primarily on his creative acts (as, for example, in Acts 17:28), nor even on his parental role in the history of Israel (for example, Hosea 11:1). It is based on his relationship to Jesus, the Lord of the Church. God is effectively redefined in terms of Jesus, and is known through him.

The consequences of such a view are tremendous. If God is now to be seen in terms of Jesus, then our understanding of Christ becomes the governing criterion for reading scripture, for living our lives and for understanding the will of God. For instance, there are parts of the Bible which ascribe actions to God that it is hard indeed to see Jesus condoning. These must be seen in the light of Christ, and as less than acceptable to Christians, rather than being used to modify our view of Jesus or to condone actions and attitudes that fall short of the example of Christ.

The God who gives

Paul's use of this particular formula may also be aimed at the troublesome teaching at Colossae. This seems to have questioned whether faith in Christ is all that is needed to know God; here Paul affirms at the outset that God is known as the Father of Jesus Christ.

This does not mean that the Colossians were lacking in faith. Paul thanks God for their faith and for the love they have for their fellow Christians (v. 4). Such faith and love spring from their hope, which is laid up for them in heaven. That is, the object of their hope, the thing hoped for, is in heaven. This is probably a deliberate point for the sake of the Colossians, who seem to have had doubts about the certainty of their future salvation. Paul's point is that the great trio of faith, hope and love (see 1 Corinthians 13:13) are rooted in the certainty of a future in the presence of God.

By this point (v. 5), Paul has digressed into a reminder of the Colossians' Christian history. They have heard the gospel and responded to it, and that is the source of their hope. They have believed the good news, which is the word of truth. Why, then, should they now start doubting parts of it? They should remember that they are in their present relationship with God simply because of the good news they have received.

It is significant that Paul describes the gospel as that which has 'come to you' (v. 6). The Colossians have not gone out to seek God (as they now seem to be attempting) but have had him visit them through his word. The gospel, as a received message, embodies the very character of God's grace. It is offered freely, coming unexpectedly with its call to faith, repentance and service. It can be rejected or it can be received, but it is not to be changed to suit the wishes of its hearers. Once it is adapted to accommodate the human desire for self-justification, it ceases to be the offer of grace and becomes merely one more technique for self-improvement, a feel-good message lacking in challenge and above all in love.

The gospel has to be a call to faith in Christ and a challenge to accept freely God's loving offer of free salvation. Otherwise it ceases to be good news and becomes one more burden, one more hill to climb, instead of the release from burdens that human beings most need. It is for this reason that Paul has responded with such depth and care to the news from Colossae. In their pursuit of spiritual experience and perfection, the Colossians are in danger of reducing their faith to something they attain through their own efforts and techniques, and losing sight of the grace of God.

A PRAYER

Father, may I come to know you more fully in Jesus Christ.

EFFECTIVE NEWS

The gospel that the Colossians have received is even now 'bearing fruit in the whole world' (v. 6). It is effectively bringing people to faith throughout the Roman empire, and perhaps even beyond. 'The whole world' is perhaps an exaggeration, but from Paul's perspective, not a great one. If it has not yet spread as far as it can, that is not because Paul and his fellow workers have been reticent about preaching it. For the Colossians, there is a reminder here that the gospel is not unique to them, and it is certainly not their property. If they are dissatisfied with what they have received, it is no defect on the part of a message which is winning converts far and wide.

Indeed, it has continued to bear fruit among the Colossians. There is a subtle change of meaning here. In the first instance, 'bearing fruit' refers to bringing new members into the fellowship of Christ. The Colossians, though, are already Christians. Yet the gospel continues to be a message that challenges converts to explore more fully their new awareness of God and its consequences for their lives.

Even today, one encounters preachers who seem to see the whole aim of Christianity as being to bring about conversions. That is hardly bad, of course, and we could do with more evangelism. But what happens when someone becomes a Christian? That is not the end of the matter. Rather, it is the beginning of a journey of faith which will take the rest of their lives. So Paul reminds the Colossians that the gospel they received has enabled their continuing growth.

That growth began with their understanding of the grace of God. Paul probably does not mean that they grasped the sheer magnitude of God's grace, much less all its implications for their lives and the future of creation. What they understood was that their salvation depended solely on receiving God's grace—an understanding that they are in danger of losing.

Epaphras

The gospel had been brought to Colossae by Epaphras (v. 7), one of Paul's missionary team, who was apparently a native of Colossae (see 4:12, where he is described as 'one of' the Colossians). Epaphras is described as a 'fellow slave' (that is, of Christ) with Paul and his helpers, and so is probably a convert who then became a helper in the Pauline mission. It is quite possible that Paul sent out local converts to neighbouring towns when he was staying for any length of time in a particular place. This is made more likely by the further description of him as 'a faithful minister of Christ on our behalf'. Most manuscripts of the New Testament have 'on *your* behalf', and are followed by NRSV and other English versions. However, a few very early ones have the former reading, and this is probably to be preferred. Epaphras, then, is an envoy of Paul who has brought the gospel to Colossae, his home town, and stayed there, probably in a position of leadership in the church. Paul is able to write so firmly to a church he has never visited because in many ways it is still one of his churches, founded under his overall supervision.

Now Epaphras is with Paul, and has most likely come to bring news of developments in Colossae and to ask for Paul's help in dealing with a problem that is threatening to get out of hand. Paul's description of him as a faithful minister serves to indicate that Epaphras is to be trusted (the gospel he brought is not his personal invention) and that Paul also trusts him to give a true account of developments in his church.

Epaphras' news is not all bad, by any means. The Colossians still bear a love for Paul (v. 8) which their leader has conveyed to him; Paul is therefore still held in respect, and can expect his teaching to be listened to. This love is described literally as 'in spirit', which could be taken to mean love inspired by the Holy Spirit (as NRSV) or simply 'spiritual'. In practice, there is little difference. Love is the supreme product of the work of the Spirit, and to describe it as spiritual merely reinforces the point.

The Colossians, then, are in danger of taking on board a teaching that threatens the gospel itself, but they have not lost their love. As long as that remains, there is hope.

One of the hallmarks of love is a willingness to listen to others, and to take seriously what they have to say. It is the very love that the Colossians have for Paul which makes it likely that they will be willing to pay heed to his message.

A PRAYER

*Father, help me to understand your teaching, but never let me
close my ears to others.*

45 COLOSSIANS 1:9–10

PRACTICAL UNDERSTANDING

Paul now returns to the subject of his prayers, which are also loaded messages to his readers. His prayer is no less sincere for that. It is public prayer, intended to be understood and appropriated by his readers or hearers, as much as it is his personal prayer. It is couched in terms that invite his hearers to share his concerns and make his prayers their own.

So, he has not ceased to give thanks for the Colossians since he first heard of their conversion and subsequent growth in the faith. ('For this reason' in verse 9 refers to the whole of the preceding paragraph, not just to the Colossians' love for Paul in verse 8.) Perhaps the most impressive aspect of Paul's prayer is its constancy. He has prayed continually for the Colossians, repeatedly returning to them in prayer. That Paul can say this about so many of his churches (see Philippians 1:4; 1 Corinthians 1:4; 1 Thessalonians 1:2) is a testimony to his genuine concern for them. He is no evangelistic scalp-hunter, counting conversions alone, but a pastor who desires to see his converts grow in faith and love.

Knowledge

The first thing for which Paul prays is the Colossians' growth in knowledge. The usual Greek word for knowledge is *gnosis*, which in Paul's day was fast becoming (if it was not already) a technical term in some religions. It denoted special, and often secret, knowledge given to the initiates of some religions, which would enable them to progress to greater levels of spiritual awareness or purity than were available to ordinary people. The extent to which gnosticism was a distinct religious tradition in Paul's time is hotly debated, so it is safer simply to speak of *gnosis* as a religious tendency rather than a distinct set of religions. Since Paul couples the mention of 'knowledge' with that of 'wisdom and understanding' (two other terms that often went with religious knowledge), it is likely that he is picking up concerns from the Colossians, who were in search of just such élitist religious wisdom.

Paul counters the Colossians' search for *gnosis* in two ways. Firstly, he uses a different but related word for knowledge—*epignosis*. This adds the prefix *epi*, meaning 'upon', to give a sense of superior knowledge. That is, the Colossians may seek knowledge of spiritual matters, but the knowledge found in Christ is super-knowledge, and far above anything they may learn elsewhere.

Secondly, this is knowledge of the will of God. Normal religious ideas of *gnosis* tended to be abstract, concerned with the realm of the spirit, with right ways of worship and contemplation and self-control. Paul's view of the knowledge that matters is about how to live and act in daily life, about how to discern the will of God for everyday matters. Spirituality is no isolated part of life, but fully integrated with the daily round. Hence it is seen in the bearing of fruit in good works, which cannot be separated from knowledge of God (v. 10).

Moreover, such practical knowledge is indeed spiritual (v. 8), a matter of understanding and wisdom. These words carried for Paul a different connotation from that of *gnosis* seekers. Wisdom in the Old Testament seeks to find ways to serve God in the material world of work, family and politics, as the book of Proverbs shows. Such wisdom and understanding is 'spiritual', both because it seeks to put into practice the will of God, and above all because it does so in the context of the guidance of God's Holy Spirit.

Worthiness

The result of true spiritual wisdom and knowledge, then, is a life lived in a way that is worthy of Jesus Christ (v. 10). This sums up neatly the distinct nature of Christian ethics. Christians seek to live a good life because they follow a Lord who has given them salvation as a free gift. Their loving response is to seek to be worthy of such a gift. Part of the promise of salvation is a call to look forward to, and to live in the light of, the coming kingdom of God. Christian life here and now aims to put into practice the way of life that is natural to the kingdom; to prepare oneself for it, and to model it before the world like a new designer dress.

Such a life both learns and demonstrates the true and superior knowledge of God.

A PRAYER

Lord, may I know you better, and may my knowledge of you be apparent to others from day to day.

46 COLOSSIANS 1:11–14

COUNTER-CULTURAL CHRISTIANITY

The difference between seeing the knowledge of God in abstract terms and in practical terms is that the latter is actually difficult. It's one thing to pride oneself on one's understanding of the Trinity, and another to be faced with the choice between spending one's last coin on a summer ice-cream or putting it in a collecting-tin; or the choice between silence and confession of faith in Christ before an angry mob.

Such an understanding of God's will requires a strength that draws on the power of God himself. It requires endurance and patience in the face of opposition and attack, and in the face of the sheer uphill effort of maintaining a way of life that often runs counter to the beliefs and values of the surrounding world. If the Colossians believed that their faith was about exalted spiritual experiences, the assumptions behind Paul's prayer would pull them up short. God's will is not often in line with the way most people think. To run against popular opinion is to court mockery at best, and persecution at worst.

Paul therefore prays for strength, but also for joy. He has no picture of grim and toilsome duty as the main characteristic of Christian living. He supposes it to be shot through with joy and thankfulness. This is because it should be lived in the awareness both of the presence of God and of what he has done for his people.

The awareness of God is signalled by the change from the simple term 'God' (1:6, 9, 10) to 'Father' in verse 12. Thanks are offered to the one who in Jesus Christ has called the Colossians to be his children. He is the one who looks to the future of his children and prepares an inheritance into which they will come in the fullness of time. This inheritance is the same as the hope stored up in heaven in 1:5. Here Paul does not spell out all that it entails; the Colossians would know that. It is the promise of eternal life, the eternal presence of God, the ending of sorrow and death, and the restoration of creation to its proper relationship with its creator. It is light compared to the present world's darkness.

Light and darkness

God has enabled Christians (the saints, v. 12) to be a part of his family, and calls them his own. That itself is cause for rejoicing and thankfulness, but there is yet more. God has rescued his people (like the exodus from Egypt) and brought them out from the authority or power of darkness and transferred them into his Son's kingdom.

There is a constellation of ideas packaged in verses 13–14. Firstly, there are two basic powers in the world, and human beings are under the sway of one or the other. The first is the rule of darkness, a term which is both moral and spiritual. Without God, there is ultimately no hope, no purpose and no final yardstick of right and wrong. This is not to suggest that followers of pagan religions or of none are necessarily wicked and immoral people (see Romans 2:14–16). Rather, it is a statement that the goal and purpose of life are hidden from them. Since eternal life is based on a relationship with God, the chance of finding eternal life apart from him is problematical. The Christian, however, has been moved away from that groping darkness, and sees clearly the path to follow. He or she is now under the rule of Christ, and acknowledges his leadership and sovereignty.

The second notion is that of the kingdom of Christ. For Paul, 'kingdom of God' is a description of the future rule of God over his renewed creation; it is the world to come. The present relationship with God, mediated through faith in Jesus Christ, is termed the kingdom, or rule, of Christ (see 1 Corinthians 15:24–28). Many scholars have argued that this marks a distinct departure from the teaching of Jesus, for whom the kingdom of God was both future hope and to some degree a present reality. However, in the Gospels, it is pretty clear that the kingdom is present in the person of Jesus himself. Seen in that light, Paul's view is merely a change of terminology, to stress both the present and future aspects of God's rule, and the fact that it is in Christ that the rule of God is encountered.

For the Colossians, this would have had particular meaning. They seem to have been questioning whether their meeting with Christ has imparted a sufficient degree of spiritual power and experience. Paul stresses that in this world, Christ is the ruler and the one who embodies the presence of God.

A PRAYER

Father, may I be subject to the rule of Christ, and know his strength for the tasks you give me.

The COST *of* SALVATION

Paul drives home his point about Jesus with the third idea in the cluster of themes related to the movement from darkness to light— redemption. This is defined with a fourth and closely related idea, the forgiveness of sins.

'Redemption' is a word used to refer to the buying back of a captive, or payment for the release of a slave. This led some early theologians to speculate on exactly who received the payment. This misses the real point of the image, which is not that a payment had to be made to anyone, but that salvation is costly to God: it took the incarnation, cross and resurrection.

It also, of course, reinforces Paul's point about belonging to either the realm of darkness or the kingdom of Christ. People may like to think that they are free agents, but in fact they belong firmly to someone or something else. They either belong to the rule of blindness or they belong to Christ. There is no middle position, no fence from which to watch the world go by. The work of Christ is God's costly way of allowing a transfer from one realm to another.

Redemption is effectively the forgiveness of sins. For Paul, sin is a state of separation from God, of which specific sins are symptoms. To be brought back to God, transferred to his kingdom, is to have sins forgiven. Even this, though, is only shorthand for the whole process of reconciliation, in which forgiveness is offered and accepted, and the once-broken relationship with God is restored.

All this has already happened to the Colossians. The tense of the verb 'transferred' in verse 13 is the Greek aorist, which denotes a single completed action in the past. To be sure, they need to grow in faith and service, in love and worship, but they do so from within an existing relationship with their Father, God. They are in the family.

There is also a hint as to when this took place. Christ is described as God's 'beloved Son', the description of him in the Gospel stories of Jesus' baptism (Mark 1:11). In his letter to the Romans, Paul reminded them of their baptism as the decisive moment at which they died to their old life (Romans 6:3, 6). It is likely that he has the Colossians' baptism in mind here also.

Paul sees baptism as the starting point of Christian life, and a fixed point to which reference can be made later in the journey of faith. It stands as an objective fact, both promise and call, and something which can be asserted with certainty.

The Christ-hymn

The next section of the chapter, verses 15–20 (or, according to some scholars, vv. 12–20) is often seen as a quotation from an early Christian hymn. It contains a good number of words that occur only here in the New Testament, it has a sort of rhythmic feel, and it can be divided into lines that look and sound poetic. To do this, one has to remove certain words or phrases, but it is quite possible that Paul, if he was quoting a hymn, would have added explanatory comments or expanded certain phrases to help to stress certain points. Much scholarly work and debate has gone into reconstructing the original hymn, and into determining what it can tell us about the theology of the church or churches where it originated.

As we noted with the suggested hymn in Philippians 2:6–11, the major flaw in this approach is that Paul would hardly have quoted something with which he disagreed, so it is hard to discover a hymn which has a very different understanding of Christianity from Paul himself. This doesn't mean that the exercise is pointless, but it does place it outside the scope of this book. Our task is to discover what Paul meant by what he wrote, regardless of whether the words originated with him or not. For what it is worth, it seems to me much more likely here that Paul is indeed quoting a hymn than is the case with Philippians 2. However, we shall approach the passage in the same way as the Colossians presumably did—as a message from Paul and a resounding affirmation of the work and place of Christ in creation and salvation.

For a church that was doubtful of the sufficiency of Christ alone, such a passage would have acted as a powerful reminder of who and what Christ really is, according to the gospel they had received.

A PRAYER

*Lord, may I also be reminded of Jesus, of who he is and what he
has done, for me and for all creation.*

GOD'S SELF-PORTRAIT

Who is this Christ who brings redemption, the forgiveness of sins? He is, says Paul, 'the image of the invisible God'. That is, God, who is beyond human sight or comprehension, has provided a picture of himself.

For long centuries the Jews had assiduously kept the commandment of Exodus 20:4, that there was to be no attempt to craft an image of God. God was too great to be encompassed by human imagination, too free to be imprisoned in a rigid form, and certainly too powerful to be controlled by human beings. Yet now he has provided his own image. The Greek word used, *eikon*, was often employed for religious images (it gives us the term 'icon'). There was a sense in which the image embodied the reality of the deity it represented. Thus a devout pagan would argue that he was no more bowing down to a lump of wood and stone than a modern Catholic would say that she was reverencing a piece of bread at Benediction.

The point here is that God cannot take up residence in a statue or painting: it is too circumscribing to be a meaningful representation. Moreover, what counts about God is not that he exists, but what he does, and what is his nature. That can never meaningfully be expressed in terms of art. It can, however, be expressed in terms of a human life. If Jesus Christ calls us to redefine God, it is because he embodies in a living person the reality and nature of God. If God has shown himself to be the saviour of Israel by bringing them out of slavery, that saving nature is made visible and present in Christ the Saviour. If God has shown himself to be compassionate, that compassion takes flesh in Christ, and is shown in daily acts of forgiveness and healing.

'Image' here means something rather different from its use in 3:10, which harks back to Genesis 1:27, where humans are created in the image of God. This is obvious from Colossians 1:16–17, where Christ is described as having a role in creation itself. He is therefore not to be seen as a created being, but someone who actually precedes creation.

In the light of the following verses, 'firstborn of all creation' cannot mean that he is the first to be created. 'Firstborn' is not necessarily a term referring to physical birth; it denotes one who stands in the favoured position of power and inheritance normally occupied by the eldest son. So the picture that emerges here is of Christ's existence before creation and of his authority over it. (Actually, time is a part of creation, so this would indicate that Christ is eternal, which is good theology but may go further than what Paul had in mind.)

Word and Wisdom

It is sometimes asked how such an idea could develop so quickly after Jesus' life-time. The basic answer is the resurrection, in which Christ is also described as the firstborn (see comments on 1:18, pp. 120–121). The conviction that the resurrection planned for the last day had, in Jesus' special case, been brought forward led his followers to seek an understanding of who he was that could explain so shattering an event. And in Jewish thought of the time, there were at least two concepts which helped that understanding.

The first was that of the Wisdom of God, which was thought of in some circles as almost a separate entity, a divine offshoot of God himself, which (or who!) became both God's tool and assistant in the work of creation (see Proverbs 22—31). A second and similar idea was that of the Word/Reason (*Logos* in Greek), the creative principle of reason and order that underlay the world in some Greek philosophy. Jewish thinkers saw it as referring to the word by which God created (Genesis 1), and which, like Wisdom, could be seen as a sort of emanation from God's divine self, with its own degree of independence. So John's Gospel begins with the assertion that 'in the beginning was the Word...' and thus ties together the story of Jesus and the opening words of the Bible.

A man who had been raised from the dead, whose death had made manifest God's act of salvation, who had shown authority over demons and sickness and had challenged the received teaching of his day, just about begged to be seen in terms of Wisdom and Word— the firstborn of creation as he was the firstborn from the dead.

A PRAYER

Open my eyes, Lord, that I may see Jesus.

The ORIGIN of ALL THINGS

If Christ is the firstborn of creation, existing before anything else (v. 17), with all that that implies, then it follows that he is superior to any other power that may exist within creation. All things have been created in him (v. 16: the Greek could also mean 'by him' but 'in' is preferable) and through him and for him.

The prepositions 'in', 'through' and 'for' are not chosen at random. The Jews who spoke of God's *Logos* envisaged the Word as the rational, logical principle which gave order to the universe and suffused it with a meaning and purpose that could be detected by the human mind. Christ, says Paul, is precisely that principle. Without him, creation would cease to be, returning to the chaos from which it was created (Genesis 1:2).

In the Jewish Wisdom (Greek: *Sophia*) tradition, God's Wisdom was the tool and vehicle for his creative purposes, and true wisdom, based on the knowledge of God, can discern God's Wisdom still at work in the world.

But finally, Paul goes even further beyond. The universe was created *for* Christ, something which was not said about either *Logos* or *Sophia*. If we take the view that God created the world for himself, to delight in it and to express his love and creativity (Revelation 4:11), then Christ is being associated as closely as possible with God's creative purpose. Only in Christ can the true meaning of the world be discovered, and only in him can it find its fulfilment.

Putting these three statements together, we find a movement through time from its beginning to its end. The origin of the world is through Christ, who brought it into being as part of God's creative act. It exists in him, held together by his very being as the one who brings order to the world (v. 17), and it moves towards him as its goal, the one for whom it exists and in which it will find its destiny. The flow of time is carrying God's handiwork towards its final destination, and whatever that turns out to be, whatever form his renewal of creation will take, it will be intimately tied up with Christ.

The powers

All this makes a powerful and resounding hymn of praise, but Paul has another reason for quoting it, which is to affirm that there is no power in creation greater than Christ. He is over all thrones, dominions, rulers and powers—all of which are terms used for angelic, supernatural beings.

In the first century, most people believed that the events of earthly history were a reflection of the actions of heavenly powers. For some, such as the Stoics, the overriding power was fate. For most Jews, the powers were angels, each controlling the destiny, or looking after the interests, of their earthly counterparts. At times they could even be in conflict. In other views, the powers were less personal, such as the stars (astrology was even more popular then than now), but the notion that invisible heavenly beings of some sort were involved in human life was almost universal.

The powers that Paul lists in verse 16 can all be found in Jewish writings dealing with visions of heaven. They are the invisible reality behind the visible world. The Colossians seem to have had a strong interest in such powers, be they angels (2:18) or the 'elemental spirits of the universe' (2:20). It seems likely that the Colossians were pursuing mystical experiences which sought to put them in touch with the heavenly realm.

Paul himself was not opposed to heavenly visions (see 2 Corinthians 12:2–4), but he was certainly opposed to any teaching which claimed that such things conferred a higher spiritual status on their recipients. All these things are unnecessary because Christians are already 'in Christ' (1:2). They are united with the one who is before and above all these spiritual forces. The powers were created in and through Christ, and exist for him. Why, then, should the Colossians be bothered about them?

Futile though it is, there seems to be a deep-seated desire in us to provide our own salvation. Whether it is through good works or initiation into hidden mysteries, the response of the gospel remains the same: Christ is all that is needed.

A PRAYER

Lord, help me to rely on you alone, and not on
what I can do or discover.

LORD *of the* CHURCH

Having established the place of Christ in creation, Paul now turns to Christ's role in the Church. The Colossians are somehow doubting the sufficiency of Christ either for salvation or for spiritual enlightenment and experience. Paul has shown that no other resources in creation (be they natural or supernatural—not that Paul would make that distinction) can compare with the one who is the origin and goal of creation itself. Now he uses a similar idea about the Church. While 'head', when used as a metaphor in Greek, can mean 'primacy of place', it can (less commonly) also mean 'source' or 'origin'—the one from which something flows or proceeds. Quite possibly Paul has both ideas in mind as he describes Christ as head of the Church. Certainly both ideas occur in the rest of verse 18.

Just as Christ is prior to creation, so he is prior to the Church, as the firstborn from the dead. The Church came into being as a result of the resurrection. Paul became a Christian as the result of a vision of the risen Christ. Therefore, just as Christ existed before creation, and had a major role in its origin and in its sustenance, so it is with the Church. He rose from the dead and called it into being; he is its present Lord and preserver. Hence, if the Colossians are to look for any spiritual experience, any further degree of perfection, it must be found in Christ. No amount of knowledge or advanced spiritual technique can improve on what is found in him, for he is the supreme Lord, the beginning and the end of the Church's life. Moreover, he is the beginning not just of the Church, but of the new creation that God is bringing about. As the first instance of the resurrection, he is the prime example of the new humanity that God is making, and the living and eternal pledge of the reality of eternal life. In him, through his resurrection, the new age has begun.

To make this point, and to draw the parallel between the original creation and the new one, Paul uses the phrase 'firstborn from the dead'. In many ways, the meaning here is the same as in 'firstborn of all creation' in 1:15. Christ precedes the general resurrection of the dead which will happen at the last day, and stands in the favoured position of the firstborn, having the 'first place' in the new creation. Where the image differs is in the fact that Christ actually has undergone death and resurrection, whereas he was not originally a part of creation, but its initiator. Now, however, through the incarnation, he has become one with his creation and undergoes its universal experience of death. At the same time, as the incarnate Word and Wisdom of God, he is able to initiate the new creation and blazes the trail of resurrection.

All this, says Paul, is so that Christ might have the first place in everything. Here Paul is being true to a deep-seated biblical tradition—that creation and salvation are not separate events, but part of the same work by the one God. In later gnostic thought, it was often held that the world of matter was evil, while that of the spirit was good. The aim of religion was to free the human spirit from the prison of matter and send it winging into heaven. Indeed, in some forms of gnosticism it was argued that the God of the Old Testament, the creator, was evil, and was the enemy of the God and Father of Jesus Christ. There is no suggestion that the Colossians believed any such thing, but the first shadows of the idea seem to be present in their search for a spirituality beyond that of basic Christianity.

Creation and salvation

Throughout the Bible, creation and salvation are held together. The world is God's good creation (see the refrain of 'and God saw that it was good' in Genesis 1) and is not to be despised or ill-treated. On the other hand, the world is also tainted by sin and marred by rebellion against God. Thus it needs a saviour. Yet the saviour is the same creator God.

This has very practical consequences. Firstly, it warns us that a spirituality based purely on creation, however that is encountered, is flawed because it ignores the need for salvation. Secondly, it reminds us that we can never set the work of Christ against that of God (for example, Jesus does not placate an angry God by offering himself on the cross)—for the creator is the redeemer. Thirdly, it reminds us that the place where Christian discipleship is worked out is this wonderful and terribly flawed world in which we live. It is here that we are called to serve God, and here that we encounter him. This in turn reaffirms what the Church has long taught, that Christianity is a sacramental religion. We meet God in the material world, through material things, because it is his world and he is working to remake it.

A PRAYER

Lord, help me to keep my eyes open, so that I may meet you in your world, and play my part in its re-creation.

51 COLOSSIANS 1:19–20b

The FULLNESS of GOD

The Greek of verse 19 simply says that in Christ 'all the fullness' was pleased to dwell, without saying of what it is the fullness. However, the best answer seems to be that which most English translations adopt: it is the fullness of God himself, as is explicitly stated in 2:9. In the Old Testament, God is spoken of as filling all things, and when his presence appears in the temple, for instance, it automatically fills the available space (2 Chronicles 7:1; Isaiah 6:1).

Once again, Paul is driving home his point about the sufficiency of Christ. God has nothing to offer which is not found in Christ, because the fullness of God himself is in Christ. There is no way that anything can be added to Christ, because there is nothing that is not already in him. God is present in Christ, bringing to bear his full saving work. Only this seems to make sense of the phrase 'pleased to dwell'.

The reconciler

Paul does not, of course, make a simple identification between God and Jesus, and it is this point that causes problems for many people. It is also the root of the doctrine of the Trinity. For some Christians, and for a good many denominations on the fringe of mainstream Christianity, such as the Unitarians, Christadelphians and Jehovah's Witnesses, the issue is simple: if Jesus was God, they argue, Paul (and the other writers of the New Testament) would simply say so.

The point that is missed, however, is that no one claims Christ to be God in the sense of being invisible, immanent, omniscient, and all the other long words that try to describe the infinite creator. At the same time he is God's rationality, creativity and saving power made present and made flesh. He is the image of God (see also 2 Corinthians 4:4), the form of God (Philippians 2:6), the radiance of God's glory and the imprint of his being (Hebrews 1:3). The New Testament writers are striving to express this new and mind-bending concept as best they can, drawing on the traditions and ways of speaking that were available to them at the time. It is the struggle to express both the identity of Christ with God and his difference from him which ultimately gives rise to the formal statements of trinitarian doctrine.

All this leads us to the opening of verse 20, where Christ's role in salvation is seen as similar to his role in creation. Through him, as agent and expression of God's saving nature, God chose ('was pleased') to reconcile to himself all things. The creator of all is the saviour of all. We have already touched on the idea of salvation as a new creation. Here it becomes explicit.

That new creation reaches throughout all the present created world, embracing both physical and spiritual powers. The main thought here is simply of the sheer scope of salvation. There is nothing that it cannot touch, no part of the world beyond the reach of God's loving redemption. There is also a slight dig at the Colossians' preoccupation with the spiritual powers. If salvation reaches into earth and heaven, it is quite possible that the powers the Colossians are counting on to provide enlightenment are themselves in need of redemption. This is not to say that Paul thinks the Colossians are deliberately trafficking with evil spirits (though that is a danger), but it places the powers firmly within a creation which is in need of renewal. They therefore have nothing to offer to those who are already set free by Christ and have a foretaste of the world to come.

If God was reconciling all things to himself in Christ (2 Corinthians 5:19), does this mean that Paul regarded the whole universe as automatically saved? The intensity of his evangelism alone suggests otherwise. Reconciliation is possible for all creation, down to the devil himself. But reconciliation is a two-sided affair. The creation will be renewed, and there will be a place in it for all. But that place has still to be taken up, the gospel has still to be preached, and God's work in Christ made our own.

A PRAYER

Lord, may I make your reconciliation mine
and share in the world to come.

RECONCILED *to* GOD

The reconciliation offered by God means peace, peace where once there was enmity between God and his creation. That peace comes about through the death of Christ, the price of redemption that God himself has paid. It is God's self-giving act of salvation, which opens the way to a new relationship with him and sets in train his remaking of all that is.

Once, the Colossians were estranged from God (v. 21). They had no notion that the God who created them was the strange God of the Jews. They gave him no thought, save perhaps as one competing voice in the clamour of the religious marketplace that was first-century Colossae. Unaware of God, they were going their own way, making no effort to bridge the gap that existed between them and their maker.

Once, they were hostile to God. Their state was one of outright enmity. This may seem a bit strong to modern readers, but it reflects the thought we met earlier in 1:13. There is no middle ground, merely the kingdom of Christ or the rule of darkness. Humanity may walk God's path or its own, but it is a choice between being for God or against him.

Their former unreasoned hostility to God showed itself not in a conscious attitude to God, but in 'evil deeds'—probably a reference both to idolatry and to immorality. From this Godless state they have been rescued, but at great cost—the cost of Jesus' death. Paul refers to that death by the rather clumsy phrase 'in his body of flesh by death' (v. 22). He stresses the physicality of Jesus, and the reality of his physical suffering, to point up the contrast between the involvement of Christ in the world and the Colossians' tendency to escape into abstract spirituality. They may seek for pure spiritual experiences, but Jesus bled real blood on a real cross to bring them back to God.

The effect of Jesus' death was to reconcile the Colossians to God, to change their relationship to him. Paul's language at the end of verse 22 is reminiscent of the law court. They are presented before God, but can stand as innocent and blameless not because of their own good merit, but because of what Jesus Christ has done. Thus they stand as holy people, marked out as God's own.

Holding fast

The new standing of the Colossians as Christians was brought about in an instant, at their baptism/conversion (see comment on 1:13, pp. 114–115), but that is not the whole story. This is all theirs, says Paul, as long as they continue in the faith. To do that, they need to be immovable and steadfast (terms used of buildings) in the faith. As long as they remember that their relationship with God depends on what he has done in Christ, all will be well. It is possible, though, to put one's faith in other things under the guise of Christianity. The Colossians face a real danger that the true focus of their faith will shift from the message they received to their own efforts at spiritual perfection. We tend to think of the main danger to faith as being the attempt to prove oneself good enough for God by good works. It is equally possible to try to prove oneself by religious effort. Once the focus shifts from God's grace, salvation becomes a matter of human achievement and is doomed to failure.

For this reason, the Colossians must keep their eyes fixed on the goal that lies ahead, the hope promised by the gospel. At this point Paul has come full circle back to the topic of 1:3. The gospel that the Colossians have received is all that is necessary for salvation. It is the source of hope for this life, and carries a promise of eternal life to come. It is the true gospel which has won converts throughout the world, a fact that bears testimony to its authenticity.

To this gospel, Paul has become a servant. As a servant, his task is to further the spread of the gospel, guard it from misinterpretation and hand it on to future generations. He shares this task with fellow workers such as Timothy, Epaphras, who founded the Colossian church, and Tychicus, who will carry the present letter to Colossae—and with us.

A PRAYER

Lord, may I also be a carrier of the gospel to others.

53 COLOSSIANS 1:24–25

SUFFERING CHRIST

Verse 24 is one which causes consternation in Bible study groups and debate among New Testament scholars. The obvious problem is the question of how Paul makes up for a 'deficiency' in the sufferings of Christ. Before that, though, there are other issues. Paul is now—at the time of writing—rejoicing in his sufferings, which are for the sake of the Colossians. How can they be for the sake of a church he has never visited and most of whose members he does not know? And what is there about suffering to make him rejoice?

The immediate cause of his suffering is his imprisonment, which is both a result of his faithful preaching of the gospel and an opportunity to spread the word of God even further (see Philippians 1:12 and comments on p. 32). Neither of these, however, is mentioned directly here, and Paul doesn't mention his imprisonment until 4:3, so it is likely that there is a wider sense to his words. He rejoices 'now', that is, in the present age, because he plays a part as the servant of the gospel in spreading God's word and helping to move the world closer to the coming kingdom of God. For all the suffering his task may bring, it is yet an immense privilege, to which he has been called by God.

However, there is another idea lying under his thought. To get at that, we need to consider what he means by saying that his suffering helps to 'make up what is lacking in Christ's afflictions'.

Paul does not mean that Christ's redeeming work on the cross is somehow incomplete and needs to be finished off by Paul. Paul makes it clear in Colossians itself that Christ's work is the full and final saving act of God and provides all that is needed in the way of salvation (1:14, 19–20). For that matter, neither Paul nor any other New Testament writer ascribes salvation to Christ's 'afflictions'. It is the death of Jesus that brings about salvation, not the pain he bore. Later Christian piety has paid a lot of attention to Christ's suffering, to the extent that the events of Good Friday are routinely referred to as the 'Passion' (meaning 'suffering'). The New Testament, on the other hand, is extremely restrained on this matter. Of course, it is significant that Jesus shared human suffering, but the amount of suffering he felt is not what counts towards salvation.

The best answer is probably found in the Jewish tradition of the 'messianic woes'. According to a lot of messianic teaching, the coming of the age of the Messiah would be preceded by a time of intense suffering by the people of God, but this suffering was to be of a fixed amount, so that there would be hope of survival (see Mark 13:20). Paul's suffering as an apostle is a part of the suffering that heralds the new creation, the birth pangs of the new age (see Mark 13:8). Since the messianic woes are of a fixed extent, any suffering that Paul endures means less suffering for others, including the Colossians. At the same time, these afflictions of Christ are for the sake of the Church, for they bring the new age and the salvation of God's people that much closer.

This may seem an odd notion to modern readers, but its implications are more immediately relevant. The suffering of Paul, and of other Christians, is the suffering of Jesus. When Paul encountered Christ on the Damascus road, he was asked, 'Why do you persecute me?' (Acts 9:4). In all that the Church undergoes, Christ is present and sharing in its pain and its joy. Paul takes seriously his own image of the Church as the body of Christ: what the Church feels, Christ feels. What individual members of his body feel, Christ feels.

Suffering servant

God's call to Paul was to service. Paul has already expressed that in terms of serving the gospel, but this may seem a little abstract. Now, in verse 25, he rephrases it as a call to serve the Church, the people of God. Paul sees his suffering both as a sharing in the pain Christ feels with his people, and as suffering borne on behalf of the whole Church, of which the Colossians are a part.

For Paul, his own afflictions are an integral part of his calling as an apostle. They are the school in which he learns to trust God (2 Corinthians 1:9) and the expression of a faith which is willing to walk in the steps of the Lord, even if that path leads to Calvary. It is a fact of Christian discipleship that it faces the possibility of suffering as well as the promise of glory.

A PRAYER

Lord, whatever I may face in life, help me to remember
that you are facing it with me.

MYSTERY

Perhaps the most striking note in the present few verses is Paul's view of his mission as service. The great temptation of any kind of leadership is to flaunt, or even misuse, authority. Paul often claims authority as an apostle, but it is never something to be enjoyed. In fact, he seems much happier describing himself as a slave of God, or servant of the Church or gospel, than as an apostle.

There is a lesson in this for church leaders today which is so obvious it hardly needs stating. The lesson is not only for bishops and clergy. All Christians are called to serve God, the gospel and each other, not to mention the world for whose renewal Christ died.

That renewal comes about through the proclamation of the gospel, which Paul here describes as a mystery (v. 26). He is probably picking up the sort of language that was impressing the Colossians. They are keen on mysteries and secret knowledge and esoteric experiences. So here is a mystery, says Paul, one that has been hidden for uncounted years, and now you are in on it!

The mystery hidden through the ages has now been revealed to the people of God through the proclamation of his word by Paul.

By simply revealing the mystery, part of its content becomes known. It is how God will fulfil his promise that he will be glorified by the Gentiles (v. 27). The gospel has come to non-Jews and made them a part of God's covenant people, bringing them to praise him. In fact, the Greek literally says that he will make known the riches of the mystery 'in' the Gentiles. While this can be taken to mean 'among', it probably goes further, and points to a change in the life and actions of the Gentiles, so that their very selves become a testimony to the glory of God's saving mystery.

The mystery itself is both simple and awesome. It is 'Christ in you, the hope of glory'. Paul generally prefers to speak of believers being in Christ, while the Holy Spirit is the indwelling power of God in the Christian's life. At the same time, for Paul, the Spirit is the mediator of the presence of Christ, who in Christian experience can be spoken of as 'life-giving Spirit' (1 Corinthians 15:45), so it is a small step for him to take in speaking of the indwelling Christ.

The Colossians need not doubt whether the gospel of Jesus Christ truly carries all they need to fulfil their spiritual aspirations. Christ has come to take up residence in their hearts and lives, and to give them assurance of the glory of God's coming kingdom. Any spiritual experience they may need is supplied by the Christ who dwells in them.

Maturity

This is why Christ is the total content of Paul's teaching (v. 28). There is nothing else that is necessary for salvation, for discovering one's true purpose and realizing one's true potential. Therefore Paul proclaims the gospel and teaches its implications, so that his hearers may stand before God as complete and mature members of his kingdom. Paul stresses that this proclamation of Christ is true wisdom, the source of right living that is based on the knowledge of God. By following it, Christians may be presented (an image of being introduced to a king's court) as worthy and mature followers of Christ (see Philippians 3:15 and comments on pp. 84–85).

Paul's teaching and warnings are not simply about the pursuit of sound doctrine for its own sake. They are about enabling Christ's disciples to become more like him because they have a clear vision of their Lord and a firm grasp of his will for them. Therefore, Paul throws himself body and soul into the task, labouring and striving to carry it out (v. 29). It is a task that would be beyond his strength were it not that God enables and empowers him.

This is a theme that crops up frequently in Paul's letters. His task is hard, but his resources are infinite because they come from God. It's one of the hardest lessons to learn, but one of the most potent: God calls us to no service for which he does not equip us, and no task for which he will not give the strength.

A PRAYER

Lord, help me to see the task you set before me,
and the strength you offer me.

55   COLOSSIANS 2:1–5

The REPOSITORY *of* KNOWLEDGE

Paul now addresses the Colossians specifically. His work is not just on behalf of the churches he has founded personally, but also for those, like Colossae and neighbouring Laodicea (v. 1), that he has never visited himself. He expends as much energy in prayer, in caring and in writing letters on their behalf as he does for his own converts.

Paul wants their hearts to be encouraged (v. 2). The knowledge that Paul cares for them is itself a boost to their self-esteem and worth. With that comes the realization that they are connected to all the other churches throughout the empire, and particularly to those of Paul's mission. More importantly, they will find encouragement in an understanding of how much God cares for them, and how much he has to offer them. This will come out of a true understanding of the Christian gospel, as it is taught to them in love.

The word translated by NRSV as 'united' in verse 2 can also mean 'instructed' or 'taught', and that probably fits the present context rather better. It is as they give up their temptation to wander away from the truth of the gospel that the Colossians will be certain of the hope God offers them. Their knowledge will not be a spurious, élitist, secret *gnosis*, but of the real mystery of God, which is Christ himself. It is in Jesus that the wisdom and knowledge sought by the Colossians is to be found (v. 3). Once again, Paul is using the terms his readers would understand, and turning them in a new direction.

What is at stake is an issue with considerable importance for the modern Church. In an age which is as religiously pluralist as the first century, can it reasonably be claimed that Christ can meet all the spiritual aspirations of everyone? The Colossians may well have argued that Jesus was all very well, but there were other powers in the world to be taken into account. Could Christ alone offer all that the others offered? Paul's answer is an unequivocal 'yes'. If Christ is not able to meet the hopes and aspirations of all people, he is not God incarnate, and he is not the saviour of the world.

Holding fast

The argument that something may exist which supplements what Christ has to offer may seem plausible. Yet if it leads to putting faith in something other than Christ, it is deadly. Therefore Paul assures the Colossians that though he is unable to be present with them because of his imprisonment, he is with them in spirit, to help combat false teaching and to rejoice at their faith. There is no need to read any mystical or metaphysical meaning into the phrase 'with you in spirit'. Paul means pretty much what we mean by the term. He thinks of them, feels for them and rejoices over them even though he is separated from them by such a great distance.

In what Paul has written so far, he has laid the groundwork for the assault he is about to make on the false teaching at Colossae. Before he begins to examine the Colossian teaching, he re-establishes his standpoint. Paul is not writing to condemn or destroy. He is writing to encourage and build up. So he reassures his readers that the news he has received, his metaphorical presence with them, is a cause of rejoicing. He is glad to hear of their morale and firmness in the faith (v. 5). The actual Greek words mean 'order' and 'steadfastness' and could refer to troops keeping formation on the battlefield. Paul may not intend a military image, but that gives the flavour of his meaning. The Colossians have been perturbed by the new teaching they have encountered, and it may have made headway among some of them, but they have not been thrown into disarray and are still holding to the gospel they have received.

Paul, then, is writing to support them in their determination to hold the true faith, and to commend them for not giving way. Even if he is being over-generous, his approach has a lot to teach us. There is no hint that the Colossians are not 'real' Christians. If only many modern Christians could import Paul's manner into their debates!

A PRAYER

Lord, let me hold fast to your word and proclaim it to others.

56 COLOSSIANS 2:6–7

KEEPING *a* GRIP

Paul has laid the groundwork for his approach to the Colossian problem: it is to be an affirmation of all that Christ offers the Church, and an attack on anything that attempts to undermine the all-encompassing sufficiency of Christ's work. In verses 6 and 7 Paul outlines his approach. These two verses mark the pivotal point of the letter, summing up what has gone before and marking the approach he is about to take.

The Colossians have received Christ, by their response to the gospel. They have opened their hearts to him and he has become a living presence in their lives. Do they, however, realize exactly whom they have received? From what has been written so far, they certainly should. This is Christ Jesus the Lord. Each word has meaning. 'Christ' is the anointed one, the chosen of God. 'Christ' is, of course, the Greek translation of the Hebrew 'Messiah', but Paul's preference for the term as a title for use in Gentile churches shows that he sees Jesus as more than the fulfilment of Jewish hopes. He is the one sent with God's blessing into the world to bring salvation. He is Jesus, a human being, sharing the lot of human beings and shedding his blood on the cross. And perhaps above all, he is the Lord. 'Lord' is the title normally given by Jews to God, and it sums up all that has been said about the incarnation and Christ's role in creation. The title also logically stresses the rule of Christ.

To receive Jesus is to receive a Lord. Accepting the gospel moves the believer into the kingdom of Christ—and that means into the rule of a King. To have Christ as Lord is to commit oneself to following him, serving him and doing his will. Hence it has consequences for the life that follows: 'live your lives in him'—literally, 'keep walking in him'. Accepting Christ is the beginning of a journey of faith, and not an end in itself.

With a blithe disregard for mixed metaphors, Paul characterizes the walk of discipleship as rooted, built up and established in Christ (v. 7). Or perhaps he is well aware of the apparent contradiction between the image of the journey and the static picture of rootedness and building. Both are necessary to delineate what it means to be a Christian. Christ is the source of strength and stability, the sure foundation on which to build, and at the same time a guide and trailblazer in a relationship which is dynamic. Christian discipleship is about learning new things about God, finding new ways to serve him and discovering new ways to worship him. At the same time it provides an underlying peace and security in the knowledge of God's love which can enable the Christian pilgrim to weather the storms of changing circumstance, doubt and fear that are likely to be encountered on the journey.

Kept by God

It is worth noting that the three images of stability in verse 7 are all participles in the passive voice. That is, they indicate something that has been done to the Colossians, rather than something they have to do themselves. The use of the passive voice is a common biblical and Jewish way of speaking of God's action. The Colossians have to walk, to live out their lives, but they have been given the basis for that life by God. He has rooted, built up and established them in the faith. This happened (and continues to happen) on receipt of the teaching that is contained in the gospel.

None of this is to say that the Colossians play no part in the process, but their part is willingly passive rather than active. They need to be ready to receive and willing to learn. The more they learn of God, and the more they realize what he has done for them and what he has to offer, the more they will abound in thanksgiving.

In these two verses, Paul outlines the two-sided nature of Christian life. It is a life that is lived by following Christ, actively putting into practice the call to service and thanksgiving. It is a life that receives from God, drawing on his strength, accepting his grace and learning from him. It is this pattern of receiving and acting, of being grounded in Christ and in the awareness of all that he has done, that Paul sets against the Colossian teaching.

A PRAYER

Father, let me learn from you, and live for you,
for Jesus Christ's sake.

PHILOSOPHY—*the* LOVE *of* WISDOM?

Since the Colossians have so much in Christ, they need to beware that they do not lose it. Or, to take up Paul's metaphor, since they have been set free by Christ, they must be careful not to be recaptured by the realm of darkness.

The current threat is described by Paul as a 'philosophy' (v. 8). This tells us little about it. Philosophy was a highly regarded discipline in the Greek-speaking world, but almost every system of belief and superstition described itself as a philosophy in order to gain a certain intellectual legitimacy. Jewish thinkers such as Philo of Alexandria recast Judaism in terms of Platonic philosophy, and referred to the *Torah*, the Jewish Law, as a philosophy. In later centuries, Christianity was to follow suit.

The Colossian philosophy is deceitful (v. 8) for two reasons. Firstly, it is based merely on human tradition. Tradition is not bad in itself. Paul was a hander on of tradition (1 Corinthians 11:2, 23) and proudly so. The problem is that this is merely human tradition, based on the speculation of religious inventors, with no basis in God's revelation of himself.

This is a phenomenon that we see a lot in the present day. In a genuine search for spiritual fulfilment, it is tempting to take bits of various religious traditions and meld them into a personally satisfying spirituality which has no roots in any particular claim to authority other than that of personal taste.

Secondly, and much worse, the Colossian philosophy looks no further than a world which is sinful and in a state of rebellion against God. It looks to the 'elemental spirits of the universe', the powers that govern human destiny and hold sway over the nations of the world. Whether they were seen as being placated or worshipped, these powers are part of the universe which is itself fallen and sinful. To look to them is merely another form of idolatry, for they are created beings and, like humans, they can find their true purpose and fulfilment only in Christ. Powerful and mysterious though they may seem, they are as nothing compared to their creator, and to suppose that they can either replace or supplement the work of Christ fails to recognize who Jesus is.

Fullness

Against these cosmic powers stands Christ, their creator and Lord (v. 9). In him, says Paul once again, the full being of God is embodied. Since there is only the one God, this is as strong a statement of the incarnation as one can get. Again, Paul emphasizes the completeness of God's dwelling in Christ: 'the *whole* fullness'. Christ is not one among many manifestations of God, comparable perhaps to the elemental spirits, who might be seen that way. He is the whole thing. That whole deity (the Greek word is *theotes*, a strong abstract noun for God—*theos*—rather than merely divine qualities) dwells *bodily* in Christ. That is, God has made himself known in an actual person, a human being who sums up the reality of God in human terms. The essence of God, that which makes him God, is fully present in Christ. Unlike 1:19, which was couched in the past tense, this is in the present. The fullness of God is still to be found in the risen and ascended Lord.

Out of that fullness, the Colossians have themselves been filled (v. 10) or perhaps 'brought to fullness'. The word-play is as obvious in English as in Greek, but the meaning is a bit obscure. It seems best to see a reference to the indwelling by Christ to which Paul has already referred (1:27). For those who are 'in Christ', Christ is also in them, filling their spiritual needs and satisfying their deepest longings.

This Christ, himself the fullness of God, the full satisfier of human need, is the head—the source and Lord—of all cosmic rulers and authorities. Those who know him have nothing to fear from any other power.

A PRAYER

Lord, may I see you as the one who fills my life
and fulfils my needs.

TRUE CIRCUMCISION

If an interest in the cosmic powers was unique to the Colossians, Paul's next target is an old acquaintance of his. The question of circumcision has been raised. It is not clear whether circumcision was being advocated by the Colossians as necessary or just as a possibly desirable option. Paul is not as vociferous in his condemnation as in Galatians, so it is likely that this was seen as one possible way to enhance one's standing with God, or as a way to deeper spiritual experience. Either way, though, Paul sees it, as always, as a threat to the work that Christ has done.

Paul's meaning in verses 11–12 is far from clear, and there are broadly two ways of interpreting it, each of which makes quite good sense. The first is to say that baptism is the Christian equivalent of circumcision. Thus, as (male) Jews entered into the covenant community of God's people through circumcision, Christians do so through baptism, and circumcision is therefore unnecessary.

The second view assumes that Paul's argument is primarily about the death and resurrection of Jesus. On this view the circumcision of Christ does not refer to his own circumcision on the eighth day after birth, but to his death, in which his whole physical body was stripped away. Christians, by being united with Christ in his death, die to their old life and live a new one.

Baptism

What is Paul's argument? Firstly, Christians already have a circumcision, one which is not 'made by hands'. This is a phrase often used in the Bible to deride idols, in contrast to the real, invisible God. Thus physical circumcision, says Paul, can be an idol, leading the circumcised to put their trust in it rather than in God himself. Christians do not need circumcision, for it marks a membership of the people of God which is already theirs by virtue of sharing in the 'circumcision of Christ'. It is difficult to imagine that Paul would expect the Colossians immediately to recognize this as referring to Jesus' death, and the phrase 'putting off the body of flesh' more naturally seems to refer to the spiritual circumcision that the Colossians already have than to the execution of Christ.

The key point is that the believer's union with Christ in his death comes about in baptism (v. 12). Thus it seems to make better sense to say that baptism is indeed the Christian equivalent of circumcision, but that baptism in itself is not something in which one can put one's faith any more than is circumcision. It is baptism, in so far as it effects a sharing in the death of Christ, that enables the Christian to put off their old life, the 'body of flesh' (compare 'body of death' in Romans 7:24). The logical consequence of sharing in Christ's death is a share in his resurrection as well. This is both a promise for the future (Romans 6:5) and a present reality in the form of a new life which is lived for God by the citizens of the kingdom of Christ.

That new life becomes real through faith in God. It is not a magical act produced by the ritual of baptism, but is part of an ongoing relationship with the living God, whose power raised Jesus from the dead (v. 12). He calls his people to new life here and now, and that life is based on faith in him.

Paul therefore contrasts the ritual of circumcision with the living relationship with God that is brought about through the death of Christ. Baptism (which Paul has already hinted at in 1:13) brings about the union with Christ and the transfer into his kingdom, but that kingdom life must be lived out by faith or it is meaningless. Baptism is therefore both an assurance of belonging to God and a challenge to live for him.

A PRAYER

Lord, thank you that I have been baptized into your kingdom.
May I grow in faith as I seek to be your servant.

59

The TRIUMPH of the CROSS

Before their encounter with Christ, the Colossians were dead to God, lacking the spiritual awareness and hope of eternal life that come from knowing him (v. 13). Firstly, their trespasses—a word which suggests the breaking of God's moral law—created a divide between them and their creator. As Gentiles, they did not have the Law of Moses, but their failure to keep their own standards, which seems to be a universal aspect of the human condition, counted against them in much the same way (see Romans 2:14–15). Secondly, they were outside the covenant relationship with God, as uncircumcised Gentiles, and so had not received any of the benefits of knowing God that the Jews had enjoyed.

All that is now in the past, for God has made them alive, bringing hope and the presence of Christ, the giver of eternal life. Paul at this point switches to the first person, 'us'. This is not just something that applies to the Colossians. It is the linchpin of Christian faith. On the cross, Jesus has done away with the demands of the Law and brought forgiveness to all who put their trust in him.

God has, says Paul, 'erased the record that stood against us' (v. 14). The 'record' or, in some translations, 'bond', translates a Greek word, *cheirographon*, which literally means a hand-written note. It was used to describe an IOU written down by the borrower himself rather than by a scribe, as a pledge of personal indebtedness. God has cancelled the debt that human beings owed to him. The human failure to obey God leaves people indebted to him and liable for whatever penalty clauses may be attached to his commands. The basic penalty clause is, of course, the breaking of relations with God, and subsequent abandonment to the consequences of sin.

All this was wiped away by the cross. The obvious conclusion from the nailing of the IOU to the cross is that Christ took upon himself the human debt and expunged it with his own death. It is frequently objected that this idea of Christ's payment of the debt makes God immoral: he takes out on Jesus what is really deserved by others. The objection has no force, however, since Paul has been at pains to demonstrate that Christ is God's incarnate self. The cross is about God taking upon himself the consequences of sin in his own creation, to bring that creation back into a right relationship with him.

Broken powers

A consequence of Christ's redeeming death is that the powers and authorities so esteemed by the Colossians have been stripped of their power (v. 15). It is likely that Paul thinks of them as the ones who held the IOU and used it to gain authority over humanity. Because of separation from God, humanity falls prey to the cosmic forces and becomes enslaved by them. Once God re-establishes a relationship with sinful people, the powers are stripped of their control and become like captives in a Roman triumphal procession, dragged along behind the triumphant Christ, their powerlessness displayed for all to see.

Can this be put into modern terms? In fact, Paul does this himself. The cosmic powers include angelic and demonic beings but also anything that holds sway over human life. So in verse 16 religious rules are effectively equated with the powers—they can become the controlling feature of life instead of being an expression of a living relationship with God. In the modern world, the constraints of work, keeping to the clock, meeting the deadline, can be the controlling power in our lives. So can politically oppressive regimes; so can poverty and hunger.

Christ still disarms the powers. In religion, he opens a direct access to God which is not dependent on observing the religious calendar or doing the necessary rituals. In daily life, he gives fulfilment in a relationship with him, rather than in the demands of the material world.

Where rulers demand that which belongs to God, God's power is yet greater, providing the inspiration, the impetus and the courage for resistance, the proclamation of peace and the struggle against injustice. Where the enslaving power is poverty and disease, the power of God is greater, waking a challenge to the economic systems that engender poverty and keep medical treatment for the wealthy. The real challenge is to those who claim allegiance to Christ but fail to recognize the powers that still seek to keep people in bondage.

A PRAYER

Lord, for all that your cross achieved, I praise you. For all that it calls me to, I ask your strength.

GOD *or* SLAVERY?

If Christ's triumph is a disarming of the powers that bind us, it is also a call to recognize the presence and danger of those powers. In the Colossian heresy, it looks very much as though Christ was seen as one among many intermediaries between humanity and God. His work could be added to, enhanced by human effort—and that was the seductive attraction of it. Grace is free, abundant and all-encompassing, but self-justification, the sense of putting someone else, even God himself, in our debt is devilishly attractive.

Colossian spirituality seems to have included rules about what sort of food to eat. This may have been an adoption of Jewish purity laws, or it may have been pagan in origin, with some foods regarded as more spiritual, less tainted with the material world, than others. The Colossians' rules seem to have included maintaining certain days as more holy, probably including Jewish festivals and sabbath observance. In themselves, none of these was wrong, particularly if they were the Jewish observances laid down in the *Torah*. But, says Paul, these observances were all pointers towards the reality that was to come, an insubstantial shadow in comparison to the solid reality that has now arrived in Christ (v. 17). Once again, the Colossians have everything in Christ. What more could they need?

Things that they see as adding to their spiritual quest end up as powers to which they are in slavery. Having had the IOU of human debt wiped clear, they proceed to write another one, which will only point up their failure.

Mysticism

A second dimension to the new Colossian teaching appears to be an emphasis on what might be termed mysticism—a quest for visions sought through abstinence. The term translated by NRSV as self-abasement (v. 18) means literally 'humility', but was used to refer to ascetic practices and especially fasting.

Part of the goal of such practices was the 'worship of angels'. It is highly unlikely that Paul is referring to worship offered to angels by the Colossians. If that were the case, he would surely make more of the issue. More probably, the Colossian mystics aimed for visionary experiences in which they joined in the worship of God that is offered by the angels in heaven. Such practices were not unknown in Judaism, in which mystics sought a glimpse of the chariot-throne of God. Indeed, Paul himself was not averse to visionary experiences, and in 2 Corinthians 12:2–4 recounts his own vision of heaven. Paul's objection is that the Colossians may be 'disqualified' by their failure to attain such experiences or, conversely, may believe that such visions qualify them for some sort of high spiritual status. At the very least they were inventing a two-tier system of Christianity, with the ascetic, visionary mystics as the aristocracy of the church. At worst, they were making salvation dependent on religious practice and spiritual experiences, and not on the grace of God.

Such a double system has been a perennial temptation for the Church. Whether it has been the exaltation of religious orders, or of clergy, or of those who speak in tongues, there has been (and still is) a tendency to see certain gifts or offices as of more value than others.

This, says Paul, is a way of thinking that is based on the flesh (v. 18), the weak and sin-prone component of human nature that needs to be overcome by God's grace. It is about self-aggrandisement and a disdainful attitude to others. Instead of mutual help and love, there is a comparison of spiritual achievements and a desire to boast. It is religion as a competitive sport, and in fact the word for 'disqualify' is, at root, about removing a prize.

As with the observance of festivals and food laws, the pursuit of spiritual experiences has become a means of slavery. Those who have been set free by Christ now find themselves tied to a hopeless quest, in which what might have been occasional and glorious gifts from God have become so many points on the score-card of spiritual achievement. The very core of the Church, its worship, has become a means of glorifying the worshippers rather than the God to whom worship is supposedly offered.

A PRAYER

Lord, may I glimpse a vision of your glory, not that I may be exalted, but that you may be more greatly praised.

The UNITING HEAD

The most damning indictment of the Colossians' new teachers is simply that they have lost their grip on Christ (v. 19). Any theology that claims to be Christian must be centred on Christ, for only in Jesus do we see the distinctively Christian understanding of God.

By cutting loose from Christ, the teachers (and any who may follow them) are denying their relationship of grace with God and thereby breaking it off. As a result, they are separated from the source of spiritual life.

Paul uses his analogy of the body again, this time seeing the head as that from which all the rest flows. (The sheer physicality of the image stands in stark contrast to the visionary aspirations of the Colossian teachers.) Here he sees the head providing the rest of the body with unity, the ligaments, sinews and nourishment all proceeding, as it were, from the head.

This ultimately comes from God, who provides the Church's growth in knowledge, love and service. It is as the Church learns love that it is bound together (2:2) and the source of that love is God.

Dead to the world

In verse 20, Paul returns to his main point. All that the Colossians need is found in Christ. Previously, they had indeed been a part of the world that is ruled by the elemental powers, the spiritual rulers of the cosmos. In their baptism, they died to the old life of bondage (2:12) and put it behind them. Why should they now seek to re-enter slavery?

Paul uses two parallel phrases to describe the same reality—'the elemental spirits of the universe' and 'belonging to the world'. This present world is marked by its rebellion against God and subsequent slavery to other powers. It is this dimension of slavery that explains Paul's next question: 'Why do you submit to regulations?' Instead of the freedom that is theirs in Christ, the Colossians are in danger of reverting to slavery, in this case slavery to religious rules.

The particular rules that Paul mentions are concerned with food, and may well reflect the Jewish dietary laws. The problem is that by being over-scrupulous about what they eat, the Colossians are returning to a mentality of fear. Instead of pursuing a relationship with God, they become concerned purely with the material world, with things that decay and vanish and so can have no lasting significance (see Mark 7:14–15). Of course, this is a complete reversal of the Colossian teachers' intentions. By seeking to live a life of ritual purity, devout religious observance and intense spiritual experience, they sought to draw nearer to God. The difficulty is that if rules could be kept to perfection, religion practised with no blemish of hypocrisy or half-heartedness, and spiritual events manufactured to order, there would be no need of salvation.

God's grace, on the other hand, cuts through all this paraphernalia. It is God's free gift of salvation, of adoption into his family and union with Christ that makes such things unnecessary. The rules and regulations by which the teachers aim to reach God are human inventions, with nothing to offer that God has not already far surpassed by his saving acts in Christ (v. 22).

Mind you, they look good and no doubt sound very impressive, claiming the wisdom of ancient tradition. None the less, it is a self-made piety, an invention with no ground in God. It puts great emphasis on asceticism, the refusal to give way to the demands of the body, and ends up indulging the flesh (v. 23). To understand this, we need to remember that 'flesh' is Paul's term for unredeemed human nature. It is that part of us which is prone to failure and sin. So by putting on a good show in their outward appearance, the false teachers are building up an attitude of pride and superiority which is simply an indulgence of their sinful nature—hence the NRSV translation that the practices of the Colossian teachers are of no value in checking self-indulgence.

We should not imagine that Paul is denying the need for self-discipline. The issue is about where the focus of our spiritual life lies. If it is centred on Christ, and based on an awareness of the overarching grace of God, then various spiritual disciplines can be useful tools. When they become an end in themselves, or are credited with giving access to God by good religious technique, then they are simply as false and dangerous as anything taught in first-century Colossae.

A PRAYER

Lord, may my life be centred on you, and all else be simply a means of knowing you and serving you.

LOOKING UP

Paul continues by exhorting his readers to 'seek the things that are above' (v. 1). Isn't this exactly what they have been doing, through their asceticism and mysticism? In fact, Paul's argument has been that whatever they imagined their efforts to do, they were in fact failing miserably.

The Colossians' new teaching ties them to the things of this world, to the fleshly desire for superiority and human approval. It is the perfect example of the type of religiosity that seeks to reach out to God while ignoring God's prior reaching out to us. As a result, seek as it may for the things of heaven, it can only remain earthbound.

Now, says Paul, as those who have been raised with Christ, you are actually able to seek heavenly things, so look for them and you will find them in Christ, 'seated at the right hand of God'. The image is borrowed from Psalm 110:1, a verse much used by the early Christians to stress the lordship of Christ. That lordship comes not just from his own character as the incarnate Word and Wisdom of God, but from his achievement of salvation through the cross and the resurrection. It is as the one who has accomplished God's act of salvation that he is worshipped as the ascended Lord, sharing the rule of God (see comment on Philippians 2:6, pp. 54–55).

The new mindset

Therefore, rather than being concerned with earthly matters, the Colossians should indeed be looking for higher things (v. 2). 'Higher things', literally 'the things above', is probably a term that the Colossian teachers used themselves. They encouraged their followers to leave the earthly life behind and reach up to heaven. In fact, they did the reverse, by forgetting the access to heaven that Christians already have in Christ, and concentrating on merely human religious techniques. Paul is effectively reversing their argument. The 'things on earth' (v. 2) are precisely those things that the Colossians were tempted to see as the means of liberating them from a worldly existence, and opening for them a door into heaven.

In reality, they already have a route into heaven. Indeed, they have a share in the life of heaven here and now. The risen life of Christ is the centre of the Christian's life. In Christ, the Colossians have died to their old, earthly life, and share in the resurrection life. This is not to say that they have reached perfection, or that the resurrection does not lie in the future, for it certainly does. At present the full extent of that life is 'hidden with Christ in God' (v. 3). That is, it will be discovered only when God transforms the world and brings to completion the new creation that he has set in train through the work of Christ (v. 4). Until then, the Colossians have a share, an interest, in the resurrection life. It has become their reality, in contrast to the earthly life of separation from God. It is the life of the kingdom of Christ, the life of those who in their baptism died to the old life (v. 3) and whose new life is summed up in devotion and obedience to Christ, the source of the life to come (v. 4).

Set your minds, says Paul, on the truly heavenly things that are yours in Christ (v. 2). Here he uses the same idea as in Philippians, of the Christian mind that is focused on Christ and transformed by faith. In this new way of thinking, the Christian patterns his or her life on that of Christ, living now by the light of the world to come.

Thus the Christian mindset has two components. It is something that might be expected to flow naturally from the new relationship with God in Christ, drawing sustenance from the life of prayer, worship and service that characterized the way of discipleship. At the same time, it is something that has to be worked on, to be put into practice by an effort of will and determination. Or, to put it another way, the Christian outlook is a matter of co-operation between the work of God's Holy Spirit and the Christian in whom the Spirit works. Hence Paul can command the Colossians to have this way of thinking, and at the same time can stress that their real life is already found in Christ. The Christian mindset is the result of living out the implications of the salvation that God has graciously given.

A PRAYER

Lord, may my mind be set on you, and may my life
reflect the world to come.

UNDERCOVER SPIRIT

In our last section we mentioned the work of the Holy Spirit. It is worth noting that while, in other contexts, Paul stresses the role of the Holy Spirit in Christian life (for example, Romans 8), he gives little mention of it in Colossians. The reason can be found in his determination to stress the completeness of what the Colossians have in Christ. He wants nothing to distract them from the central message that Jesus Christ offers all they need. This does not mean that he considers the Spirit to be dispensable. The Spirit is the means by which Christ is present in the Christian's life, and to those who have read Paul's other letters it is clear that the idea of the Spirit's work lies very close beneath the surface of Colossians as well.

Flesh and Spirit

Having told the Colossians to set their minds on things above, Paul seems to come down to earth with a bump. Yet this is exactly what he means by having a heavenly outlook. For Christians, there is no escape from everyday reality into a realm of the spirit. The result of a mind set on things above is a renewed life in the day-to-day world.

Dying with Christ therefore brings its own command: the Colossians are to put to death 'the members that are on earth'. 'Members' is almost certainly a reference to bodily organs, though Paul is neither suggesting the removal of real body parts nor saying that the body is sinful. It is his way of stressing that life is lived physically by physical bodies in the material world. What we do, we do with our bodies, and our actions reflect our relationship with God and affect the lives of other people.

Paul therefore presents a list of five typical sins that characterized the pre-Christian life of the Colossians and of the pagan world in general. The first is 'fornication', which translates the Greek word *porneia*. *Porneia* refers to any kind of illegitimate sexual intercourse, and, depending on its context, can cover pre- and extra-marital sex, prostitution and various sexual perversions. Christians and Jews were much less casual in their attitude to sex than were most of the peoples of the Greco-Roman world. This is in part because of the place that the Hebrew scriptures give to marriage in God's ideal plan of creation (see Genesis 2:23–24). For Jews, sexuality was an integral part of a total relationship, and not lightly to be separated from it. Moreover, marriage reflected the relationship of God to his people, and unfaithfulness was a major image of idolatry.

The seriousness of sexual sins is underlined by the next word, 'impurity', which refers to moral uncleanness and usually carries sexual overtones. It also stresses another reason for taking sexual sins seriously. For Christians, the body is the self. There is no separate soul sitting inside, unharmed by what the body does, and waiting to be released upon death. What is done in the body has spiritual as well as physical consequences, for body, soul and spirit are simply different ways of speaking of the whole person, the human being who belongs to God.

By 'passion', the third of the five sins, Paul means unbridled human desires, be they sexual or otherwise. It is the attitude of indulgence, of 'going for it' no matter what the consequences, and is closely linked to the fourth, 'evil desire'. Here Paul speaks of a life which is governed by the search for pleasure, or which sees no reason to abstain from whatever is on offer. Desire in itself is not necessarily sinful, and in the New Testament it can refer to a longing for what is good. Where it goes adrift is in the assumption that whatever is wanted must be good, or it would not be wanted.

Finally, Paul adds covetousness, or 'greed'. It is, he says, tantamount to idolatry. Covetousness is the desire to have more—and then more. It can never be satisfied, by its very definition, and so the pursuit of ever greater acquisitions becomes the main goal of life and hence a god.

All of these things are characteristics of a life that looks no further than the present world and seeks its fulfilment within it. Those whose eyes are fixed on the things of heaven will have other priorities and other goals to pursue. Conversely, those who live this way show by their very behaviour that the life of heaven has passed them by.

A PRAYER

Lord, may my life show yours, and my eyes remain fixed on you.

TRUST

In view of the sort of vices that Paul has outlined, the wrath of God is coming. Talk of judgment is unpopular in the modern age, even among Christians. Yet if we are to be entrusted with freedom and moral responsibility, we must accept the consequences. In verse 6 Paul looks at the final result of disobedience to God—his wrath. The wrath of God is not, for Paul, a capricious or bad-tempered anger. It is a statement of his implacable incompatibility with evil, and so is a matter not of legal reward and punishment but of relationships. Those who have no place for God are effectively keeping him at arm's length. They are pushing away the source of eternal life.

That was the way in which the Colossians used to live (v. 7), before their own encounter with God. Their new life now requires a daily decision to walk with Christ, to live in a way that reflects his character, and to put away the characteristics of the old life.

One area where the change should be obvious is in the way Christians speak (v. 8). Outbursts of temper (anger and wrath), malicious speech, defamation of character (slander) and abusive speech are things which have no place in Christian living. Such sins damage the Christian community more than any other. That is why Paul ends this second list of sins with lying (v. 9). Telling lies is always tempting: it avoids the necessity of being humble and having to admit failure, it shifts blame on to others, and sometimes it can be seen as a kindness. On the other hand, once one is found out as a liar, the possibility of future trust is severely diminished. In a community that is called to work together in the spread of the gospel, in worship and prayer and in mutual encouragement, trust is a necessity. If Christians cannot trust each other, the possibility of being a community evaporates, and the church's task of demonstrating the kingdom of God to the world cannot even begin.

Dressing up

This is something the Colossians put behind them when they came to Christ. They are like people dressed in new clothes, presenting a new appearance to the world (v. 10). In their baptism, they have stripped off their old lives as they stripped off their old clothes to enter the water. We know from later writings that this was a common practice at baptism, and it is virtually certain that it took place in New Testament times as well (see Galatians 3:27). Candidates for baptism stripped naked and after baptism were dressed in a new white robe.

Note the double action in this stripping and reclothing. It is something that the Colossians have done themselves, and must continue to do (v. 12). By repentance they have cast off the past, and through faith in Christ they have dressed for the future in the new humanity which will find its completion in the coming new creation. At the same time, this is something that God has done and continues to do. Note the use of the passive voice in verse 10: the new self 'is being renewed', that is, by God, in the image of its creator.

According to Genesis 1:27, God created human beings in his own image. Exactly what that image consists of is debated, but that is not important here. The point is that humans are meant to bear the family likeness of God. That likeness has been marred by sin. Now, in Christ, the image is being renewed, as God carries out the ultimate makeover and transforms the present sinful human nature into the new one that is found in Christ. Thus, the 'image of its creator' in verse 10 is a reference to Christ, through whom and for whom all creation came into being (1:16). In Jesus is found the true image of God, the new humanity, and he is the pattern for the lives that are being renewed by God.

Paul describes that renewal as a renewal in *knowledge*. The new self is one that is aware of God and constantly growing in knowledge and understanding of his will and purpose. To be clothed afresh in Christ (see Romans 13:14) is to be given the ability to discern what is appropriate to Christian life and what is not. The renewed nature of the Colossians will instantly recognize that the sins Paul has listed in verses 5 and 8 are incompatible with the worship and service of God.

So once again Paul ties together the ideas of spiritual growth and transformation with practical living in the material world. To be baptized is to be renewed, and that renewal shows itself in the ability to discern the path of discipleship.

A PRAYER

Lord, help me to dress in the new life and to live it for you.

BREAKING *the* BARRIERS

Baptism into Christ, and hence into the new humanity, brings about a radical change of status. From the point of view of the Christian, there is now no distinction between the different members of society. For Paul this was an important point, and he says something very similar in Galatians 3:28 and 1 Corinthians 12:13. In Colossians 3:11 he lists differences which were very real in the social world of his time, but which make no difference at all within the Church.

There is no longer any Greek or Jew, circumcised or uncircumcised. The great religious barrier between the ancient people of God and the Gentiles has been broken down. Anyone can now belong to God's people, through faith in Christ. Those who have been baptized have entered into the same relationship with God that was for so long the preserve of the descendants of Abraham. Hence Paul stresses the role of circumcision, which was apparently tempting to the Colossians. It is redundant, for Christ has removed the need for the old sign of covenant membership.

There is also no distinction between nations. There is no longer a difference between Greeks, who prided themselves on their culture, philosophy and history, and the barbarians, among whom the Scythians were legendary for their uncouth language and behaviour. This was a particularly Greek way of thinking. 'Barbarian' is a Greek word for anyone who didn't speak Greek—to the cultured Greeks, they just made 'bar-bar' noises! The Scythian tribes from around the Black Sea were seen as the lowest type of barbarian, despised as the most menial of slaves and least cultured of peoples. Whatever previous prejudices one may have held, says Paul, each person is someone for whom Christ died, and each is an equal member of the Church.

Indeed, there is no longer a distinction between free and slave. In Paul's time this was a more fundamental difference even than that between Greek and barbarian. Slavery was an intrinsic part of the social order. It was important in economic terms, but perhaps even more so in terms of defining society. Slavery was so much a part of life that almost no one thought about it, in much the same way as we today accept motor cars. Slaves were legally objects, living tools of their masters. In the Church, though, this was not to be the case. In the new humanity instituted by Christ, the difference between slave and master should disappear.

Changing the world

To what extent Paul thought that the equality found in Christ should make a difference in wider society is debatable. Christians were a small, politically powerless group who for the most part expected the world to end fairly soon. It is unlikely that Paul or any other Christian of his time gave much attention to wider issues of social reform. However, it is clear that in the Church, social distinctions were expected to be meaningless, and in that alone, Paul provides the seeds of much of the Christian inspiration which eventually would lead to the great social reformers of the 18th and 19th centuries, the American civil rights movement and the issues of justice to the poor that exercise many Christians today.

The reason Paul gives for this radical equality in the Church is that in the new humanity Christ is 'all in all'. Christ is all that matters, the defining core of the Church's being, beside which all other concerns fade into insignificance. If he is the focus of each Christian's life, the one thing that matters above all else, then those Christians have so much in common that any differences become trivial. Christ is in all, the indwelling presence in each Christian's life, the guide and goal of that life. If Christ is equally present in slave and master, Greek and Jew, Greek and barbarian, then there are no grounds for human divisions. If another is deemed a suitable person to be the dwelling place of God, who am I to despise that person?

A PRAYER

Lord, help me to recognize that you have broken the barriers that humans erect, and so to live as though they did not exist.

The WELL-DRESSED CHRISTIAN

In verse 12, Paul returns to the image of dressing in the new life. Sometimes the language of reclothing makes Paul's modern readers uneasy. They object that it seems to reduce Christian living to mere play-acting or, even worse, to hypocritical pretence. Like children dressing up in adult clothes, Christians dress up in the costume of the kingdom of heaven. But then, that is precisely what it is. By putting on the role, and making the conscious effort to live it out, we align ourselves with the work that God is doing in our lives. What begins as a role becomes second nature, and in the fullness of time becomes our only nature, as God and we work together to make us into the image of Christ. The hypocrite pretends to be something he is not, so as to make a good impression. The Christian strives to be something he is not, in order eventually to become it.

Virtues of the kingdom

Hence Paul goes on to list, as a contrast to the vices mentioned in verses 5 and 8, some of the virtues that make up the heavenly costume. The first is 'compassion', literally 'bowels (or internal organs) of compassion'. In the ancient world, the guts were seen as the seat of emotion (as we have 'gut feelings'), while the heart was seen as the seat of reason. Compassion denotes the ability both to feel for others and to put those feelings into action.

Then comes 'kindness', which is a benevolent attitude to others. It goes with 'humility', which is the same word as the one translated 'self-abasement' in 2:18. Here it means having the realistic attitude to oneself that neither seeks a false lowliness nor demands more credit than one is due.

'Meekness' is thinking of others rather than of oneself—the ability to give way to the needs and hopes of someone else. It goes with 'patience', the ability to put up with exasperating or annoying behaviour in others. Literally it means something like 'long-tempered' and is the exact opposite of short-tempered. All these are qualities that go towards building up a community. They require the grace of God, and hard work!

Paul drives home his point in verse 13: 'Bear with one another.'

Paul is a realist in his understanding of the Church. It is the community of God's saints, but also a collection of people who may have nothing in common but their faith in Christ. Some would need to be encouraged to speak for themselves and to take responsibility where none was given in daily life. Others would be only too used to calling the tune, and would need to learn silence and humility. In fact, Paul's churches contained the same rag-bag of humanity that the modern Church contains, and perhaps even more so. Learning mutual respect and care was and is the priority for any congregation that wants to be more than a brief weekly meeting. Hence a core characteristic of the local church has to be forgiveness.

Forgiveness is a key element in the Lord's Prayer, and it is embedded in the creeds that were formulated in the centuries after Paul, all of which points up both its necessity and its difficulty. This may be part of the reason why Paul does not use the normal word for 'forgive', but one which is related to the word for 'grace', and stresses the abundant, unmerited nature of forgiveness. Forgiveness is not about being right but about restoring relationships. Thus Paul envisages situations in which church members will have (probably quite legitimate) grievances against one another. In that situation, they are to forgive—to wipe the slate clean and carry on.

There is no need to suppose that Paul is against discussion and the working out of difficulties. Many Christians make the mistake of assuming that any kind of conflict must be avoided at any cost. This is both unhealthy and far from Paul's own example. What must be done, however, is to keep forgiveness uppermost in any difference or disagreement. We can hammer out our differences, but at the end of the day we must forgive those who offend us.

The great example of this is, of course, Christ's own forgiveness of us. (Paul uses the title 'Lord', which is almost certainly a reference to Christ rather than to God.) When the whole purpose of God in Christ was to bring us forgiveness and restore us to himself, how can we fail to do likewise?

A PRAYER

*Lord, may I dress my speech and my relationships
in a forgiveness that mirrors yours.*

LOVE

The final and most important garment in the Christian wardrobe is love. The characteristic Christian virtue, the one that should define God's people and stamp the family likeness on the whole diverse membership of the Church, is love.

Love is the spring from which flow the compassion, kindness, humility, meekness and patience that Paul has exhorted the Colossians to show. It is love that binds the disparate membership together —and here Paul slides out of the analogy of clothing and back to his image of the Church as a body. Like muscles and tendons (see 2:19), love joins the various organs together and enables them to work towards perfection. Love binds the community together and enables it to grow towards the completeness and unity that is its final goal, as it is made over into the image of Christ.

Like the other virtues, love is both a gift of God, growing from the experience of his grace, and an act of will, a decision to behave that way. That is one reason why the New Testament writers use the relatively rare word, *agape*, for 'love'. They needed a word that could be virtually redefined in terms of a love that was not about natural affection or attraction. No one can be commanded to fall in love or to feel affection. But they can be commanded to act in a way that is best for others. And of course, once you start acting with love towards someone, you may well end up actually liking them!

Peace

Alongside love stands the peace that comes from knowing God (v. 15). Once again, it is the deep-seated sense of wholeness and well-being that is the result of a life based on the awareness of God's promise of salvation. In the immediate context, though, Paul is certainly thinking of peace as the dominant attitude between members of the Christian congregation. Peace is to rule in the Colossians' hearts, which means the seat of their reason and will rather than their emotions (see comment on 3:12, p. 152). It is the way they are to behave towards each other, not necessarily the way they are to feel.

An attitude of peacefulness to others is part of the Colossians' Christian calling. To be a Christian is to adopt a certain approach to others that reflects the way Jesus behaved. Paul's phrase goes further than this, however. The Colossians have been called into peace. The peace of Christ is seen here as more or less equivalent to salvation. It is the realm of wholeness and well-being that is the antithesis to the realm of darkness from which they have been called. Peace, with God, with each other and with oneself, is the characteristic of Christ's kingdom. That kingdom is the place of security and healing.

Called to belong

Christians are called into the realm of peace 'in one body'. Given the way Paul has so far used 'body', this is certainly a reference to the body of Christ, the Church. The Christian calling is not an individual call (though of course it comes individually to each member) but a call to be a part of the Christian community. At the same time it is a call *to* the Christian community.

Those who enter the realm of Christ's peace also enter the community of the saints. Then, that community has to make real the calling to be a place of peace, of wholeness and well-being, which has been Paul's exhortation through this chapter.

All this has a direct bearing on the false teaching at Colossae. Where the Colossian teachers sought the experience of God outside the world and the Church, through fasting and religious ritual, true peace is found through working out the call of salvation in the Christian community, and indeed in the world at large.

It is appropriate that Paul's next admonition is to be thankful. Instead of ceaselessly seeking to approach God, the Colossians need to recognize all that they have already received. Salvation is theirs, and the new creation lies ahead. In Christ they have all they need; indeed, they have all there is to have. Their outworking of the virtues of the kingdom in their daily and congregational life should be a glad act of thanksgiving for all that God has done.

A PRAYER

Lord, may I never lose sight of your gift or your call, but gratefully live as one of your people.

68

WORSHIP & TEACHING

Paul's call to thanksgiving at the end of verse 15 forms a bridge into a new area of teaching, as he turns his attention to the worship at Colossae.

His first concern is with the gospel the Colossians have received. This is the word of Christ; that is, the teaching about him, which must dwell among the whole community. The word of Christ has come to the Colossians and borne fruit (1:5–6), but it must continue to do so, dwelling in them richly; that is, bringing further blessings and gifts as it continues to take an ever surer grip on their lives.

As they grow in understanding, they will have more insights to share among themselves, both in teaching and in admonition. The task of teaching and putting each other on to the right path is the work of the whole congregation, not only of designated teachers and pastors. Such a task must be exercised with wisdom, however. For the Colossians' false teachers, wisdom was an esoteric mystery. For Paul, it is a practical matter, the exercising of discernment in speech, knowing when to impart new insights and how to offer correction in a way that is both helpful and loving rather than destructive and domineering.

Significantly, Paul envisages teaching and admonition as coming through the medium of worship. It is highly likely that meetings at Colossae would have contained elements of biblical exposition and preaching, as well as prophecy and other forms of inspired speech. These, though, were for those with particular gifts. The way in which everyone would be able to impart their share of teaching was through the medium of praise and thanksgiving, and particularly by their contribution of hymnody. As they expressed their gratitude to God in songs of praise, those very songs would be a vehicle of teaching.

Nowadays we tend to make a distinction between worship and teaching, and some modern liturgists are firm in their belief that teaching should be distinct from worship. Paul would disagree. Hymns, psalms and spiritual songs are to be sung to God as the expression of thanksgiving that springs from a heart set on him. At the same time, the content of those songs, the way in which they are introduced into worship, and their suitability to particular occasions cannot help but impart understanding. It is probably fair to say that in present-day churches, more teaching is imparted through the liturgy (of whatever kind) than through sermons—and certainly more than through small teaching groups or Bible studies, which are usually attended only by a small proportion of the congregation.

Sharing faith

The style of worship that Paul seems to envisage is one in which individual members make their own contributions to the service as it is in progress. Within a relatively short time, the Church would develop fairly set liturgies, and that is the norm today (even in churches that pride themselves on not having a written liturgy!). There is much to be said for a well designed and balanced service, as anyone who has suffered from a badly led 'free' service will know. However, Paul's view of worship does raise the question of the place of individual contributions to services. What opportunities for mutual teaching and encouragement (yes, and admonition) do we provide today?

It is hard to distinguish between the three types of musical contribution that Paul mentions. What does he mean by psalms, hymns and spiritual songs? It is unlikely that each word denotes a particular type of song (unlike the rather vague distinction between modern 'hymns' and 'worship songs'). Each of the words in Greek could denote any type of song, and it is likely that Paul lists the three to stress the range of songs sung. These could well have included biblical psalms, previously written Christian hymns and impromptu Spirit-inspired songs, but also anything else that might be on offer. The main criteria are that they express a real sense of thanksgiving and that they edify the congregation as well, being chosen wisely.

It must be stressed, though, that they are first and foremost directed to God. It is worship that teaches the congregation, not teaching that can also double up as worship!

A PRAYER

Lord, may the thanks and praise I offer draw others to you.

LIFE *as* WORSHIP

Just as the call to thanksgiving at the end of verse 15 formed a bridge into a brief discussion of worship, so verse 17 now carries us into the next section of Paul's practical advice.

If worship is the expression of Christian gratitude to God, it is also the undergirding of all Christian life. Therefore, just as songs of praise and thanksgiving mark the Christian assembly, so an attitude of thanksgiving should run through all that Christians do or say. Their lives are to be lived for Christ, which means that anything that is done is done as an offering to him. Daily tasks, even the most menial, can and should be acts of worship, offered in the first place to God. This is the basic idea behind Paul's exhortation to do everything 'in the name of Christ'.

God of paper-clips

This can be a rather difficult idea to grasp. As I once heard someone ask, 'Is there a specifically Christian way of ordering a new batch of paper-clips?' In fact, there is, in two ways. The first is to recognize that all the world belongs to God and exists to give him glory. That means that God is glorified simply by the normal processes of nature, by the normal daily life of human beings. If God's presence pervades his creation, he is present in all things, and is even present in the act of ordering paper-clips. When his presence is recognized and acknowledged (even unconsciously), then it is fair to say that worship and prayer are taking place—not, admittedly, in the focused way of a church service, but simply by the fact that the job is done well, as part of a life dedicated to God.

God of justice

The second aspect is a moral one. To do something in the name of Christ is to do something that is in accordance with his will and character. So if the paper-clips are available cheaply because they fell off the back of a lorry or were made by slave labour, buying them, in the knowledge that a crime is being aided and abetted, is hardly an act of worship, glorifying God. Thus the awareness of God, and a spirit of thankfulness in daily life, provide a necessary moral check on a

Christian's actions. Again, it need not always be a conscious one. Simply forming the habit of doing what is right is part of the daily process of self-offering and worship that glorifies God in the acts of his people.

Like all worship, this daily offering of thanks is made to God through Jesus Christ. The common formula expresses the reality of Christian life and worship. It is aimed towards God, and the way to God is always through Christ, who forms the bridge between humanity and God, and who, by his incarnation, death and resurrection, permanently opens the way from the human world into the presence of the creator and Father.

One thing Paul does not say is that either daily life is a substitute for formal worship or vice versa. He would be surprised at today's common view that 'you don't have to go to church to be a Christian'. Daily life can be worship because it is lived in the light of that conscious and formal self-offering which is the Church's worship. 'Sunday worship' is meaningful because we go out from it to put into practice what our hearts and minds have said.

A PRAYER

Lord, may I, in my daily life, be always aware
that I live and work for you.

HOUSEHOLD RULES

At first sight, the list of household members' duties that forms this passage appears to sit uncomfortably in the midst of Paul's letter. In the Greek there is no linking word at the beginning to form a grammatical connection with what goes before. However, there is a very clear connection of idea. Paul includes these concrete examples from daily life because he wants to stress the reality of worship and service in the real world, as opposed to the Colossian teachers who seek it in a rarefied spiritual realm. The question is, where did Paul get this list from? There are many contemporary examples of lists of duties for members of households. The Greek-speaking world produced handbooks on the duties of householders, while Jewish writers similarly gave advice on household matters. This is hardly surprising, since the household was seen as the basic unit of ancient society, with 'family life' as the backbone of civilization. We need to remember, though, that the household/family of Paul's time was very different from modern Western models. It could have included slaves and servants, as well as what we would call an 'extended family', and was traditionally ruled by the male head of the household.

Various writers have therefore suggested that Paul adapted an existing Greek or Jewish list of household duties. This is unlikely, though, because these tended to be written simply as advice to the head of the household, whereas Paul addresses all members. Other writers have suggested that Paul had previously made up the list to counter radical social innovations that had sprung up in some churches as a result of taking too literally his own teaching on equality in Christ. There is no evidence for this, however, and the very fact that Paul addresses each family member, in mutually responsible pairs, is quite an innovation in itself. It is probably best to imagine Paul writing the list specifically for the Colossians, for the reasons given above. Other New Testament writers also modelled teaching on the basic household unit of the ancient world (see 1 Peter 2:18 to 3:7; 1 Timothy 2:8–15; 6:1–2; Titus 2:1–10—assuming that the letters to Timothy and Titus are, as most scholars suppose, not by Paul).

Paul therefore continues his teaching on doing all things in the name of Jesus by focusing on the area of the household, as most first-century writers would.

Christians in a pagan household

Before we look at the first of Paul's examples, we need to ask one question. What sort of household does he envisage? New Testament scholars seem to be in agreement that Paul is thinking here of a Christian household; that is, one in which at least nominal allegiance was paid to Christ by all its members. While this view is widespread, it needs to be challenged, for two reasons.

Firstly, while household conversions did happen (see the case of the Philippian gaoler in Acts 16:32–34), it is by no means certain that this was the norm. Is it realistic to suppose that everyone in a household would become converts at the same time? Indeed, in 1 Corinthians 7:12–16 Paul explicitly addresses the situation of a Christian man or woman whose marital partner is an unbeliever. It is therefore likely that many, if not most, of the Colossian Christians dwelt in households whose members were not uniformly Christian.

Secondly, the advice to husbands and wives in verses 18–19 seems a far cry from the radical equality in marriage that Paul outlines in 1 Corinthians 7:3–4 (and the rest of that chapter). It is possible, of course, that Paul changed his mind, or that a different church situation called for different advice, but neither of these seems very likely.

What is more likely is that Paul has in mind a household in which a Christian may find himself or herself living among non-Christian relatives, slaves or masters. This is both a more realistic picture of the likely situation of the Colossians and a better test case for Paul's argument. It is, after all, one thing to see daily life as lived for Christ in a Christian environment, and quite another to attempt the same thing in a pagan one.

A PRAYER

Lord, a lot of my life is lived in a pagan world.
May I live it to your praise and glory.

WIVES & HUSBANDS

In the ancient world, women were expected to be under the authority of a man. Unmarried women would be subject to their fathers, and wives to their husbands. Women could not, in Roman law, own property or run businesses. In practice, there were ways around these restrictions, so that in Paul's day there were many examples of independent, business-owning women. Technically, though, there was almost always the name of a male relative on the necessary bank and business documents. Certainly, in popular expectation, and probably for most women in reality, life revolved around the home, with the husband as the household's authority figure.

Paul's first admonition (v. 18) simply accepts this social norm. Wives are indeed to be subject to their husbands. Yet there is a difference. For wives who are Christians, this becomes their proper sphere of Christian service, their offering to God; it is fitting in the Lord. 'As is fitting' is a phrase that suggests a proper duty. That duty is not necessarily to be subordinate but to recognize that where a wife is subordinate, her position can still be lived out for Christ and be offered to him as an act of worship. Paul says nothing about situations in which the wife had considerable power or influence, though these did exist. His point is merely that in the traditional wifely role (on which he passes no judgment, either good or bad) Christ can be served.

Turning to husbands (v. 19), Paul has more latitude for advice. The husband had considerable power in his household, and the way that power was used was an area in which Christ could be honoured. Thus the first command is for a husband to love his wife. That may not seem too strange to us, but the word Paul uses is once again the Christian word for love, *agape*. Other words would normally have been expected, which conveyed the ideas of affection, friendship or sexual attraction. For Paul, though, the main sort of love to be shown was the self-giving, undemanding love that mirrors the love of God. Such a love will not show itself in harsh treatment, but will look for the best interests and well-being of the beloved. In short, a husband is to care for his wife and always to seek her good. Again, this is a command that can be put into practice irrespective of the faith of the wife. It is a minimum requirement which is possible in any situation. It certainly does not rule out the equal partnership that 1 Corinthians 7 envisages in a Christian marriage.

Children and parents

The same sort of advice is given to children and fathers. Today we would say 'parents', but in the ancient world the official power lay with the father, though it is likely that mothers dealt with their children on a day-to-day basis. Children should fulfil their expected role as a service to Christ. In practice, they had little option, since they had virtually no rights until they came of age (if they were boys). Girls, of course, simply passed from the authority of the father to that of their husband, at least in theory.

Again, this is said to be the proper, or acceptable, duty of children 'in the Lord'—that is, as Christians. Once again, it is a minimum requirement, which could make even the most traditional childhood into an opportunity for service. Paul's injunction does not rule out the possibility of a much freer and more responsible role for children. The point is that even in the apparently limited sphere open to children, the possibility exists for a life that is offered to God. As with wives, children may be powerless, but by living out their roles as a free offering, those roles can be transformed into an act of worship.

Unlike children, fathers had considerable power. And so they have a much greater responsibility—to ensure that their children are not 'provoked'. This word implies nagging, denigrating and even bullying. Children must not be belittled or made to feel worthless, or they could lose their sense of worth. The implication is that they are to be cherished, encouraged and loved. The power of the Christian parent is to be directed towards bringing out the best in their children and building up their self-esteem in preparation for adult life.

A PRAYER

Lord, may I always use what power I have to build up,
and not to tear down.

SLAVES & MASTERS

So far, Paul has established a pattern. Those with little power or room to manoeuvre in their lives receive few instructions. Wives and children are to live out their roles as a free offering to God. With slaves and masters, the situation is at first sight reversed. Slaves receive the longest piece of teaching in this section.

This is because, although their condition could often be pitiful, slaves could also hold positions of considerable responsibility within a household, and their opportunities to cheat their masters were notoriously plentiful. The first injunction is therefore to be obedient to their earthly masters (the same word, *kyrios*, as is used for the Lord). Paul knew, as everyone did, that slaves were prone to work their hardest only when watched. After all, it isn't as though they were paid for their work. Actually, this is not quite true. Slaves often had opportunities to gain money which, while technically the property of their masters, was customarily treated as the slave's own property. Household slaves could also expect to be released at some point and to live out the rest of their lives as freedmen and women, using their accumulated savings, together with whatever their masters gave them on parting, to set up their own businesses. Many of the wealthy merchants of the empire either began life as slaves or were descended from slaves. It was therefore in their own interests to serve their masters well, so as to gain their freedom that much sooner.

This, however, is not Paul's point. Slaves are to work diligently not because they want their freedom (though Paul had no objection to their being freed) but because the life they live and the work they do is their offering to God. Thus they work in the fear not of their masters' displeasure, but of God. By fear of the Lord, Paul could mean fear of his judgment, but it is more likely that he means the sense of awed awareness of God that the term denotes in the Old Testament. It is as they are aware of God that they are enabled to transform their daily work into something offered to him (v. 23). Once again it becomes their service and their daily worship.

By the same token, the reward they get comes from God (v. 24), and is greater than anything their human masters can offer. Once they see themselves as slaves of Christ rather than of earthly masters, they can indeed look forward to ultimate freedom—the gift of salvation itself—as long as they remain diligent in their service of God. Now a note of judgment does come in. It could be tempting to think that as the poor and oppressed, slaves would find God on their side. Paul does not comment on that. What he does say is that God judges everyone impartially, and a slave who has not fulfilled his potential as a slave of Christ will have to answer to God as much as any slave-owner.

Having said that, the same warning could also apply to slave-owners, and leads quite naturally to the words to them in 4:1. There, masters are to treat their slaves fairly and justly, with exactly the same motivation as the slaves themselves: all, whether free or slave, are slaves of Christ. The slave-owners have their own owner in heaven, and they will have to answer to him for their behaviour.

Reward and punishment

Is Paul being inconsistent in resorting to talk of rewards and punishments in heaven (3:24), while maintaining that salvation is God's gracious gift? If he is, it is an inconsistency that is shared by much of the Bible. Salvation is consistently presented as God's free gift, while judgment is on the basis of works done. The biblical teaching seems to be that those who belong to God are saved by his grace, but still have to answer for their actions when they meet him face to face.

A PRAYER

Lord, as you call us all to be equal in your kingdom, may I count all others as equal to me.

SLAVERY?

Finally, what about the concept of slavery itself? Should Paul not simply have told Christian masters to set their slaves free? Can Christians own slaves? The answer is, no—not now. But then, they could. Paul lived in an age when slavery was so much a part of the social setting that it was unquestioned by all. Even when slaves rebelled, they did not question slavery as such, merely their own participation in it. Should Christians keep pets? Is it even a question we ask?

Moreover, Paul did not expect the present age to last that long. Christ was expected to return shortly and bring the kingdom of God to fruition. Even more than that, the power of the Church to change society was strictly limited. It had no voice, no force of arms and no economic power. Nowadays, all that is very different, and the teaching of equality that Paul laid down for the Church has borne further fruit in a desire to end the ownership of one human being by another.

Household rules

To sum up, in the rules for the household, Paul is not setting out his vision of an ideal Christian household. Instead, he is showing how all Christians, no matter what their social status, may offer their lives as an act of worship and service to God. Each hypothetical person addressed could carry out the duties that Paul outlines, irrespective of whether or not other members of the household were Christians.

This drives home Paul's main point to the Colossians—that the service and worship of God are not to be found in the spiritual spheres where the angels dwell, nor are they attained through religious rules and discipline, but are found in the ordinary life that faces Christians day by day.

At the same time, there is a quite radical emphasis on the use of power. Those who are powerless, as were traditionally wives and children, can make their very powerlessness an offering to God. Those who have power must not abuse it. The power of slaves was limited, and found mainly in an ability to cheat their masters. That power should not be used, for a power that exists only in dishonesty is at odds with the life to which Christians are called.

The powerless, by seeing their work as God's work, find a new dignity that has nothing to do with social status but everything to do with an awareness of their own worth as beloved children of God. They are therefore treated as responsible individuals, answerable to God for their actions and with the personal worth that such a responsibility gives. For this reason, they are addressed first, wives before husbands, children before fathers, slaves before masters.

Others, though, have real power to affect the lives of others for good or ill. Husbands, fathers and slave-owners had it in their grasp to destroy lives. They also had the ability to offer encouragement, protection, justice and support. For a Christian, the true use of power lies on the latter path. Thus power, of whatever kind, brings with it a corresponding degree of responsibility to God, and God will demand an answer for how it has been used. Indeed, where power is used to build up, it is to some degree transferred. The task of the powerful is ultimately to empower the powerless.

A PRAYER

Father of mercy, God of justice, support all who work to bring
equality, those who fight for the downtrodden,
and those who bring hope to the hopeless.

PRAYER

Having finished his concrete examples of Christian living, Paul rounds off his practical advice with a few final thoughts. The first is a reminder of the necessity of prayer (4:2). A life lived for Christ, in which daily life is offered to him as worship and service, is not an alternative to conscious prayer, but is rather supported by it. So to live as his followers, the Colossians must be diligent in their prayers. Unlike Jews, Christians had (and have) no set times of prayer, but are expected to pray spontaneously and often. (This, of course, does not rule out the useful discipline of set prayer times; it simply removes their legalistic necessity.) So Paul tells the Colossians to devote themselves to prayer, or to persevere in prayer.

It is not clear what Paul means by 'keeping alert' in prayer. It could be a recognition of the tendency to let the mind wander, or even to fall asleep, when praying. Or it could be a reminder that the kingdom is coming. With each moment passed, and with each prayer for the coming of God's final victory, the return of Christ draws nearer. Neither of these is clear from the text, though, and perhaps what Paul has in mind is the need for a mental engagement with prayer. Prayer is not a rote job to be ploughed through with dogged determination, but an exercise in awareness—awareness of God's gracious acts, so that thanksgiving is genuine; awareness of others' current needs, so that intercession is focused; and awareness of oneself, so that there is honesty in confession and supplication.

Once again, Paul explicitly mentions thanksgiving. Worship and praise spring from the constant awareness of what God has done and continues to do, both in bringing salvation and in particular aspects of the life of the individual Christian. The stress on thanksgiving also has special relevance to the Colossians, who are tempted to think that they can add to what Christ has given them. They cannot, and their proper attitude is not to seek for more but to give thanks for all that has been done for them.

Support your local apostle

While praying, the Colossians should also remember Paul (v. 3). They can play a part in his mission by asking God to provide opportunities for him to preach the gospel. Some commentators suppose that this is a prayer for his release from imprisonment, but Paul does not seem to have regarded imprisonment as a hindrance to the gospel (Philippians 1:12) and, for that matter, freedom does not seem to have guaranteed good opportunities for preaching, for when such opportunities came it was good news worth sharing (see 2 Corinthians 2:12; 1 Corinthians 16:9). Paul is therefore asking for opportunities to preach while under close arrest, and in chains.

The Bible does not provide a philosophical rationale as to how prayer 'works', but it consistently assumes that God hears and responds to the prayers of his people. If the Colossians pray, Paul's mission will be different from what it will be if they do not, and he regularly requests prayer from his readers (Romans 15:30–32; Philippians 1:19; 1 Thessalonians 5:25; Philemon 22). Prayer is also the way God includes people in his work. Distance is no hindrance to a shared ministry if that sharing is expressed through prayer.

A PRAYER

Lord, may I too be given opportunities to tell others about you.

PREACHING *in* CHAINS

The gospel Paul proclaims is the same one that the Colossians have already heard and received—the mystery of Christ (v. 3), which is God's plan of salvation, bringing the possibility of a new relationship with God through the indwelling presence of his Son (1:27).

It is for preaching this gospel that Paul is in prison (literally, 'in chains'). This is Paul's first mention of his imprisonment, though presumably the Colossians would have known that he was in gaol, so this was hardly news to them. Even if Paul's present imprisonment is not the one mentioned at the end of Acts, it is clear from his own account that his imprisonments were all a result of his work as a Christian missionary (2 Corinthians 11:23).

Paul seems much calmer about the outcome of his imprisonment than in Philippians, but this could be for a couple of reasons. Either it comes from a different period of his time there, when his hopes of release were higher, or, as he did not know many of the Colossians personally, he was reticent about baring his soul to them.

Clear preaching

Whatever the place and circumstances of his captivity, Paul's main concern remains the preaching of the gospel. So he asks for prayer that he will be able to explain it clearly (v. 4). Like all good communicators, he knows that the way the message is delivered is as important as its content. Nor does he assume that years of experience will take the place of good preparation and delivery. Each place where the gospel is preached has its own concerns, its own culture and its own needs. The job of the missionary, evangelist or preacher is to know what those are, and to address the gospel to them. This is a fact that the Church needs to rediscover in each generation, as it seeks to find how the gospel message speaks to the people among whom the Christian community lives, serves and proclaims its message.

Indeed, how Christians relate to the world around them is of paramount importance for their effectiveness as messengers of God. So Paul reminds his readers of the need for wisdom in dealing with their unbelieving neighbours (v. 5). Here, wisdom is the awareness of God's will that enables the believer to live a life that is above criticism (see 1 Corinthians 10:32) and does not put off the outsider from wanting to know more of what goes on inside the church.

Christians are to make the most of the time available to them. The word that Paul uses to mean 'make the most of' is a commercial one, meaning 'to buy at every opportunity'. Christians are to snap up the available moments. The word for 'time' is *kairos*, the moment of opportunity. Christians, then, are to seize every available moment. But for what? On one level, Paul is no doubt stressing an aspect of the Christian's stewardship of time. The time we have is a gift of God, to be used as wisely as any other gift, and not squandered pointlessly. (Think how much time we spend doing neither what we should nor what we really want.) In the present context of dealing with outsiders and the proclamation of the gospel, Paul is probably thinking specifically of opportunities to share the news about Jesus Christ.

No opportunity should be wasted to show compassion, courtesy and a loving awareness of others. Nor should one miss the chance to let the reality of one's own faith be known. This does not mean that Christians should buttonhole complete strangers and subject them to a one-sided discourse on the need for salvation. That would hardly be wise!

Nor would it be gracious. Part of the normal witness of Christians to the world should be their interesting and courteous speech (v. 6). Those who seek to put on the virtues of the kingdom of Christ should be people whose company is worth having, whose speech is respectful but full of conviction. Paul likens Christian speech, both private conversation and public proclamation, to well-seasoned food: it is something to be savoured. This certainly does not mean the same thing as the English expression 'salty language', which comes from the vocabulary of seafarers rather than from Paul.

Finally, Paul expects the Christian's life to raise questions. Why do you hold these strange beliefs? Why do you act with such graciousness? Why do you treat all your members alike, be they slave or free? To these there should be ready answers. Christians must be prepared to explain their faith and, by their attractiveness of life, draw others towards the one who can reclothe us in the new humanity.

A PRAYER

Lord, may my life be a witness to your transforming power.

FRIENDS *in* CHRIST

Paul rounds off his letter with personal greetings from his companions and to the few people he knows personally in Colossae. A similar section ends the letter to the Romans, and it is perhaps significant that Paul had not visited Rome either. The greetings serve to cement a sense of solidarity among Christians who are strangers to each other, but who are united in devotion to Christ.

Two particular names lead the list. Tychicus (v. 7) will be bearing the letter to Colossae, and he is commended on several counts. Particularly, he is dear to Paul and has proved a trustworthy, or reliable, servant or minister, like Paul himself (1:23). He is also a fellow slave (again the English translations shy away from the literal meaning, and have 'servant'). He, like Paul, belongs lock, stock and barrel to Christ. He is a slave 'in the Lord', which here probably means 'in the Lord's work', a sharer of the task of bringing the gospel to the Gentiles.

This accolade suggests that Tychicus is Paul's right-hand man at the time, and is being entrusted with the important task of bringing the letter to Colossae. 'I have sent him' (v. 8) is written from the standpoint of the recipients, who will hear it read some weeks after Tychicus' sending. He is far more than a postman—he will bring news by word of mouth, no doubt answer questions, and encourage the Colossians. That encouragement will be by bringing news of Paul, but it will probably also mean that he can expound Paul's message and add his own weight to the argument against the Colossian teaching.

With Tychicus comes Onesimus, who is almost certainly the same runaway slave who is the subject of the letter to Philemon. He will be bearing that personal note to his master, but that is a private matter, not mentioned here. What is public is the good news of Onesimus' conversion. He is now the faithful and beloved brother, one of the Colossians both in the sense of being from their city, and now also as one of their Christian community. Perhaps, too, Paul does no harm to Onesimus' case by introducing him in such terms to the church as a whole. Philemon would be less likely to have a rough welcome waiting for his slave if his fellow Christians had heard Onesimus commended publicly by Paul. Onesimus too will have news of Paul and his team.

Jewish friends

Aristarchus is a friend who has shared Paul's imprisonment. It is difficult to decide whether he is also officially under arrest or has voluntarily shared the apostle's confinement. Assuming Paul to be writing from Rome, the latter is more likely, as we know Aristarchus joined Paul on his trip to Rome (Acts 27:2), and presumably has stayed on to help out. He was a native of Thessalonika, and was presumably one of Paul's converts.

Mark (v. 10) was yet to gain fame as (probably) the author of the earliest biography of Jesus of Nazareth, the Gospel that bears his name. Here he is introduced as the cousin of Barnabas, which suggests that Barnabas was known to the Colossians. Perhaps the Pauline churches had heard of how Paul and Barnabas had quarrelled over what Paul saw as Mark's defection from a missionary journey (Acts 13:13; 15:36–41). Now the rift is healed, and Mark is once again working with Paul. None the less, the Colossians are told to welcome Mark (that is, without any hesitation or doubt of his worthiness) should he make his way to them. Comments such as these are a salutary reminder that much more was happening in the world of first-century Christianity than we now know. There are hints here of networks of churches, joined by letters and by visiting missionaries, of whom no historical trace remains but whose work was used by God to spread the gospel and build up faith. It may indeed have been from such a channel that the Colossians received some instruction about Mark of which Paul is aware and endorses—though what it was, there is no way of knowing.

Mark and Aristarchus are two of a trio of Jewish Christians with Paul. The third is Jesus, also known as Justus (v. 11). The presence of these three was a great comfort to Paul, perhaps because they could understand both his thought and his emotions better than could his Gentile friends. It is an irony of Paul's life that while he was called to be the apostle to the Gentiles, he would have given anything to be able successfully to evangelize his fellow Jews (Romans 9:1–3).

A PRAYER

Lord, in your service, may I do what you call me to do,
and not what I prefer.

GAOL *in* ROME

At this point, it may be becoming difficult to imagine Paul in prison, yet surrounded by helpers and fellow missionaries, some of whom have moved in with him. Paul is not strictly in prison, and he accurately describes his condition when he writes of his chains. As a prisoner awaiting a personal review by the emperor, Paul was under what we might call close house arrest. He was manacled, and probably shackled to a guard. But he would almost certainly be in a house, and his food and other necessities would be provided out of his own pocket, or by friends and fellow Christians. In those circumstances, he would be allowed to receive visitors and even to have others live in the same house. Paul's freedom was curtailed, but as he was a Roman citizen who had been convicted of no crime, he was free to communicate with whomsoever he chose.

Man of prayer

Epaphras (v. 12; see 1:7) apparently will not be returning with the letter which has been written in response to his arrival in Rome. There is a whole sermon in that for church leaders and pastors. Although he founded the church, he is aware that others can lead it through its present problems, and that the church can flourish without him. A mark of a good pastor and leader is to know when his or her job is done and to let others take over.

Although he is distant from Colossae, that does not mean Epaphras is uninvolved with the church. He prays constantly for it, striving (literally 'agonizing') in his prayers. Prayer carried out diligently and sincerely is no easy task. There is an almost physical exertion to prolonged intercession. The most obvious example in the Bible is the prayer of Jesus in Gethsemane. Luke 22:44 describes Jesus as being in anguish—the related noun to the verb Paul uses to describe Epaphras' prayer and his own toil in the service of the gospel (1:29).

The goal of that prayer is the same as Epaphras' goal as pastor to the Colossians—that they may stand fully mature (see 1:28) in their faith, assured that they are doing the will of God. This is, then, a continuation of the work that Epaphras has done in person in the churches of the Lycus valley, not only at Colossae but also at neighbouring Laodicea and Hierapolis.

Luke (v. 14), described as the beloved physician, was a frequent companion of Paul on his journeys, and was eventually to write the two-volume account of the origins of Christianity which we know as Luke's Gospel and the Acts of the Apostles. We know very little about Demas. 2 Timothy 4:10–11 says that he deserted Paul because of love for the world, but what this actually refers to is an insoluble mystery.

Church leaders

Now, Paul sends greetings to people he knows. He is taking the opportunity to write to the church at Laodicea (v. 16), and each church should read the other's letter, since they could presumably benefit from knowledge of each other's situation. Paul greets a church leader in Laodicea, Nympha (feminine) or Nymphas (masculine). The best manuscripts are divided over whether this church leader is a woman or a man. Certainly there were women in leadership positions in the Pauline churches and in missionary activity. Several are named in Romans 16.

Churches at this time had no special buildings, and met in houses that could accommodate them. Presumably Nympha/Nymphas was wealthy enough to host such a meeting, as was Philemon at Colossae (Philemon 2). Archippus, presumably another prominent member of the Colossian church, is reminded of a service he has to carry out, but what it was is unknown to us.

And finally...

At the end comes Paul's personal signature. He asks for his chains to be remembered, both as a subject for the Colossians' prayers and as the mark of his service to Christ. The one who writes is an apostle who is prepared to back his teaching with suffering for his Lord.

The very final words are a prayer and a blessing: 'Grace be with you.' Without it there would be no church, no faith, and no salvation.

A PRAYER

Lord, may I too know your grace and be your servant.

78

OLD FRIENDS

Paul's short letter (335 Greek words) to Philemon is the closest we have to a personal letter from the apostle. It has close links with Colossians. Archippus, greeted in Philemon, is also mentioned in Colossians 4:17; and the subject of the letter, Onesimus, is to travel with Tychicus to Colossae (Colossians 4:9), no doubt bearing this very letter. Those who argue that Colossians is not by Paul see these links as having been inserted to lend colour and realism, but if that were the case, it is strange that Philemon is not mentioned in Colossians. If Colossians is Pauline, as we have supposed, it makes sense, since Philemon had his own personal letter.

Paul describes himself as a prisoner of Christ Jesus. He means that he is imprisoned on account of preaching the gospel. There is probably also a slightly deeper meaning. He is Christ's prisoner because all aspects of life, and every situation within it, can be offered to Christ as an act of worship and an opportunity for service. Just as slaves can serve Christ through their situation (Colossians 3:22), so can Paul, even in prison. Paul does not mention his calling as an apostle, for he is writing as a friend and requesting a favour. Timothy is also named as the sender, for he would have been known to Christians in Colossae, but he is not the co-author and has no part in what follows.

The letter is addressed primarily to Philemon, who is apparently known to Paul and is greeted as a beloved brother and co-worker. Presumably Paul met Philemon during his two-year stay in Ephesus (Acts 19:8–10), and Philemon was probably converted at that time (v. 19). He is therefore a brother in Christ as a fellow believer, and as a sharer in Paul's mission he is a fellow worker. That he is also described as 'beloved' may point to a closer friendship, especially as Paul repeats 'brother' in verse 7, suggesting that this is a term of friendship as well as Christian solidarity.

Greetings are also offered to Apphia, who is probably Philemon's wife, and to Archippus, but Philemon is the intended recipient of the letter. Archippus may also be a member of Philemon's household. He is described as Paul's fellow soldier, which is a rare term for one of Paul's co-workers. Perhaps it refers to some particular task or ministry that Archippus was charged with (see Colossians 4:17). Such tantalizing glimpses remind us that these were real people, with complex lives of which we have only the briefest snapshots through the pages of the New Testament.

Church and churches

A final greeting is sent to the church that meets in Philemon's house, which suggests that Paul is referring to one house church that met there, and not to the whole Colossian church. Christian places of worship were not built until the third century. Before then, worship took place in private houses. As the church in a particular place grew, it would need more than one meeting-place. Paul's use of the term 'church' is not very helpful, since for him it could mean the Christians in a particular city, or the whole Church in the world, or simply an assembly (the basic meaning of *ekklesia*) like the one that Philemon probably led, as well as hosted.

To all those he greets, Paul wishes his usual benediction of grace and peace which come from God and from Christ (v. 3). (For further comment on the opening greeting, see pp. 22–27 and 104–105 on Philippians and Colossians respectively.)

Paul now begins the main part of his letter. From now till verse 21, he addresses Philemon alone, and 'you' takes the singular form in the Greek. He begins by assuring Philemon that he is remembered with thanksgiving in Paul's prayers. Philemon is reported (perhaps by Epaphras, Colossians 1:7–8) as showing love for the Christian community and faith in Christ, from which such love springs. A cynical view might suppose that Paul, since he wants a favour from Philemon, might be expected to say nothing less. However, there is no need to be cynical, and the letter as a whole seems to expect that Philemon is the sort of person who would respond to such a request: he is a man of love and faith. Also, in verse 6, love is mentioned before faith, which is unusual for Paul. Perhaps love was the first thing to spring to mind as he remembered Philemon.

A PRAYER

Lord, may love be the first memory people have of me.

NEWBORN CHRISTIAN

Paul's account of his thanksgiving for Philemon leads easily into an account of his intercession for him. However, exactly what Paul is praying for is far from clear. The Greek of verse 6 is extremely ambiguous. The prayer is in essence that Philemon, who has received so much from Christ in the way of spiritual blessings, should put them into practice in his own act of generosity, and thus gain an experiential knowledge of the grace and love he has seen in Christ.

Paul himself has been encouraged by the love that Philemon has shown in his Christian ministry (v. 7). He is a source of refreshment to the church. While the specific ways in which this happens are not spelt out, it is clear that Philemon's love is an encouragement to the Christians in Colossae. Paul is therefore sure that Philemon will seize the opportunity to bring him the same refreshment (v. 20).

Now Paul comes to the main point of his letter. He is able, as an apostle, to command Philemon to do what is his obvious Christian duty (v. 8). Indeed, he has the double authority of being an ambassador of Christ and a prisoner of Christ. That is, he has the authority granted by his call to be an apostle, and the moral authority of one who has suffered in Christ's service. (This takes the Greek *presbytes* in verse 9 to mean 'ambassador' or 'envoy' rather than its literal meaning of 'old man' which is represented in NRSV.) There is obviously no doubt how Paul wants Philemon to act! On the other hand, such a duty, which is essentially to show love, can only be carried out freely and willingly. Therefore Paul leaves the decision to Philemon, who may rest on his legal rights or respond with the generosity that springs from faith in Christ. Therefore, Paul's appeal is simply to love (v. 9).

The object of the appeal is Onesimus, Philemon's slave (v. 10). The name means 'useful' or 'beneficial' and is typical of names given to slaves. In the Greek, the name comes at the end of the sentence, after the news that a new Christian has come into being. Philemon might not have been expected to react terribly happily to the name of Onesimus, so Paul first says that he has a new 'child', someone who through his ministry has come to faith in Christ. Paul uses the idea of fathering or bearing children as a metaphor for being the instrument of conversion in 1 Corinthians 4:15 and Galatians 4:19. Here Onesimus has become Paul's spiritual son, as indeed is Philemon. Already the implication is clear: Philemon and Onesimus are brothers.

Worthless slave

From this it would appear that Onesimus had run away, as slaves often did, and made his way to Rome, but instead of seeking anonymity in the great city he had instead sought out the imprisoned Paul, whom he knew to be a friend of his master. Penalties for absconding slaves could be severe, and the number of fugitives bears testimony to the harsh treatment some slaves could receive. There is no indication, however, that Onesimus had been badly treated. In Rome, he had heard the gospel and committed himself to Christ. Now Paul is sending him back to put things right. In fact, he is sending back a new and improved version. Previously, it would seem, Onesimus was not a very useful slave at all. Certainly he was unhappy in his situation. Now he is useful indeed, because his attitude has changed, making him a useful slave to Philemon, and also making him a useful companion and helper to Paul. The pun on Onesimus' name is no doubt quite deliberate (v. 11).

Paul does not want Onesimus to return, and sends him back with a heavy heart. Onesimus has become dear to him ('my very heart', v. 12) and Paul would like nothing better than for Onesimus to remain, fulfilling the role that Philemon evidently had during Paul's Ephesian ministry (v. 13). But there is no choice. It was illegal to harbour a fugitive slave, and dangerous for Onesimus to remain a runaway. More important even than legal considerations, which are not mentioned explicitly, is the point that love and honesty demand openness with Philemon. Paul will not do anything behind Philemon's back, and if Onesimus is to continue helping Paul he will do so as a result of his master's love and generosity, which must be willingly given, neither forced nor assumed (v. 14).

A PRAYER

Lord, may I serve you in generosity and love.

HIDDEN PURPOSES

A further reason for Paul's return of Onesimus is that he might possibly be going against God's plans. It could be that the whole episode of the slave's visit to Paul was (at least in part) for Philemon's benefit. The temporary separation now means that he can possibly have Onesimus back for ever (v. 15). This is more than a simple assurance that he will not run away again, but looks forward to the next verse. Onesimus now has an everlasting relationship with his master, for he shares the eternal life that God gives to those who put their faith in Christ.

Paul makes no claim to be able actually to see what God's plans are, but he is sure that God does work in people's lives and circumstances. Paul's own meeting with Christ on the Damascus road was the most spectacular example, but his letters show that he was aware of God's activity and communication through the events that came his way (2 Corinthians 1:9–11).

Onesimus is therefore returning to Philemon as much more than a slave. He is now a brother, and indeed a beloved brother (v. 16), the same term that Paul has used for Philemon himself (v. 1). 'Beloved' here is also a subtle reminder to Philemon that love is the prime command for relations between fellow Christians. It might be thought that a leader of the church would hardly need reminding of so basic a teaching, but Onesimus could well be too close to Philemon for him to realize that it also applied to runaway slaves! As a small boy once put it, 'Jesus told us to love everyone, but did he mean our sisters as well?'

Onesimus is dear to Paul, who converted him, but he should be even dearer to Philemon. He is both a brother in Christ and a brother 'in the flesh' (v. 16). This refers to his normal earthly relationship as a member of Philemon's household, in which he should still be valued as a human being, whatever his legal status. Paul is not addressing the issue of slavery here, or in the letter as a whole, but the issue of brotherly love. His statement that Onesimus is not returning 'as a slave' is not a demand for Onesimus' freedom, but simply a recognition of the altered relationship brought about by the slave's conversion.

In verse 17 Paul comes to the main point. Philemon and Paul are partners (*koinonoi*) because of their fellowship (*koinonia*) in Christ.

'Partner' often meant business partner, but here it is partnership in the shared venture of preaching the gospel, a task to which both partners are drawn by their love of Christ. Since Philemon is bound to recognize this fact, he will surely welcome Onesimus as he would welcome Paul, for Onesimus is also now a member of the fellowship of Christ. He has become Paul's partner, and must therefore be Philemon's too.

Practical love

The use of a business term leads neatly into Paul's practical offer of support for Onesimus. If Onesimus has wronged his master or owes him anything, Paul will make good the debt (v. 18). The offer is couched in commercial language, and signed in Paul's own hand (v. 19). He includes a formal and legally binding IOU, as a father might when faced with damage caused by his son. Verse 18 has led many commentators to assume that Onesimus had stolen from his master in order to fund his escape. This may be so, but if he had, Paul might be expected to make a more forthright statement of it. Onesimus certainly had wronged his master, as such things were thought of then, simply by running away, and Paul effectively offers to make up for any expense that the loss of work may have caused. There is, though, a sting in the tail of Paul's generosity. I hate to point this out, he writes, but you do, after all, owe me your very existence. Paul had brought Philemon to know Christ. If there was to be talk of debts, then there was an unpayable one on Philemon's side.

This is not to say that Paul's offer of recompense was spurious. Paul has stated his love for Onesimus, and love which is unwilling to pay a practical price is hardly love at all. However, if Philemon were to demand payment, he would have missed the whole point of Paul's letter. The three of them—apostle, master, slave—are now brothers in Christ and partners in the Church's mission. To talk of debts was legally possible, but ridiculous in practice.

Paul therefore calls on Philemon to exercise the very ministry for which he was famous. As he has refreshed the hearts of the Christians at Colossae, so he can give encouragement and respite to Paul, by granting the apostle's request (v. 20).

A PRAYER

Lord, let me recognize opportunities to share your love—even the ones close to home!

The BASIC COMMANDMENT

Verse 21 at first sight strikes a jarring note in the letter. Paul has carefully not pressed his apostolic authority, and has been deferential to Philemon's rights all through the brief epistle. He has stressed that Philemon must act freely out of love (v. 14) and that he, Paul, is making a humble but heartfelt request. Now he says that he is confident of Philemon's obedience. Does this mean that, after all, he is throwing his apostolic weight into the argument? If he intended to do that, he might as well have saved his ink on all that has gone before.

On the other hand, there is one great command which is never explicitly stated but which lies under the whole letter—the command of Jesus to show love. For Paul, it is the fundamental commandment, written in the blood of Christ himself, and so much assumed that it is rarely made explicit. It is to this command that Philemon must be obedient. If he fails in this, his whole understanding of God and the nature of Christ (v. 6) is faulty. When someone calls on a Christian to show love, it may well be a request from that individual but it is a resounding command from God.

Paul goes even further. He has made no other request but he certainly has a hope, and is sure that will be met as well. Philemon will do even more than he is asked. Precisely what that may be is tactfully not spelt out. Some commentators take it to be a hope for Onesimus' manumission (his formal release from slavery). Much as this may appeal to modern sensibilities, it is probably wrong. The whole thrust of the letter has been about the brotherly love that should be shown between Christians, and Onesimus' legal status has certainly not been challenged. Paul has, on the other hand, stated his desire that Onesimus might remain with him to help in Paul's ministry (v. 13), and it is most likely that Paul wants him to return to Rome for that purpose. No doubt it would be easier for him to do so as a freedman, but there was nothing to prevent Philemon from sending a slave on such an errand.

Final greetings

Paul, though in prison, still hopes to be released, but if he is, it will be by the grace of God, in response to the prayers of Christians such as Philemon and his church (the 'you' of verse 22 is plural, as Paul ends his personal business and includes others in his greetings). It is difficult to tell whether Paul is less certain of his release than in Philippians, since as far as he was concerned, all things were in the hands of God. At any rate, he hopes to visit Colossae and asks for a guest room to be prepared.

Meanwhile, other Christians in Rome send their greetings. Epaphras, who founded the church in Colossae, is named first, as one whom Philemon would know well. He shares Paul's imprisonment, either voluntarily or not. Mark would be known of in Colossae, as perhaps were Aristarchus, Demas and Luke. (On all these, see the comments on Colossians 4:10–17, pp. 173–175.)

Paul ends (v. 25) with a benediction that is identical to Philippians 4:23 (see the comment on that verse, p. 103).

Philemon and slavery

We have already briefly commented on Paul's apparent failure to engage with the issue of slavery (see pp. 164–165, on Colossians 3:22—4:1). That he does so even less in Philemon, a letter about a slave, is only superficially surprising. Even if Paul were a convinced abolitionist (and hardly anyone in the first century was), it is clear that Philemon was not.

Paul writes a delicate and diplomatic letter, carefully respecting Philemon's rights while expecting much more of his Christian convictions. To weigh in with a denunciation of the institution that Philemon implicitly supports would merely be read as condemnation, and would be counterproductive.

Moreover, the point of the letter is that Christian love and fellowship transcend social distinctions. Because of the love demanded between believers, the relationship of master and slave becomes of little point. Nowadays, we would quite rightly demand more. But if we do, it is because of the very gospel of equality in Christ that Paul himself proclaimed.

A PRAYER

Lord, in all my dealings, may I see only human beings,
and your image in them.

FROM WHOM?

The first word of Ephesians is probably the most problematic of the whole letter: 'Paul'. Most modern scholars doubt very strongly whether it was written by Paul at all. For the reasons given in the Introduction (pp. 13–14), we shall assume that Ephesians is not by Paul. On a purely practical level, this will make little difference to our reading of it, so anyone who strongly disagrees can easily read 'Paul' where we have 'the author' and still gain something from our study.

If we assume that the author is someone other than Paul, several questions need to be addressed. The most obvious is who the real author was, and why he wrote it. The answer is that we have no idea of the writer's identity. Some have suggested Tychicus, as he is the only other person mentioned in the letter, and this would make sense; although, on the other hand, the bearer of the letter to the Colossians may simply be mentioned to add a bit of colour to the writing. As to why it was written, the best explanation seems to be that the letter is an attempt (and a successful one) to show that the thought and teaching of Paul have much to offer to a later generation of Christians for whom the situations that Paul directly addressed now lie in the past. In particular, the expectation of an imminent second coming seems to have faded, and while the writer does not fall into the trap of assuming that Christians already have all that God has promised, there is a strong stress on the present experience of the new life that Christ brings.

The author of Ephesians develops Paul's thought on the resurrection, and draws out the implications of the apostle's teaching on the Church to show the role and nature of the universal Church. Overall, the letter is a treatise of encouragement for Christians who must discover afresh what it means to be the Church.

To whom?

A second question is to whom the work was written. The address to the church in Ephesus is missing from the best and earliest manuscripts, which read, 'To the saints who are also faithful in Christ Jesus'. The address to Ephesus was added later, on the assumption that the letter was written to a church in Asia Minor. What evidence we have (and it is fairly slender) seems to suggest that it was indeed written to that province, or that it originated there, but we have no original name of a church. It is possible that the original address was removed to make the letter more general in its application (something similar has been done to some early copies of Romans, where the specific greetings of chapter 16 have been left out) or it could indeed have been simply addressed to (all) the saints, in keeping with a work that deals with the nature of the Church universal.

This raises the third question of whether Ephesians should be read as a letter at all. The answer is simply, yes. Whether it was intended to be seen as a genuine letter of Paul, or whether its first readers were aware of its origin, it still takes the form of a letter. It is intended to be seen as the letter Paul would have written if he had still been alive.

A fourth question follows. Is it right to assume that a forgery found its way into the Christian scriptures? This actually begs several questions. The practice of writing in the name of an author of the past was widespread in the ancient world. The followers of Pythagoras continued to write in his name, as, probably, did the disciples of Plato. Jewish and Christian writers often wrote books that were couched as prophecies from long-dead heroes of the faith.

None of this was seen as forgery in the modern sense, but as an attempt to honour the supposed author by continuing to state his relevance for changing times. At the same time, a work in the name of a great writer or teacher explicitly claimed his authority as an appeal to the readers to take the work seriously and to give it the same attention as they would if it were really from the supposed author. Certainly, in the ancient world, the notions of plagiarism, copyright and intellectual property were either absent or far more fluid than they are today, and any judgment we make on ancient authors should not demand more honesty on their part than would normally be expected by their contemporaries.

Ephesians certainly gained wide acceptance because it was thought to be by Paul. It lasted, however, on its own merits, unlike other early pseudonymous writings and, indeed, some of Paul's own letters. And as to whether it could be regarded as inspired, that too is no problem. After all, if God cannot use human failings, he has little to use at all.

A PRAYER

Lord, thank you for your word, whoever wrote it!

APOSTOLIC TEACHING

Ephesians, then, claims to be the words of Paul, applied to a situation later than Paul's own life. It is modelled particularly on the letter to the Colossians, and expands many of that letter's emphases. As it stands, it is addressed simply to the saints who are faithful in Christ Jesus. It is explicitly addressed to all Christian readers, for to be a Christian is to be marked out as belonging to God and called to be a faithful follower of Jesus Christ.

It comes, via the author, from Paul, and stands in continuity with the gospel that was given by God to Paul himself (see Galatians 1:11–12). This is one of the most important touchstones of Christian teaching. With the passing centuries, followers of Jesus have tried to put into practice the call to be his people. They have sought in many different ways to communicate the gospel to their neighbours. Each time, their way of being the church, and the message they proclaimed, has been different from what went before. Sometimes it has lost all links with the past and with the teaching of the Bible, and become a heresy. Mostly, though, it has preserved its links with the teaching of the Bible and the historic Church, and found new ways of expressing old truths. It is that ability to see both the connection with the past and at the same time the newness of its expression which has kept Christianity alive.

In typically Pauline fashion, verse 2 is a benediction to the readers, who are wished grace and peace. This should not be seen as merely a stylistic flourish, to make the whole work seem more Pauline, but a genuine wish of the writer, a part of the continuing message for a new generation. Grace (*charis*) replaces the usual Greek 'rejoice!' (*chareite*) and indicates the selfless self-giving of God. It is God who becomes incarnate in Jesus Christ and goes to the cross for the salvation of the world. Then he calls for a response of faithfulness and love. In short, grace is the word that stresses that God acts first and then demands a response. He does not offer salvation as a response to human worthiness.

The result of God's grace is a new relationship with him which brings all that is implied in the traditional Hebrew greeting, 'Peace!' (*shalom*), although here the Greek is used (*eirene*). It is a word that encompasses the absence of conflict—especially, in Christian thought, of the conflict between humanity and God (see Romans 5:1)—and goes on to include notions of safety, wholeness, well-being and healing. All this is included in the new creation that God is bringing about through the work of Christ.

Therefore, the benediction is not just a general wish for grace and peace, but a statement of their origin in God, who is now our Father.

Lord of the Church

The notion of God's fatherhood comes from Jesus' own experience. He referred to God as his father, and called his disciples to share that relationship as God's children. Thus the fatherhood of God as known by Christians is dependent on recognizing Jesus for who he is. Grace and peace come not only from God but from Jesus Christ, who makes God known and defines our way of seeing God.

As in the genuine Pauline letters, the title 'Christ', which means 'anointed one', is treated virtually as a name here. The significant title is 'Lord'. Jesus is Lord of the Church, the master of those who acknowledge him, and the one through whom God's grace and peace come to his people. Where Jesus is the focal point of the Christian message, that message remains Christian. Where Jesus becomes one among many ways to encounter the grace of God, the Church has begun to lose track of its identity and of the channel through which God is made real.

This is something to bear in mind in today's world, where our consciousness of the multi-cultural, multi-faith nature of society makes a genuine temptation to seek a lowest common denominator in religion, and so runs the risk of producing a religiosity with neither content nor integrity.

A PRAYER

Lord, may my knowledge of your grace call out
my love and commitment.

LONG-TERM PLANNING

The pattern of God's grace evoking a response of love and faith lies behind the extended outburst of praise that follows the opening greeting. 'Blessed be the God…' reflects a Jewish formula of blessing directed towards God as a result of his great works, and can be found throughout the Old Testament and in later Jewish worship (see for example, 1 Kings 8:15). This *berakah* (blessing) has a Christian slant, of course, for it defines the God who is blessed as the Father of Jesus Christ, and the grace he bestows is explicitly the salvation that Jesus brings.

God has given to his people all that he has to offer. Every blessing that is to be found in the spiritual realm is now theirs. In the genuine Pauline epistles, there is an equal stress on the unimaginable riches of God's grace (see 1 Corinthians 2:9), but much of this lies in the future. Here our author stresses the present experience and availability of those riches. They are blessings which are to be found in Christ. They are thus for those who by faith are 'in Christ', and they come to the world from God 'in Christ'.

They are the outworking of God's choice of his people from the very beginning (v. 4). In later Christian theology, this sort of language was to evoke a debate that has still not been resolved. It can be read as a statement that God, even before he created the universe, decided who was to be saved and who was not. Or it can be read as a statement that God decided beforehand that the Church would exist and be blessed: that is, what was foreordained was the blessing rather than the individuals who would receive it.

If we have to make a choice, the best is surely the one that does justice to the preaching of the gospel with its call to repentance. In other words, to say that God decides beforehand who is saved and who is not would empty the gospel proclamation of meaning. Therefore it seems safer to say that the salvation of the people of God is part of his plan from the beginning, but who is a part of that people (and it could in theory include all people) is left to our response to his call. The destiny of those who respond to that call is to be able to stand before God as a people who are truly his and whose sins are finally wiped away—they will be holy and blameless. Here in verse 4 the word 'holy' has the sense both of belonging to God and of moral purity.

Gracious Father

God's plan from the start was that the Church, the people of God, should be adopted as his children (v. 5). This, says the writer, was God's plan all along—that people should relate to God as his children. The lengthy phrase 'according to the good pleasure of his will' is typical of the author of Ephesians, who never uses a single word when a whole phrase will do. It stresses almost over-emphatically the fact that all this originates in God's purpose.

For those who take seriously the biblical story of fall and redemption, this may seem to raise a problem. Does it mean that God willed human sinfulness in order that he might bring about a greater salvation? However, the author of Ephesians is not expounding that idea. Probably it didn't actually occur to him. What he is stressing, once again, is the overarching grace of God, which God has always intended should be enjoyed by human beings.

The purpose and end result of that grace is that people may praise God for his free and overwhelming gift (v. 6). The purpose of creation is to praise God, not because God demands or needs such praise but because creation finds its meaning in a relationship with God, and the only meaningful relationship with God is one of praise and worship. It is as human beings go about the task of being human, the task of giving and loving, caring and sharing, that they reflect their creator, and so praise him in the same way that a work of art reflects on the artist. Since they are thinking beings, people who know God will also consciously offer him thanks and praise for their existence, for his love and for his self-sacrifice in the salvation brought by Christ.

All this is possible only to those who have accepted the gift of salvation, recognized God as their creator, and ultimately been transformed into the image of Christ. In that sense it lies in the future, but as those who have already been brought into union with Christ, it is already to some extent a reality in the life of the saints.

A PRAYER

Lord, may my life reflect you, and so give you praise.

85 EPHESIANS 1:7–10

The GOAL *of* SALVATION

Ephesians uses the typically Pauline phrase 'in Christ' much more frequently than any of the other letters that bear the apostle's name. For Paul, it usually indicates the relationship of believers to Christ— they have become united with their saviour in one body. In Ephesians, it also means that Christ is the instrument by and in which God acts. So, in verse 7, 'in him' means that he is the one who brings salvation and, at the same time, that salvation is found by those who are united in him.

To bring his people out of slavery to sin, Jesus has paid the high price of his own death. As in Colossians 1:14, the meaning of redemption is cast in terms of the forgiveness of sins.

But why is such a high price necessary for God's forgiveness? After all, when we forgive, no one has to shed blood, let alone die. In fact, the New Testament writers see the act of atonement as much more complex than simply forgiving. It involves a debt that has to be paid, a conflict that has to be won, and a process of resurrection that can only be reached through death. One way into the question might be to ask in turn whether even our small forgivenesses are really bloodless. When we seek to forgive a real wrong, there is real anguish involved. Perhaps it is not too much to say that the pain of God's forgiveness takes physical form in the death of Christ. As God becomes incarnate, so too does his anguish over sin.

Wisdom and insight

Whether that approach appeals to us or not, the author of Ephesians is certain that Jesus' death is the sign above all others of God's lavish grace poured out on us (vv. 7–8). With that grace comes the wisdom and understanding to appreciate the immensity of what God has done. (NRSV takes 'wisdom and insight' as describing God, but it makes better sense to take it as part of the preceding phrase.)

This wisdom, which is the understanding of God's will, allows Christians to see into his purposes and understand his plan of salvation. It can be understood only through entering into a relationship with Christ, for that transforms the mere intellectual knowledge of God's purposes into a living experience. God's plan has to be understood by experience, simply because it is the remaking of creation. It cannot be observed from a neutral position, because there is no neutrality. One is either a part of it or outside of it for ever.

The plan of salvation finds its fulfilment in Christ, because he is the one who both brings it into being through the cross and becomes the goal of creation. All things, whether physical or spiritual, are to be 'gathered up' in him (v. 10). The word translated by NRSV as 'gathered up' means 'summed up', in the sense of 'gone over again'. That is, all of creation is to be worked over and remade in Christ. This plan is for the fullness of time: it is the final goal towards which the universe is moving, and is the purpose that underlies all of history.

Underlying this image is the notion that the universe is fragmented, or out of kilter, due to the effects of sin. The proper relationship between the creator and creation has been fractured and, as a result, all other relationships are also damaged and askew. In Christ, the relationships are restored and drawn together in him. One might picture the spokes of a wheel, which draw closer together as they approach the hub. So all creation is drawn together and becomes one as its parts are drawn towards Christ. This does not, of course, mean that the separate parts lose their individuality—without individual characteristics there can be no relationships, and it is the proper relationships that are restored in Christ.

The scope of God's plan is stressed by the final words of verse 10. It applies to all things, on earth or in heaven. Heaven here, as in most of the New Testament, does not mean what most modern Christians have come to understand by the term. It refers to the hidden realm of spiritual reality rather than the dwelling-place of God and his angels. It is a realm where evil may be encountered as well as good, and is as much in need of redemption as the human world. Indeed, the book of Revelation ends with a vision of the renewal of both heaven and earth (Revelation 21:1), which is exactly what the writer of Ephesians has in mind.

This is an audacious vision, which holds out the hope of restoration to everything and everyone, even the rebellious spiritual powers that we will encounter later in the letter.

A PRAYER

*Lord, may I find my true relationship with you in Christ, and my
final home in your renewed creation.*

SOMETHING *to* LOOK FORWARD *to*

As adopted children (see 1:5), the Church has an inheritance to look forward to. Of course, the inheritance comes about not when the Father dies, but when he brings to completion his plan of salvation. Those who belong to Christ share a destiny that is certain, for God always achieves what he sets out to do. His work in Christ is no random event, but part of a purpose that stretches across time and beyond.

This is not just a one-sided arrangement, though. God's choice of his people carries with it a responsibility for them to live in faith and to be a light to the world. That responsibility will be a part of the worship and praise that the Church offers to God, which is its final goal and purpose (v. 12). Christians, who have already (better than NRSV's 'first') set their hope on Christ, aim now to put something of that worship and praise into action in their own lives.

One consequence of verse 12 should be to make Christians rethink the nature and purpose of their own worship. While, as we saw in Colossians, all of life can be offered to God, the church's gathering together for worship is our time of rehearsal for the life to come. How seriously we take our rehearsals is open to question.

The Holy Spirit

As the writer draws his lengthy *berakah* to a close, the trinitarian structure of the blessing becomes clear. Throughout, he has stressed the origin of salvation in the purpose and plan of God. That salvation has come into the world in Christ, is encountered in a relationship with Christ and will find its fulfilment in Christ. It also has a present dimension which is brought to us by the Holy Spirit, who is himself the gift of God in Christ. So the work of salvation is seen to be the work of God the Father, the Son and the Holy Spirit.

Salvation is grasped when the word of truth, the gospel, is received. The gospel is not just a story that helps some people get through life, or makes them feel good for a while. It comes with the claim to be true, and has to be received as a true picture of how the world is and as a call to faith and commitment. It draws out the response of belief, of both acceptance and trust in God, and God responds to that trust with the gift of the Holy Spirit (v. 13).

Christians have therefore been marked with God's own seal, his brand of ownership. The presence of the Spirit in the lives of Christians is the sign that they belong to God.

The Greek tense indicates that the sealing took place at a specific time in the past, so the readers of Ephesians are expected to know when that was. The most likely answer is that it refers to baptism.

There has already been a likely reference to baptism in 1:6, where Christ is called the Beloved, which calls to mind the words that accompanied Jesus' own baptism, 'You are my Son, the Beloved' (Mark 1:11). Moreover, the coming of the Spirit is frequently associated with baptism (as in Acts 2:37–39; 19:5–6). We should not rule out the possibility, however, that the writer assumes that the Spirit's coming was always accompanied by visible or audible signs, such as speaking in tongues (Acts 8:17–18; 10:44–46; 19:6). In any case, a close association between a profession of faith, baptism and receipt of the Spirit is definitely the norm in the New Testament, and any attempts to divide the three reflect modern theological debates rather than the experience of the early Church.

The point for the writer of Ephesians is that Christians have received the Spirit, who is a down-payment, or first instalment (v. 14), with a guarantee that the rest is to follow. God has put a deposit on us. The Spirit is a bit of heaven working in Christians now in order to prepare them for the world to come.

Here redemption is seen as lying in the future, while in 1:7 it was seen as the present possession of believers. This illustrates well the New Testament's tension between the present experience of Christians, who know themselves to be redeemed, and the future promise when they will experience all that redemption means. For now, we live out our lives as God's people, but do so imperfectly in a world that still needs redemption. We are God's possession and, with the Spirit's help, aim to live as such, but we will fully know the benefits of salvation only in the world to come.

A PRAYER

Lord, pour out your Spirit on me, that I may live for you now,
and one day see you face to face.

PRAYER *for the* SAINTS

The writer ended his *berakah* in 1:14 with a final reminder that the goal of human existence is the praise of God. Now he returns to the persona of Paul, envisaging what the apostle would say in the next section of one of his epistles—the report of his prayers.

The author no doubt does pray for his readers, and at the same time provides a counterpart to the blessing of 1:3–14 as he turns to the effect that grace should have on those who accept it.

The first characteristic, over which the author imagines Paul's rejoicing, is the pairing of faith and love (v. 15)—faith in Christ, and love towards fellow Christians. The two go together, since faith must show itself in the believer's attitude to others, or it is no faith at all.

The Church is called to be a community that grows together in shared faith and caring, not just a group from which individuals gain teaching and sustenance for their personal lives. We live in an age that prizes the individual, and in which concepts of community or citizenship come low in our awareness. In the first century, belonging to a household and to a city were among the most important aspects of a person's life. So a major claim that the Church made was to be able to provide an alternative community, and an alternative citizenship—of heaven itself. This remains a major part of the Church's calling—to set before the world an alternative view of community and belonging, one that is centred on Christ and made manifest in love.

If it is hard to communicate the need for community in the 21st century, it is paradoxically the Church's best hope for evangelism. In an age of individualism, the longing to belong can also surface strongly, and a community that offers a genuine attempt at mutual love provides its own appealing alternative to a competitive society.

Such a community is not easy to form, and requires the support of prayer, both from its local members and from other Christians in the wider church. The author prays for his readers both with thanks for what they have attained so far (v. 16) and with supplication for their needs as they continue in faith (v. 17).

The intercession is for the whole Church. It is addressed to the God who is encountered and understood in Christ. Like Paul, the writer does not make a simple equation between God and Christ—

God is the God of Jesus Christ; that is, the one Jesus worshipped and served. At the same time, he is the God who is uniquely met in Jesus and whose fatherhood is known through his relationship with Christ, while Christ himself is titled Lord, the designation for God in the Old Testament and in Jewish tradition.

Verses such as this are the foundation for working out a way of talking about God that does justice to the full range of biblical expression and of Christian experience. At the end of the day, Christians keep coming back to the view that God is three persons in one being—Father, Son and Holy Spirit.

Wisdom and revelation

The prayer continues with a desire that God, the Father of glory, will give a spirit of wisdom and revelation to the readers. Probably we should take 'spirit' as a reference to the Holy Spirit, whose indwelling presence brings that wisdom which is the awareness of God and his will for Christian living. It also makes more sense of the idea of revelation. The Holy Spirit is the one who reveals God to believers and enables them to see his glory and wonder. God ceases, in the light of the Spirit's revelation, to be a distant possibility, and becomes a shining reality in the lives of his people. They are enabled to know him for themselves and so be aware of all that he has done for them in Jesus Christ.

In verse 17, then, we see once again the trinitarian formula that sums up the Christian understanding of God. He is the glorious Father, who in Jesus Christ is revealed as the redeemer, and who through the Spirit opens our eyes to his grace.

A PRAYER

Lord, may my eyes be opened by your Spirit, that I may see all that you have done for me, and all that you call me to do for you.

ENLIGHTENMENT

With the Holy Spirit at work in them, Christians should gain an awareness of what lies in wait for them. The phrase 'with the eyes of your heart enlightened' (v. 18) refers to the result of the revelation that the Spirit brings. It opens the 'eyes of the heart', and, as elsewhere in the Bible, the heart is seen as the organ of reason and thought rather than of emotion. So the result of the Spirit's enlightenment is knowledge, a knowledge of what God has to offer his people. It will affect the way they live, the way they view the world and their relationships with others, both inside and outside the Church.

Hope

This new knowledge focuses here on three things. The first is the Christian's hope. This does not mean a sort of wishful thinking, but an awareness of the promise of that new creation in which all things will be brought together in Christ (see 1:10). It is the gift of God to all who respond to his call (v. 18). It is therefore not only a looking forward but also a way of life for the present. A life lived in hope of God's final rule will be a life that lives under that rule now. It will show day by day the signs of the presence of God, and put into practice the love, justice and compassion that mark the kingdom of God.

Riches

The second aspect of a Spirit-enlightened mind is an awareness of 'the riches of his glorious inheritance among the saints' (v. 18). This is not the inheritance of God's children, which we saw in 1:11. It is God's inheritance, and actually consists of the saints. God has taken possession (as when one receives an inheritance) of his people, and it is a treasure indeed.

God does not need anything from human beings. He is absolutely self-sufficient, and in the interplay of love and mutual giving between the persons of the Trinity he already has the experience of relationship which might be one thing he could be expected to gain from his creatures. However, to say he needs nothing is not the same as saying that he gains nothing from us. The scriptures speak of God delighting in his people (see, for instance, Isaiah 65:18–19; Jeremiah 31:20), rejoicing over them as a parent delights in his children or an artist rejoices at his handiwork. The basis of his dealing with us is love—and love, no matter how self-sacrificing, comes to fulfilment when it is appreciated and returned.

The Spirit brings an awareness of the depth of God's love and of the delight with which he treasures his children. No one should feel valueless, worthless, a burden or a hindrance to others, who knows their worth to God.

Power

The third insight the Spirit gives is into the power of God. The Greek of verse 19 piles up four words for power in a bid to convey the awesomeness of God's might (literally, 'what is the immeasurable greatness of his *power*… according to the *working* of the *might* of his *strength*'). It is a power which is available to his people now, and which lies behind the preaching of the gospel (see 3:7). The strength of God is available to support, encourage and equip us in our daily lives, in the preaching of the gospel and in our fight against the forces of evil (see 6:10).

If the writer is thinking of any particular exercise of God's power, it is one which has already been carried out, in raising Jesus from the dead (v. 20). Death is the one final experience that is unavoidable and common to all. Death spells the end of dreams, of achievements and hopes. There is an ancient Greek epitaph which is heart-rending in its stark simplicity: 'Philip, a father, laid here his twelve-year-old boy, his great hope, Nicoteles.' It can be echoed from cemeteries around the world. Death is the incontrovertible end of hope.

Yet in Jesus, death was smashed apart, time rolled on to the day of resurrection, and a body destined to rot was transformed into something as unimaginable to us as a butterfly would be to a caterpillar. What sort of power does it take to do that? Whatever it may be, it is found only in God, and has been brought into play on our behalf.

A PRAYER

Lord, give me the insight that recognizes your might, and the faith that claims your power.

89

The WAY *of* GLORY

The power of God has not only raised Jesus from death, but has exalted him and given him a place at the right hand of God himself. This image is a common one in the ancient world. In the Old Testament, the right hand of God is the place of favour, a sign that his blessing rests on the king. In the New Testament, one such statement about the king of Israel (Psalm 110:1) is applied frequently to Christ, and probably lies behind the imagery here. Indeed, Christ's exalted rule is a major focus for the writer of Ephesians, and governs much of the rest of the letter.

The mighty saving act of God is seen in the resurrection and exaltation of Christ, which should be seen as a single action. Jesus is exalted to share the power of God in the very action of being raised from the dead. It is notable that there is no mention here of the cross. The emphasis is on glory, power and exaltation (though see 2:13— the author does not pretend that resurrection and glorification are separable from death and pain). This points up a permanent tension in Christian thinking. On the one hand there is the way of the cross, with its stress on the need for humility, for failure in the world's eyes and for death. On the other is the affirmation of God's power, the victory of Christ and the glorious rule of the saints. Ephesians definitely leans towards the latter viewpoint, with its language of glory and power.

It is vital, though, that the two be placed side by side. Those who stress the victory need to remember that it comes through suffering and humility. Those who stress the pain and humility of discipleship need to remember that they are promised the victory. Perhaps each part of the message speaks to different situations. Where the Church is persecuted, beleaguered or ignored, the victory song needs to be sung all the louder. Where it is rich, numerous and powerful, the way of the cross needs to be asserted in the face of complacency and self-righteousness.

Power and the powers

The writer, like Paul in Colossians (and influenced by him), stresses that the power of Christ is far greater than that of the powers which rule the world. The powers mentioned here are once again those we met in Colossians 1:16, the spiritual beings that rule the world. Through his triumphant resurrection and exaltation, Christ has been placed far above all of these, and they, like all other things, must be subservient to him.

There is no mention here of the role of Christ in creation, and he rules over the powers by virtue of his work of salvation. This has the effect of strengthening the writer's emphasis on the Church and the status of the people of God. Since the powers are placed under the authority of Christ, there is no chance of seeing them as in any way equal to him. Hence they do not provide an alternative or complementary route to God, nor do they exist as an equal and opposite force to Christ. There is no notion of a balance of good and evil forces in Christianity, but an assertion of the one God who in the end will rule over all and bring all things together in Christ.

The powers are undoubtedly seen as hostile to God, enemies who, while defeated, still remain dangerous (6:12). The writer undoubtedly thinks of the powers as real spiritual beings, which are essentially demonic in nature. At the same time, they are the powers that lie behind many of the systems of this world. It is therefore no great step to translate them into modern terms as whatever powers oppress human life and keep people from the true worship of God. Those modern theologians who recast the New Testament language in terms of present-day political, economic and commercial systems would have been readily understood by the writer of Ephesians. For him, the spiritual and physical worlds are the opposite sides of the same coin, and what goes on in one is reflected in the other.

The rule of Christ extends over all other powers 'in this age and the age to come' (v. 21). With this phrase, the writer encompasses the totality of creation. He also recognizes that at present that rule may not be fully apparent. The age of the new creation is coming, and has dawned in the life of the Church, but its final consummation lies in the future.

A PRAYER

Lord, may I serve only you, and not be misled
by any other claim to power.

HEAD & BODY

The last two verses of this chapter, and of the writer's prayer of thanksgiving and intercession, pose a good many questions and are the subject of much scholarly debate. The first part, however, is fairly straightforward. God 'has put all things under his feet'. This is a quotation from Psalm 8:6 in which human beings are seen as having been placed over the rest of creation. The wording differs from the Greek version of the Old Testament, the Septuagint, and instead matches Paul's quotation of the verse in 1 Corinthians 15:27, which suggests that 1 Corinthians is the inspiration here. In 1 Corinthians 15, Paul argues that Christ is the representative of the new humanity that God is bringing about. Therefore, what can be said of human beings in general can be said specifically of Christ. He is the one who sums up all that it means to be truly human.

Whereas in Psalm 8:6 it was the rule of humans over the rest of creation, what is in view here is the rule of Christ over all things, including human beings. God has therefore 'given him as head over all things to the Church' which is a simpler translation than NRSV. Christ is first of all the head over all things. 'Head' here is influenced by the Hebrew use of the term, which can mean both 'origin' and 'ruler' or 'leader'. Since the stress of the passage is on the rule of Christ, and there is no mention of Christ's role in creation, it is the rule of Christ which is in view. The ruler over all things has been given to the Church by God.

In Colossians 1:18 Christ is the head of the body which is the Church. This marks a combination of two different images that Paul used. The image of the body was an image of the Church in which the head was no more significant than any other part (1 Corinthians 12:12; Romans 12:4). It was the whole body that made up Christ. The image of Christ as the head was a picture of him as origin and possibly ruler (1 Corinthians 11:3; Colossians 2:10). Here in Ephesians 1:22 the headship of Christ is once again a reference to his rule over creation.

God has given Christ to the Church as its Lord and saviour, which is a way of saying that the Church has a special place in his plan of salvation and a special relationship with Christ, the Lord of all things.

Indeed, it is 'his body, the fullness of him who fills all things' (v. 23). Here, 'church' (*ekklesia*) is used to denote the universal Church, the company of all the faithful, wherever they may be. Originally the word simply meant 'assembly' but was used in the Septuagint to describe the assembly of God's covenant people, Israel. In the genuine Pauline letters, it generally refers to local congregations, but is sometimes used in a wider sense (see Galatians 1:13; 1 Corinthians 10:32; 12:28; Philippians 3:6). Verse 22 is the first occurrence of the word 'church' in Ephesians, but it has been in sight from the beginning, with the address to 'the saints'.

The Church is the body of Christ and is therefore his way of continuing to work in the world. This is a metaphor, and should not be pushed too far. The writer does not imagine that the Church and Christ are the same, or that the Church somehow continues the incarnation. Christ's risen body is with God, and he works through the Church by the power of his Spirit (1:13).

It is this last idea that gives us the way into the most difficult part of verse 23. In what sense is the Church the fullness of Christ? He himself is the fullness, the completion and goal of all things (1:10). The Church is not the fullness of Christ in the sense of summing up and completing him. 'Fullness' should be taken here in a passive sense, as being that which is filled by him. The Church is filled by Christ, who pours out his Spirit on it, enabling it to worship and serve him (see 3:19).

Finally, while the images of head and body are essentially separate in these two verses, they do come together in 4:15–16, so it is likely that the writer also is thinking of Christ as the head of the Church, as in Colossians 1:18. The two images are not fully merged, however. The relationship of Christ to creation and to the Church remain distinct. He is head of creation by virtue of his rule, and of the Church by virtue of its being the body through which he works by the power of the Spirit. Creation as yet does not necessarily know him as its Lord and Saviour. The Church, however imperfectly, does.

A PRAYER

Lord, may I know you as my saviour,
and seek to serve you in your Church.

91 EPHESIANS 2:1–3

A TALE *of* TWO WORLDS

The reference to Christ and the Church in 1:22–23 leads into a reflection on the nature of salvation and of the people of God. Before their meeting with Christ and inclusion in the Church, the readers were dead. Compared to life in Christ, life without God is no life at all. Indeed, it is a life that is cut off from the source of eternal life by its sins ('trespasses' and 'sins' are synonyms—another example of the author's preference for multiplying terms for the same thing). For Paul, individual sins are merely the symptoms of the underlying condition of sin (Romans 5:12–13). In Ephesians 2:1 it is sins themselves that bring about spiritual death. Yet the thought is not all that far from Paul's, for the people's sins were symptoms of their slavery to the ruler of the present age (v. 2).

The ruler of the world

They followed the course of this world by living a life that was in actual fact devoted to a false god. Like Paul, the writer of Ephesians does not imagine a neutral position from which one can choose good or evil, God or Satan. Those who steadily live out their lives by the standards of the world around them, with no thought for the God who is their creator, are actually in bondage to a power that opposes God. That opponent is the 'ruler of the authority of the air' (v. 2). Here, authority ('power' in NRSV) is the area under the ruler's power. The 'air' is the region between the heavens and the earth, the lowest (and therefore closest to earth) of the heavenly regions.

The writer therefore envisages a spiritual power who rules over the world (and therefore over the vast array of other spiritual powers), and who is responsible for the present Godless climate of human life. Paul preferred simply to say 'Satan'. The second part of verse 2 is best taken as a reference to the human spirit, living in disobedience to its creator. The ruler is the ruler not only of the realm of air, but of the rebellious human spirit, so that those who do not recognize God may be characterized simply as 'the disobedient'.

It can quite reasonably be objected that the human spirit is not universally opposed to God. Paul acknowledged that there were Gentiles who followed the precepts of God's law by following the testimony of their own hearts (Romans 2:14–16). Thoughtful modern atheists argue that they are just as capable of moral life without acknowledging God as are Christians. However, it is not a question of whether there are good pagans or bad Christians. Salvation does not come through legal uprightness, but through a relationship with God which enables him to work in partnership with the believer. The essential question of obedience or disobedience is not about the keeping of particular laws or the committing of particular sins, but about response to, or rejection of, God's call to a relationship of mutual love.

Of course, there is a moral quality to that relationship. Responsibility for behaviour and attitudes is a vital part of human nature, and moral failings do indeed incur the judgment of God, so that those who live apart from him can be characterized as 'by nature children of wrath' (v. 3). This term does not characterize God as intrinsically angry or vindictive, but recognizes his implacable opposition to evil. Nor does it say that human nature is intrinsically wicked, since sin is always seen as an abnormality. 'Nature' here means the way things happen to be, rather than the way they are meant to be.

Ephesians 2:1–3 is not essentially about the behaviour of individuals so much as the realm, or ultimate authority, under which they live. Those who live apart from God dwell in a realm characterized by the passions of the flesh and the following of desire. 'Flesh' here is being used in the common Pauline sense of the sinful tendency of human nature. Given free rein, it leads to a life lived for self and self-gratification. In general terms it leads to a world of inequality and pain, as those with economic and political power walk over others in their pursuit of self.

This world, so readily recognizable in terms either of the Roman empire or of the modern world, is one to which the readers and the author of Ephesians once belonged, but do so no longer.

A PRAYER

Lord, may my life be worthy of my membership of your realm.

GRACE & HOPE

The plight of those who live apart from God has been painted in dark tones. They are under God's condemnation, ruled by Satan and naturally disobedient. Yet two words bring hope: 'But God' (v. 4). God is the great exception to human failure, the opposition to human death. In the face of a predicament that seems insuperable, God acts to bring salvation.

That salvation springs from deeper wells than any condemnation; it pours out of his mercy and love, which reach out to those whose sinfulness has cut them off from life and hope (v. 5). It is the characteristic of God's love that he loves those who are intrinsically unlovely. Other forms of love are based in some way on the attractiveness of the beloved, be it their appearance, their character or their relationship to the lover. God's love reaches out to bring good to those who in themselves appear to be the antithesis of all that God stands for. As a result, God becomes the hope of the hopeless.

As people put their faith in Christ, they come to share in his resurrection life and his conquest of death, and find a new hope and future. They become alive again. This is what God has done for the Church, for the readers addressed by Ephesians.

As an aside, the reminder is driven home: you are saved by grace (v. 5). This is the core of the Christian message, that God's love issues in a free gift of salvation. It is offered on a plate, and needs only to be received in faith.

In being made alive with Christ, Christians have been exalted and enthroned with him as well. Some Christians seem to have believed that the fullness of new life was now theirs, and that they already had the full experience of the resurrection (1 Corinthians 4:8). This is not the meaning of the author of Ephesians, as becomes clear in verse 7, but it does point to the dangers of such language. A church that sees itself as partaking in the victory of Christ can easily become blandly triumphalist, forgetting how far it has to go.

On the other hand, a church that forgets what it has in Christ will soon lose heart. While the world, and the church's members, may see a group that struggles and often fails, God sees it as part of the vast company of saints that shares in the rule of Christ over creation. This spiritual reality underlies the worship of the church ('with angels and archangels and all the company of heaven') and will ultimately be its only reality.

All this has been accomplished 'in Christ' (v. 6), that is, by the union of believers with their Lord. What God has done to Christ, raising him from death and seating him on the heavenly throne, he has done to him as the first instalment of a new humanity. Those who share that humanity necessarily share in some degree in the exalted status of their head.

Looking forward

The full completion of that process of raising up and the creation of God's new humanity lies in the future (v. 7). Yet the age to come began when Christ was raised from the dead. (The plural 'ages' in verse 7 probably reflects a liturgical style—its meaning is simply 'eternity'.) With his resurrection, the new age has dawned, though its full light has yet to shine. Thus the Church lives in a sort of in-between time, living now in the light of the age to come.

In this respect, the author of Ephesians is in full agreement with Paul, who also saw Christ as bringing in the new age and the Church as living in expectation of God's final victory. The difference is one of emphasis. Paul tended to stress the future dimension of Christian hope, while Ephesians focuses on the present aspect.

All this shows the immeasurable riches of grace (as the writer piles up his characteristic superlatives), of God and of his kindness. In fact, it is done deliberately to demonstrate his grace (v. 7) so that, by implication, he may be praised and worshipped (1:6, 12, 14). It would take a particularly cynical mind to suggest that God does this only so that he may be praised. In fact, he does it out of love, to restore human beings to the proper relationship of praise and worship, love and service for which they were created and in which we find our true selves.

A PRAYER

Lord, may I praise you now in preparation for
an eternity in your presence.

GRACE & FAITH

The writer now reiterates his parenthesis of 2:5: it is God's grace that has brought salvation. He now expands this by adding its necessary corollary, that grace has been received by faith. Being put right with God has two components. The first is God's gracious act of love and forgiveness which takes physical form in the incarnation, death and resurrection of Christ. God, true to the biblical pattern, acts first and asks questions afterwards. That is, he carries out his saving work and then asks that it be received. The biblical writers seem all to agree that God's work demands a response. He does not save against our will. Salvation has to be appropriated; the gift must be received and unwrapped before it can be of any use.

Ephesians offers little support to those who wish to claim that all are saved whether they respond or not. The reason is once again the biblical stress on relationships. Salvation is not a matter of juggling laws and punishments, though the language of law and judgment is common. At root, it is about entering freely into a relationship of love and trust with God. Hence the message is one not of mere cancellation of debts, but of reconciliation, the bringing together in peace and harmony of two parties who once were at enmity (2 Corinthians 5:18–20).

At the same time, Ephesians (and the Bible as a whole) offers no encouragement to those who wish to stand in judgment over others and declare who is or is not saved. The most that is said here is that those who have received the gospel in faith know of their standing with God, are part of Christ's resurrection life, share in his rule, and will one day stand in the presence of God. That should be enough to be going on with. We are not encouraged to speculate about other ways in which grace may be received and faith exercised.

In its own way, the gospel of God's grace is a great challenge to sinful human nature. The essence of sin is the failure to recognize God, and to do things one's own way. It requires a certain humility to accept that the path to heaven is not our reward but a free gift, and the perennial heresy that the Church faces is the teaching that salvation is a reward for good works.

That was as true in the first century as the 21st, and the writer drives the point home twice in two verses. It is not your doing, it is not the result of works, so no one has anything to boast about (vv. 8–9). 'Works' in Paul refers to obedience to the Jewish Law. Here it should be given the widest possible meaning: it refers to anything that human beings may do to justify themselves to God, or to convince themselves that God is more or less obliged to respond favourably to such good folks.

Good works

There are indeed good works to be done, but they are the response of faith to God's grace. Christians are God's adopted children, sharers in a new humanity, co-rulers with Christ and his servants on earth, but they are all this because God has willed it so.

He is working in his people to bring about a new creation, and what they are is the result of the first act of that re-creation (v. 10). This creation has come about 'in Christ Jesus', by the work that God has done through Christ and applied to believers by their union with Christ. In the midst of a world that the writer has characterized as being under the Devil's rule, a new creation is coming into being.

This new creation has a purpose—to perform good works. That purpose is indicated by the idea that God has prepared the works in advance. The goal of salvation is that the redeemed might do good works, and as such the works are all part of God's plan of salvation. This is the exact opposite of salvation by works—it is salvation *for* works. In everyday experience, the works that Christians do are the response of those who know they are saved by grace and in glad thanksgiving offer themselves to God's service.

These works will include the worship of God and the proclamation of the gospel, but they are not restricted to these. They will include acts of love and compassion, showing mercy and standing up for justice. They will be the works of a people who are called to show in their own lives (literally, 'that we may walk in them', v. 10) the quality of life of the kingdom of God.

A PRAYER

Lord, in my daily life, may I walk with you and do your works.

GENTILE CHRISTIANS, JEWISH HISTORY

The discussion of the great change that salvation brings leads into another aspect of God's saving work, the breaking down of the barrier between Jew and Gentile. This is a major issue in the genuine Pauline letters, as Paul argued fiercely against the teaching of Jewish Christians, who held that in order to belong to Israel's Messiah, Gentiles must become fully Jews.

Ephesians seems to envisage a situation where Gentile Christians are far in the majority and Jewish Christianity is no longer a strong force. Jerusalem has been destroyed (in AD70) in response to a Jewish revolt, and no longer houses the mother church. Jews and Christians have more or less completely parted company, and see each other as different (though closely related) faiths. If there is a problem, it is perhaps one of identity. Gentile Christians have embraced the new faith but find themselves cut off from their own past and, to some extent, from their local communities. Do they therefore have a history they can call their own? The answer is a qualified 'yes', for they now belong to the covenant people of God, though the nature of that people has radically changed.

Making peace

Taking up the thought of God's new creation, the writer goes on to approach it from a different direction. Physically and by descent (literally, 'in flesh') the readers of Ephesians are Gentiles (v. 11). This gives us a strong suggestion that the writer is a Jewish Christian, for a Gentile would hardly write in such terms, and would certainly say 'we' rather than 'you'. That at least is the term used by Jews, who categorize humanity into two groups, the circumcised members of God's chosen people, and 'the uncircumcision' (literally 'the foreskin', but 'uncircumcision' is a better translation, as it takes note of the real issue).

Circumcision, much as it may have marked out the members of God's people, is a merely physical sign. It is 'made by hands'—a phrase used to denote the merely outward rather than the spiritual. Those who count on their circumcision as denoting their status before God are in serious danger of forgetting that the real mark of God's people is faith in him.

None the less, the history of the Gentiles is one of separation from God. Before their conversion, they were without a relationship to Christ (v. 12), and they were strangers to the people of Israel. The word that NRSV translates as 'commonwealth' means Israel as a state. The Gentiles were foreigners. They had no share in the promises of God. The writer uses the plural 'covenants' to denote the several different occasions when God made an agreement with his people—with Abraham (Genesis 15:7–21; 17:9–14), with Isaac (Genesis 26:2–5), with Jacob (Genesis 28:13–15), with Israel as a whole (Exodus 24:1–8) and with David (2 Samuel 7).

They had no hope and no God. They worshipped their own gods, and no doubt looked forward to whatever form of afterlife their own religion offered them. Yet they did not know the one true God, and their hopes were based on nothing substantial. Now, through their encounter with Christ, they have been brought near. This term is borrowed from the language of Jewish proselytism. The word 'proselyte', used of converts to Judaism, comes from a Greek word meaning 'to draw near', which in turn translates a Hebrew word with a similar meaning. The Gentiles have been brought to the presence of God by the blood of Jesus.

As in most other places in the New Testament, the blood of Christ is a reference to his death and the benefits that it brings, among which is peace (v. 14) between Jew and Gentile. In his death (his actual physical death is stressed by 'in his flesh'), Christ has broken down the wall of hostility that existed between Jew and Gentile. Some commentators take this as a reference to the balustrade that separated the Court of the Gentiles from the Court of the Women in the Jerusalem temple. Though Gentiles were allowed into the outer precincts, to pass beyond the barrier was to incur death. A better view is that it is a reference to the Torah, the Jewish Law, with its rules of separation from those outside the community of Israel. The Law functioned to create hostility, causing Jews to regard Gentiles as unclean and Gentiles to despise Jews as antisocial and élitist. In Christ, all Christians are equal, whatever their origins.

A PRAYER

Lord, may I never despise my fellow believers,
whatever their background or circumstances.

95

LAW & RECONCILIATION

Christ has broken down the dividing wall between Jew and Gentile by abolishing the Law. This stark and simple statement seems almost to go too far. Surely it means that he removed the ceremonial and sacrificial aspects of the Law, but left the moral ones intact? What it says, though, is much simpler. Christ abolished the Law, with its rules and regulations. Presumably these are specifically the rules that acted to distance Jews from their Gentile neighbours, but the statement is not limited to any particular regulations. In Christ the Law is no longer binding.

This does not mean that Christians are free to do as they will. It means that they are free to live as God wills, out of love rather than a need to keep rules. The writer of Ephesians will later appeal to one of the Ten Commandments, the core of the Law (6:3), and so it seems that while he does not consider it binding on Christians, he still sees it as a useful measure of Christian behaviour.

The abolition of the Law (v. 15) is necessary in order to bind together a new people of God, drawn from Jews and Gentiles alike. This is more than a mingling of two separated strands of humanity; it is the creation of a new kind of human being. It is the first instalment of the re-creation of the universe (1:10). By bringing together two seemingly incompatible groups, Christ signals his work of reconciling creation to God. Both Jew and Gentile are transformed into a new humanity of which Christ is the prototype, and which is embraced by union with him.

The result of the new creation is that both Jew and Gentile are reconciled to God. This seems to fit uneasily with what has previously been written about the Gentiles' pre-Christian condition. If they were far from God and separated from the promises to Israel (2:12), does that not imply that the Jews at least were near to God? Undoubtedly, but the new creation is such a surpassing change that in relative terms both Jew and Gentile are found to have been far from God compared to their status in Christ. As they find themselves together in the Church, the body of Christ (v. 16), they discover that God offers such an experience of himself and of human transformation that whatever they had before pales into insignificance (see Paul's account of his own experience in Philippians 3:7–10).

The gulf that had existed between Jew and Gentile was so great that it took the re-creating power of Christ's death to bridge it (v. 16) by putting it to death. This is the sort of language that Colossians 2:14 uses of sin (and it is probably drawn from there). It suggests that the hostility between Jew and Gentile is seen as part of the sinfulness of the world for which Christ's sacrifice atones. Even though the Law was good, it could have sinful effects by creating a division that actually kept the Gentiles from meeting God, though it also paved the way for the coming of Christ.

Building barriers

If the great division between Jew and Gentile was already becoming something of a theoretical issue by the time of Ephesians, it seems a strange and distant concern to most modern Christians. Yet humanity is still divided into many groups, ethnic, cultural, religious and national. In the Church there should be no such barriers, but all too often there are. In Britain, the 1950s and '60s saw an influx of black immigrants from the West Indies, and of Indian Asians from Africa and Pakistan. Many (especially amongst the West Indians) were Christians. When they attempted to join churches in Britain, they were often rejected, and ended up forming their own Christian communities.

The story can be repeated time and again for various groups. And it can be applied more widely than in the Church alone. As populations become more mobile, societies find the arrival of newcomers to be a regular occurrence. If they are the same colour and class as the indigenous population, they may pass unnoticed. Otherwise, they tend to get short shrift. A church that glories in the reconciliation of opposites in Christ should surely be in the forefront of welcome and the proclamation of tolerance and understanding. But is it?

A PRAYER

Lord, I belong to a people that once was far from you.
Thank you for bringing me home.

96

The RECONCILER

In 2:14–16 we have seen how Jesus' death on the cross is the means of reconciling both Jews and Gentiles to God, and of doing away with the hostility that existed between the two groups. Hostility between humans is a result of the hostility they demonstrate to God by their sin. Those who live in the realm of the ruler of this world (2:2) live in opposition to God (though they may not realize it) and this transfers into the area of human relationships.

Thus the coming of Christ, and specifically his death, expounded in the previous three verses, is seen as proclaiming (the verb used in verse 17 is the one normally used for preaching the gospel, and can be translated as 'evangelize') peace to Gentiles and to Jews. The very death of Christ is God's potent message of salvation, a promise of peace between humanity and God.

Verse 17 is modelled on Isaiah 57:19: 'Peace, peace, to the far and the near, says the Lord; and I will heal them.' Although the far and near originally referred to those in exile in Babylon and those still in Judea, this verse came to be applied as a promise of salvation to those who had wandered away from God, and also to Gentile proselytes. The writer of Ephesians has modified the verse to stress the promise of peace to each of the two groups. In his understanding, both Jews and Gentiles have been given peace with God, and hence end up in the same camp. As we find peace with God, that peace transfers into a peace with others who have also encountered it.

As verse 18 explains, both groups now have the same access to God the Father, and hence find themselves united with each other. The application of this simple fact to modern church life is so obvious that it hardly needs stating. This access to God comes through the 'one Spirit', a term which deliberately stresses the unity of shared faith and worship (compare 1 Corinthians 12:13). The Christian community is bound together in one body (2:16) by the one Spirit (4:4). Through verses 17 and 18 we have the specifically Christian formula of approach to the Father through the Son in the Spirit. It is this consistently threefold action of God that underlies the doctrine of the Trinity.

A new identity

The Gentile Christians to whom the letter is addressed are therefore no longer cut off from the people of God. They have their own identity as part of the kingdom of God. The image of citizens (v. 19) looks back to 2:12, where the Gentiles were foreigners outside the nation of Israel. Now they are inside it, though not by the old route of proselytism. Instead a new people of God has been formed, of which they are fully fledged members. They are one with the saints, the holy ones of God. The 'saints', as elsewhere in Ephesians, means all Christians, of whatever racial or national origin. There is no longer any distinction between Jew and Gentile, or indeed any other group in the ancient world (Colossians 3:11).

In another image, they have been adopted (1:5) as children of God, and so are members of his household. God calls us into a relationship with him, which turns out to be the home we have always been looking for, often without even realizing it.

The Greek word translated as 'household member' in verse 19 is *oikeios*, which is formed from *oikos*, 'house'. This enables a smooth move into yet another image, for *oikos* can also mean 'temple'. So in verse 20 the household becomes a house whose foundation consists of the apostles and prophets, with Christ as the keystone, which holds the whole structure together (see 1 Peter 2:5–6). In Paul's use of a similar analogy (1 Corinthians 3:10–15), it is Christ who is the foundation, but there the building is the edifice of good works that believers build on the foundation of faith in Christ. Here the Church is compared to a building, held together by Christ, and firmly grounded on the teaching of the apostles and prophets.

This in turn reinforces the impression that Ephesians belongs to a generation in which the time of the apostles is past. Together with the first generation of prophets, they set in motion a movement that continues to grow, a building that is still under construction in each generation. Once again we see the need for continuity (see comment on 1:1–2, p. 186) with the founding generation of Christianity.

A PRAYER

Lord, enable me to take my place in your household
and live under the rule of your kingdom.

97

BUILDING *the* TEMPLE

The building of God's temple is currently under way. With a firm foundation on the work of the first generation of teachers—the apostles who bore witness to Christ, proclaiming the gospel and founding churches, and the prophets who communicated his living word—the building comes to unity in Christ. The cornerstone, or keystone, which is Christ, is probably envisaged as acting like the keystone of an arch or the pinnacle of a spire. It is the highest point, and also holds other pieces in place. The image functions like that of the head in 4:15–16 (compare Colossians 2:19), as a picture of Christ as the unifying principle of the Church.

The use of temple imagery is a rich vein in the New Testament. For Paul, both individual Christians (1 Corinthians 6:19) and the local congregation (1 Corinthians 3:17) can be described as the temple in which God's presence, the Holy Spirit, dwells. In Ephesians, the whole Church is the dwelling of God. God is present in each situation and takes up residence in individual lives, in local communities and in the universal Church.

The idea of the Church as God's temple is both a fulfilment and a radical reworking of an Old Testament hope, in which the temple of Jerusalem would one day become the centre of worship for all the nations (Isaiah 56:6–7; Zechariah 8:22–23). Now the prophecy has come true, but finds its fulfilment in the people of God, drawn from all nations, who themselves constitute the temple.

The author has a double vision of the Church which recurs throughout the letter. The presence of the pinnacle suggests a building that is finished, just as 1:23 declares the Church to have the fullness of Christ. At the same time, the building is still growing, just as the Church is still growing into fullness (4:15). This double picture represents the spiritual reality behind the Church, in which God has won the victory through Christ and made the Church his own. At the same time, in this world the victory is being worked out, and the Church is called to put into practice the vision of its inner reality. Thus the Church already is the temple of God, the place where he dwells, yet must strive to become the worthy dwelling of God.

Ongoing work

This picture of the temple as a work in progress is the main emphasis in verses 21–22, and it provides a necessary *caveat* to the author's high view of the Church. For all that it is the dwelling-place of God, consisting of saints who share the heavenly throne with Christ and who possess every blessing that God can bestow, the Church is not perfect. Improvement is a vital part of its work and its life. This means, for instance, that any pronouncement of the Church, any practice of the Church, must be provisional. As it grows further in its knowledge and understanding of God, it must be open to change, for without change growth is impossible.

Such growth comes from Christ and is found only in him. Verse 21 begins with 'in him' (Christ) and ends with 'in the Lord' (Christ), and verse 22 insists that growth is 'in the Spirit' (NRSV's footnote is the better reading here). The growth of the Church can come about only as the Church is united with Christ by the Holy Spirit.

It should be fairly clear by now that the growth that the author has in mind is growth in quality rather than quantity. We tend to stress growth in numbers, and this is important. The Church is called to proclaim the gospel and to make disciples, so a church that is faithfully performing its task should expect to see new members arriving. However, the task of evangelism is one part of the Church's growth, and one suspects that it cannot take place in a congregation which is not also seeking to grow in faith, understanding and community. For that matter, the task of making disciples is not only about conversion, but includes encouraging spiritual growth as well.

It is probably fair to say that a church that seeks to grow into a fitting dwelling for God is one that will also grow in numbers, as God's power is seen to be at work within it. One that stifles spiritual growth for whatever reason (and there do seem to be many reasons!) will not see new disciples being made, any more than it will see older ones grow.

A PRAYER

Lord, may we grow in knowledge of you and seek
ever new visions of your glory.

98

CHRIST'S PRISONER

Chapter 3 begins with a sentence that is never completed. Writing in the persona of Paul, the author begins, 'For this reason I, Paul, the prisoner of Christ on behalf of you Gentiles…' and then goes off at a tangent to discuss Paul's ministry and the gospel he preached. The original thought is probably taken up again at 3:14 where 'for this reason' is repeated and leads to a prayer for the readers. NRSV supplies the missing word, 'am', after 'Paul' but there is no reason to do this. The breaking off of sentences is something that is very easy to do with a dictated letter: a similar 'anacolouthon' can be seen in Romans 5:12–13.

Because of what he has written so far, about the building of the Church into a community that worships and serves God, the writer is about to offer a prayer for the strengthening of the Church in its task. He introduces Paul again, and this leads to a reflection on the significance of Paul and his ministry, which seems to draw its outline from Colossians 1:23–29.

Paul is a prisoner of Christ. As in Philemon 1, the term is literal, in that it envisages Paul as being in prison, but at the same time it is an image of his relation to Christ. Like 'slave of Christ' (Philippians 1:1), it shows his full allegiance to his Lord. It is also a description of his understanding of his captivity. It is part of his service to Christ: whatever comes his way is an outworking of his relationship to God and an opportunity to continue his ministry.

Moreover, Paul is a prisoner for the sake of the Gentiles. His imprisonment is a result of his work in bringing the gospel to the world outside of the nation of Israel, and if he is envisaged as being held captive in Rome, it is a direct result of his championing of the Gentile cause, which led to the attempt on his life in Jerusalem (Acts 21:27–30).

Apostle to the Gentiles

The thought of Paul's special mission to the Gentiles now leads the writer off in a new direction. The readers will no doubt have heard of Paul (who could not?), and by reference to his special calling, the writer draws attention to the continuing importance of Paul's teaching, as expounded for a new generation of Gentile Christians (v. 2).

Paul was given a particular 'stewardship (NRSV 'commission') of grace'. God graciously came to Paul and called him to be his own. That calling was for a specific purpose, so that his energies and gifts could be directed towards the conversion of the Gentiles. Paul did not see the gift of salvation as separate from his calling (1 Corinthians 15:8–10). To be saved by Christ was to be commissioned by Christ, and the grace of God that was poured out on Paul was something to be used in his service and shared with others.

Paul's experience was one of exceptional calling, but the pattern of it was not unusual. To be a Christian is indeed to receive grace and the gift of salvation, but it is always to receive a call to serve.

Paul's gospel had its roots in his encounter with Christ on the road to Damascus, and so was not simply something that had been handed on to him by normal human channels (v. 3; compare Galatians 1: 11–12). Of course, Paul also received tradition which was handed on by his fellow Christians (1 Corinthians 15:3) but the burning core of his message was his own personal calling. This underlines the import- ance of Paul's message for the writer of Ephesians: Paul had received a message for the nations from Christ himself, and such a revelation has an abiding significance.

The core of that message has already briefly been outlined in the previous chapter. In Christ, God has given salvation to the whole world, in a message that can be received and accepted by Jew and non-Jew alike.

It is this message that is described as 'the mystery of Christ' (v. 4). It is a mystery not because it is hidden, but because the veil that hides the mysterious mind of God has been drawn aside and we have been given a glimpse into the purposes of God, who in Christ has made known his will for humanity.

A PRAYER

Lord, may I glimpse an insight into your purposes
and hear your call to serve.

FOUNDING FATHERS

The mystery of the inclusion of the Gentiles is something that God had not made known in the past and has only now been revealed. The Old Testament had a hope that the Gentiles would come to know God. The way that has been brought about, by the creation of a new humanity, in which Jew and Gentile alike find salvation, is a new departure and something that has only now been revealed.

The ones to whom it was revealed were the apostles and the prophets. The apostles are those individuals who were specifically called by God to bear witness to the resurrection of Jesus (1 Corinthians 9:1; Acts 1:22) and to be the founders of the Church. They are described as 'holy', which suggests not only their special calling, for its basic idea is of being set apart, but also a degree of veneration by later Christians. It was the apostles who were the first to realize the scope of Christ's work in bringing together Jew and Gentile in one new people. The revelations of God would also be seen as coming through the prophets. These are Christian prophets (2:20) who played a major role in the early Church as receivers of words from God (1 Corinthians 14:1, 29–32) which could convey teaching or inspired interpretation of scripture and tradition.

The author probably envisages the apostles as providing the link with Jesus, the historical continuity of the message, and the prophets as keeping open the channel for God's living word to continue to illuminate the life of the Church.

It has sometimes been argued that the author sees the gift of prophecy as belonging only to the founding generation of the Church. This has often gone alongside a general argument that gifts of the Spirit belong to the apostolic period alone. There is nothing in the passage to suggest this. The apostles, of necessity, belong to one particular time. (Whatever use may be made of the term today, the dimension of witness to the resurrection is hard to duplicate in the 21st century.) Prophets, however, may belong both to the founding generation and to later ones.

The revelation to the apostles and prophets came through the mediation of the Holy Spirit, who ensures that God is not confined to the past but remains active among his people.

In verse 6 the content of the mystery is made clear. It is indeed the inclusion of the Gentiles. They are fellow heirs (1:11), sharers in the inheritance that God has prepared for his people. They are united in the body of Christ, the Church (1:23), and have a share in the hope that is promised by the gospel (1:12). In all this, it is clear that they are equal partners. There are no second-class citizens in the kingdom of heaven, for these riches are the gift of God to all who are in Christ.

Servant of the gospel

This is the message that Paul was called to serve (v. 7) and for which God's grace and power set him apart. Verse 7 effectively repeats the thought of verse 2, with the additional mention of God's power. 'Working' and 'power' take us back to 1:19–20. The power at work in Paul, and indeed in all believers, is the power that raised Jesus from the dead. This work of God continues in the Church and still brings new life as the followers of Jesus are transformed into the new creation and testify to the truth of the gospel.

The grace that called Paul to be an apostle came to one who was 'the very least' of God's people (v. 8). Here the writer takes up Paul's claim to be the least of the apostles (1 Corinthians 15:9) because he had persecuted the Church. The sense of humility is made stronger, not to highlight the penitence of Paul but to stress the greatness of God's grace. One who had been a fierce opponent of Christ, a harrier of his followers, could still receive God's forgiveness and power, to be used as the spearhead of the gospel mission.

Christians can become so used to the idea of God's acceptance that they forget the power of its message. It is the core of the gospel. No matter who we are, what we have done, God holds open the possibility of forgiveness and a new life. For human beings (and all too often within the Church) there are limits to what we consider forgivable. There are none for God, and we should be grateful for that.

A PRAYER

Lord, I do not pray for justice, but for mercy for all.

The VICTORY *of* GOD

The grace of God was given to Paul for a purpose. The point has been made before (3:2) but is driven home with an intensity that reflects his single-minded pursuit of his calling. He has touched on the riches offered by Christ, and found them inexhaustible. Paul was always keenly aware of God's call, but nowhere does he give the impression that he is striving to merit favour with God. Nor does the author of Ephesians. Paul's mission grows out of God's grace. He cannot resist the call of God, simply because it comes in a package of undeserved love and forgiveness.

So the riches of Christ that he preaches are boundless, unsearchable. The word suggests that one can explore all that Christ is and has to offer, and never come to an end of them. To encounter Christ is to lose oneself in the endless love of God.

As a result, Paul seeks to make clear to everyone God's plan of salvation (v. 9). The word for plan is *oikonomia*, 'stewardship', which here means the way God puts into practice that mystery which is salvation. Paul is called to explain, to demonstrate, how God brought about his new creation in Christ. That plan has been a mystery for time immemorial, locked away in the innermost thoughts of the creator and hidden from human understanding. The mention of God as 'the creator of all things' reminds us that God's plan of salvation has been there all along, part of the destiny of his creation (1:4). It also reflects the biblical insistence that creation and redemption are the work of the one God. Christians are often tempted to divide the world into the life of the spirit and the life of the material world. It cannot be done. God made the world, God is active in the world, and God will remake the world in Christ.

This is the content of the mystery of salvation. Earlier (3:5) the mystery was the fusion of Jew and Gentile into a new humanity. It still is, but the significance of that new humanity takes on an even greater dimension. Now, at this very time (v. 10), the rulers and powers in the heavenly places, the spiritual beings who are opposed to God and exercise their influence over the world, under the ruler of the power of the air (2:2), can see their authority shaken and emptied of meaning.

The sign of their defeat is the revealing of God's wisdom, the mystery of salvation. It is rich and varied, encompassing all of creation, but finds its expression in the created world and takes physical form as the Church. The staggering thought is that the rebellious cosmic powers look at the Church and see their defeat.

New world, new life

Later in the letter, the writer will envisage the Church engaged in a struggle with those powers (6:12) but that is not mentioned in the present passage. Nor is the Church's preaching of the gospel. These are part of the Church's mission, but they are not what spells the defeat of the powers. That has already been achieved through the work of Christ. It is the simple existence of the Church that is the sign of God's saving wisdom. By bringing into being a company of people who are the beginning of the new creation, God has declared that the process of salvation is under way. The remaking of all that is has begun and the sway of the cosmic powers has been undermined.

It needs to be stressed that this role of the Church says nothing about its perfection or its authority. We have already seen that the Church is imperfect and still needs to be built up into the true temple of God. It still gets many things wrong, and consists of people who are weak and often sinful. Yet it is being built, and is in the process of becoming what God has destined it to be. Since the new creation is in progress, the powers that seek to lord it over the existing creation can see that their days are numbered.

The soaring wonder of the vision that the writer has set out in these few verses now returns to earth and to the vision of Christians. God has achieved all this through what Christ has done (v. 11), for in him God's plan of salvation has borne fruit. Planned from the beginning, it is now plain to see. From the viewpoint of Jesus' followers, it has meant a change of allegiance. From being in bondage to the powers, they have moved into the realm of Christ and confess him as their Lord. They have changed masters and been called to his service.

A PRAYER

Lord, in my life, in my small way, may I be a sign
of your new creation.

101 EPHESIANS 3:12–16

ACCESS *to* GOD

Verses 11–12 draw the digression on Paul's ministry to a close in a flurry of language which has a liturgical feel to it. God has brought his plan of salvation into the world in Christ (3:11) and through Christ, and those who have faith in him now have access to God ('to God' is not in the Greek, but is the obvious meaning). This access, the ability to engage with God in worship and prayer and to stand in his presence as adopted children, is no half-hearted concession. Christians approach God boldly and in confidence, knowing his love and the immensity of his grace, sure of their welcome from the one who sent his Beloved to shed his blood on their behalf (1:6–7).

Confidence and boldness are terms often associated with prayer, so the thought leads back to that subject, and the delayed prayer of 3:1 is resumed in verse 14. First, though, there is one other thing to say about Paul, also couched in terms of prayer. The apostle is envisaged as encouraging the readers not to be dismayed about his imprisonment (v. 13). Far from his imprisonment and death being a cause for shame or dismay, they should be seen as a further example of the progress of God's work of salvation. Indeed, Paul's sufferings are on behalf of the Church.

This is fairly obvious in the sense that his imprisonment was a result of preaching the gospel that brings salvation and calls the Church into being. There is probably also a deeper sense that draws on the thought of Colossians 1:24. Paul's sufferings are a part of the pangs that bring the new creation into being, and he takes upon himself a portion of the messianic woes which in Jewish thought herald the coming of the new age. Hence his sufferings are the glory of the Church, for they bring closer the time when believers will share in the glory of the world to come.

Praying for strength

Now the writer returns to the thought that he began in 3:1. 'For this reason' refers in 3:1 to all that was written so far about the great work of God's salvation. The same phrase now takes in that subject and also what God has done through Paul for the Gentiles (v. 14). He has called the Church into being to offer him worship and service.

Therefore, the writer prays that the Church will be granted strength to fulfil its role.

He bows the knee, a posture indicating particularly fervent prayer and supplication (Jews and Christians tended to pray standing) before God the Father from whom all families are named. There is play on words between Father (*patera*) and family (*patria*—a group with a common ancestor), which reinforces the notion of each family taking its name from God. The idea of naming links to that of creation and of power. Adam's dominion over the other creatures was expressed by his naming of them (Genesis 2:18–20) and God as creator was said to have given names to all things (Psalm 147:4; Isaiah 40:26). God is seen as Father, not just by virtue of his relationship to Jesus but also as the maker of all things.

The families in heaven are the different groups of the spiritual powers, or angels, which in first-century thought came in many classes. They include both the angels who serve God and the powers who oppose him, for all owe their existence to him. This use of the term 'family' need not suppose that angels reproduce (Mark 12:25), though some Jewish writings speculate about the gender of angels. 'Family' is used as a means of classification rather as it is in modern biology.

In the same way, each family on earth will include human families and households, the basic units of society, but may well include the different classifications of other creatures. The writer is not in fact interested in saying much about families, either earthly or spiritual, but in stressing the greatness of God, who created all things and rules over all things.

Out of his great power, his glory and riches (v. 16), God is asked to strengthen believers in their inner selves, the innermost place of thoughts and feelings, where God works to draw us to himself and from which spring all actions and attitudes. The power of God, which raised Jesus from the dead (1:20) and which was at work in the ministry of Paul (3:7), is called upon to work in the innermost lives of his people. That power is conveyed by the Spirit, who dwells in the people of God and works in and with them in the service of God.

A PRAYER

Lord, may I know your power at work in my life.

FIRM FOUNDATION

The first part of verse 17 effectively repeats the thought of the indwelling Spirit, and makes clearer what the author has in mind. Like Paul himself, the writer of Ephesians sees no distinction between the presence of Christ in a believer's life and the presence of the Spirit. Christ is now experienced as Spirit, and the Spirit is nothing less than the one who makes Christ present. To experience the Spirit is to experience Christ (1 Corinthians 15:45). Indeed, to separate the work of the Spirit from Christ is to run the risk of losing the core of the Christian faith, which is found in Jesus Christ.

Strengthening by the Spirit therefore means intensifying the presence of Christ in the Christian's heart. The heart, in biblical thought, is not the centre of emotions but of thought and reason. The writer sees Christ as increasingly governing the outlook, attitudes and behaviour of his people. This new outlook is closely connected with faith. Faith is a relationship of trust between two parties. Christ does not invade a person or force himself upon us. He comes in response to trust, to build a partnership in which he shines out from the life of his follower to the extent that faith allows.

The primary characteristic of the presence of Christ is love. A life that allows Christ full reign will be one that is built on love. Characteristically, the writer uses two terms, 'rooted' and 'founded', from trees and buildings respectively. Each one stresses the firmness of a life that is based on the love God gives.

Measuring the immeasurable

For one whose life is rooted in Christ, there is a further dimension to the prayer, that he or she may know the breadth, length, height and depth (v. 18). But of what? Interpreters have supplied a bewildering array of possible ideas. Perhaps it is wrong to choose a specific object. Words are piled up here to give an impression of hugeness—the all-encompassing greatness of God which finds its manifestation in his love, his creative power, the scope of salvation, indeed all the mind-boggling vastness of the themes that Ephesians has presented so far.

Certainly they are beyond the scope of human comprehension unless aided by the power of God himself (v. 18). He alone can enable us to begin to grasp the extent of his grace, his love and his wisdom. In fact, what there is to know passes the possibility of human knowledge. So the very prayer that his readers may know the love of Christ (v. 19) includes the recognition that that very love surpasses human knowledge. But it can be known in a very different sense, in which a lover knows himself to be loved while struggling to understand why or how. Christ's love is beyond knowledge, yet its impact is such that it calls forth a desire to know it more and more, to journey ever onward into the inexhaustible richness of divine mercy.

To acknowledge that there are limits to knowledge does not denigrate knowledge. It is important, as this very prayer makes clear. Yet, faced with the infinite, there must come a point where mystery remains and the only response is worship.

As if recognizing this fact, the prayer ends in a benediction addressed to God on behalf of the church (vv. 20–21). None the less, the worship of God is not simply a response to his awesomeness. It is grounded firmly in a recognition of what he has done. God does not demand that we simply worship him for his sheer lovableness, though a vision of God will no doubt evoke that response. Worship here springs from an awareness that God's power is at work in his people (as it was at work in the resurrection of Christ and the ministry of Paul) to bring about that new creation which surpasses human imagination and goes beyond the scope of human petitions. All that is known about God, about his work of salvation, about his love and power, evokes a response of praise.

Perhaps it is in worship that a different kind of comprehension is found. Where knowledge fails, adoration carries us on. Thus glory is given to God in the Church, where worship is offered and where his power of re-creation is at work. Glory is given in Christ, by those who have come into union with Christ and in him have discovered the immeasurable love and power of God. So the doxology ends with a vision of praise, of glory, being offered to God throughout history and onward into eternity. So be it—that is, 'Amen'.

A PRAYER

Lord, may I know you as fully as possible and beyond that worship you for ever.

WALKING *the* TALK

An obvious feature of Paul's letters is the section of advice on practical issues of morality and appropriate Christian behaviour. For Paul, a faith that does not show itself in lifestyle is no faith at all. Ephesians follows the same pattern, and has the longest section of practical teaching of any of the letters ascribed to Paul in the New Testament. The section of ethical teaching occupies half of the letter. A comparison of this section with the corresponding one from Colossians 3:1—4:6 shows many similarities, and it is likely that the author has used Colossians as the outline for his teaching here.

The key word that introduces this long section is 'Therefore'. The writer of Ephesians, like Paul himself (see Romans 12:1), sees the ethical exhortation as arising naturally from what has gone before. Because of the great grace of God, the formation of the Church and particularly the need to build up the Church, he gives a call to practical church building. The lives of Christians must show the grace of God in word, deed and the formation of a community that shows the presence of God's new creation.

The origin of Christian ethical teaching cannot be stressed too much. It is the response to God's gift of salvation. For this reason, the Church should be wary of calls to be an instrument of moral stability in society. It may or may not be able to function that way, but it is certainly not a tool of social control. Those who see the value of religion as lying in its moral teaching (a claim heard both from politicians and from non-churchgoers who request the baptism of their children) miss the whole point of the Christian message. While Christians share many of the moral concerns of their unbelieving neighbours, their rationale for moral behaviour is different. Christianity is not a self-help course in good living. It is a call to worship and serve the God who comes to us in Jesus Christ, and without that dimension it ceases to have meaning.

None the less, an upright life should be the characteristic of those who serve and worship God. God himself is portrayed in moral terms in the scriptures, which call attention to his faithfulness and love, his implacable opposition to evil and his love of truth and justice. The qualities that most people at most times have valued are not mere accidental by-products of their social development, nor are they simply evolutionary strategies that allow the survival of human genes. They reflect the characteristics of the Creator himself, which he has put into his creation so that it may reflect its maker. The image of God in human beings, marred though it may be by sin, still enables us to show some of the divine family likeness. In Christ, the hope is held out of the full restoration of that image, and in the present time, before the fullness of the new creation, his Church is called to reflect as truly as possible the image that is being restored in Christ.

Prisoner's plea

Therefore, because of all that has been written so far, the writer calls upon his readers in the name of Paul, who suffered imprisonment to bring them the gospel, to lead a life worthy of their calling. The word used for that call is *parakalo*, which can mean 'plead' or 'beg' (as in NRSV) but here is better translated as 'exhort'. 'Lead a life' brings out the force of the Greek, which simply says 'walk', a common biblical expression for life as it is lived. It is a dynamic image, picturing life as a journey on which, for Christians, Christ is the leader and constant companion.

That walk is to be worthy of the calling to which the readers were called. The double use of 'call' stresses the need for a response on the part of the hearer. The initial call was God's call to salvation, to which the hearers responded through faith and baptism (1:13, 18), but that call was into a continuous state of calling, demanding a response day by day of faith and worthy living. The Christian's life is one of responsibility to live up to the immense privileges that have been heaped upon him or her. The letter so far has stressed the privilege— the state of being part of God's people, the first instalment of a new creation, and the recipients of immeasurable grace and love.

Now comes the challenge: will your life measure up to all that has been given to you? Will you recognize each daily situation as a call to demonstrate in your own life the wealth of God's grace, and an opportunity to draw on his power to serve him in the world?

A PRAYER

Lord, may I hear your call each day, and in your strength respond.

BINDING TOGETHER

The long exhortation which is the second half of Ephesians does not fall into easily divisible sections. Chapter 4:1–16 could be headed as advice on being the Church, and how to build it into a temple for God. First of all, life is to be lived with humility, gentleness and patience (v. 2). The word for humility was encountered in Colossians 1:18 with the sense of self-abasement, and probably referred to ascetic practices. Here it has its more usual meaning of willingness to serve, and to put others first. In pagan thought, this 'lowliness of mind' which is the literal meaning of the word *tapeinophrosune* was not highly regarded, except in slaves. It denoted a contemptible servility. In Jewish thought it was more highly regarded as the attitude of the humble who do not flaunt their arrogance before God, who is likely to lift up the humble and cast down the mighty.

It reminds us that not everything that is regarded as a virtue by God will be admired by those who do not know him. The humility of God himself, and the ignominy of the cross, were a folly to Greeks and a scandal to Jews (1 Corinthians 1:23). In particular, the Christian teaching of forgiveness will seem foolish to many today, yet it lies at the heart of our understanding of the nature of God.

Gentleness is the word *prautes*, traditionally translated as 'meekness'. It denotes courtesy and consideration, and a willingness not to stand on one's own rights. It is a hallmark of the kingdom of God in the Beatitudes (Matthew 5:5).

Patience, *makrothumia*, is literally 'long temper' and is obviously the opposite of a short temper.

All three of these qualities combine in the ability to bear with one another in love. Love is, in fact, the necessary prerequisite for all the other virtues. When we desire the best for another and see them as someone dear to God, a willingness to serve, to hold our temper and to act with courtesy becomes more likely and more achievable. It enables us to affirm the worth of others and to give room for them to be themselves.

In exercising these virtues, believers are to spare no effort to keep the Church in unity (v. 3). That unity already exists, for all are sharers in the Spirit of God and he works to draw the community together.

Such unity, though, runs the danger of being purely theoretical, much as different denominations today affirm an underlying unity while joint worship remains a distant dream.

The binding force of such unity will be peace. In this context, peace probably refers to a sense of reconciliation and acceptance between members of the community, in which each finds his or her place. It is part of the outworking of the Spirit's presence in Christian lives and in the community as a whole.

The sign of one

The unity of the Church is driven home by an acclamation of oneness which focuses on those things that the Church has in common (vv. 4–6). The seven examples of oneness are possibly drawn from creeds or hymns with which the writer was familiar.

There is one body, that is the body of Christ, the Church. Here it applies in practice to any given local congregation, which was its basic meaning for Paul (1 Corinthians 12:12; Romans 12:4) but it also applies to the universal Church, in which Jew and Gentile have been joined in one new people of God (3:6). To speak of a single holy people and not to put that into practice would be nonsense.

There is one Spirit (v. 4), who works in the Church and in the individual lives of believers to bring unity and bind the one people together (2:18). There is one hope, which is the goal of creation, and in which all who trust Christ will share (1:10). With God acting to draw all things together in Christ, and the Church called to be a demonstration of the new creation, how can it not strive for unity?

There is one Lord (v. 5) who is the source of salvation, and in whom all things are to be united and find their true destiny. There is one faith, which here probably means the faith as set out in creed and scripture, rather than faith as a quality. There is one baptism, in which faith is given its outward sign and through which formal entry is made into the Church. All these, believers have in common, and each again constitutes a call to unity, to put into practice the obvious oneness of Christian belief and experience.

A PRAYER

*Lord, may your Church still genuinely seek the unity
to which it is called.*

ONE GOD

Arching over all the other signs of unity is God himself. There is only one God, the creator of all things. This was the standard Jewish affirmation about God, repeated daily in the recitation of Deuteronomy 6:4, the *Shema*. Their affirmation of YHWH as the one and only God was a source of pride to Jews and a puzzle to many Gentiles. Christians asserted the same thing (1 Corinthians 8:6), though with the characteristic addition that he was known as Father, through Jesus Christ. Here, as in 3:14, the fatherhood of God extends over all creation, though it needs to be remembered that his fatherhood is made known in Jesus. God's transcendence and immanence are both stressed. God is above all, beyond the comprehension and reach of his creatures, yet at the same time is present throughout his creation and to be found in the least part of it.

The fact that God's title of Father finds its origin in Jesus, the Lord of the Church, and yet applies to God as creator, is a vivid reminder that the Church cannot be separated from the world in its ministry and worship. Christians affirm the world as God's area of activity, and should seek to see him acting there as well as within the Church. At the same time, this resounding affirmation of the one God is intended as a call to unity within his people.

One Church?

While, in the present day, growth into a viable community is not beyond the reach of any single congregation, the unity of the world-wide Church seems ever more distant. Indeed, I have so far avoided the Church's original term for universal—'catholic'—simply because the word has become the designation for one surface of the multi-faceted Church that exists today. Is there a realistic hope that the Church can display to the world the unity which is so important to the writer of Ephesians?

On the face of it, the answer would seem to be 'no'. Even Ephesians' list of indicators that the Church must be one contains sources of contention. The Church agrees that there is one Lord, but argues over how he is to be encountered. There is one Spirit, but there are differences about what he does and whether he is channelled by human authority. All agree that there is one baptism, provided that baptism is administered to the right candidates, at the right age and at the right stage of their pilgrimage to faith. We agree that there is one body, but some are certain that it is theirs alone, and, as a joker once most seriously said, 'We spell ecumenism "you-come-in-ism".'

There is a sense in which perfect unity belongs to the new creation and not the present age (see 4:13), but that does not negate the call to unity here and now. It seems to me that the way forward in this world must be one of unity in diversity. The unity of the Church must be one that recognizes and even celebrates its differences. If unity is built through humility, gentleness and patience, the unity of the truly catholic Church must be one which is self-effacing about claims to authority and truth, and must be one in which its members accept one another with courtesy and compassion. Perhaps above all, it must be one which is patient in recognizing that differences will always remain, and may even be a sign of the greatness of God, whose truth cannot fully be contained in any single tradition.

Grace and gifts

The diversity of the Church's members comes into view in verse 7: 'But to each has been given grace according to the measure of Christ's giving.' As a student, I used to have a theory that grace came in different amounts to different people. After all, there were those who were clever, handsome and talented. Then there was me. This is not quite what is in view here, however. Grace in the sense of God's love and gift of salvation is poured out without favouritism. In verse 7, 'grace' (*charis*) is probably intended as the equivalent of Paul's use of 'gift of grace' (*charisma*), which is often translated in the same way as 'gift of the Spirit' (*pneumatikon*) which is used with the same meaning (1 Corinthians 12:4; 14:1).

Christ gives grace to all, but grace manifests itself in certain gifts or abilities whose purpose is the building up of the Church. The Church attains unity when its variously equipped members work together and use their abilities for the common good.

A PRAYER

Lord, may I be humble to those who differ from me, and accepting of those who see you differently.

VICTORY'S GIFTS

Like a triumphant king, Christ gives gifts to his supporters. This seems to be the thought behind verse 8, in which the writer quotes Psalm 68:18. In the psalm, Yahweh ascends Mount Zion in triumph to take up residence in his temple. As often happens in the New Testament's use of Old Testament texts, the wording has been altered and applied to Christ. The biggest change is that in the psalm, it is God who receives gifts of tribute, whereas here Christ is said to give them. It could be that the writer is aware of the *targum* version of the psalm. The *targums* were Aramaic translations of the Hebrew scriptures, and contained lots of interpretative notes, so that they were paraphrases rather than true translations. In the *targum*, Psalm 68:18 is applied to Moses, who ascends Mount Sinai to receive the *Torah* and then gives it to his people.

In his ascent, Christ is said to have 'made captivity captive'. The word translated by NRSV as 'captivity', *aichmalosia*, can also mean 'a captive multitude' and that is probably its meaning here. The author is taking up the thought of Colossians 2:15, which presents Christ as leading the defeated cosmic powers in his triumphal procession. Christ has triumphed over the spiritual powers and freed his people from bondage to them, opening the way to a new life in which they receive his grace and the church-building gifts that his grace entails.

The quotation from Psalm 68:18 includes the assertion that Christ has ascended. So the writer pauses to explain what that means (vv. 9–10) but does so far from clearly! The ascension is undoubtedly Christ's ascension into heaven, as part of his resurrection and glorification. It is the affirmation of his victory over sin, death and the cosmic powers. Ascension, says the writer, implies a descent as well. However, it is not at all clear from the Greek whether the descent is seen as coming before or after the ascent.

Early Church writers assumed that the descent referred to Jesus' descent into the realm of the dead, but this is unlikely, since Ephesians seems to envisage a two-layered universe of heaven and earth (notice that the evil spirits are found in the air, not under the earth). The New Testament writers do not present a single picture of the world's structure. Several views were current at the time, and different writers seem to work with different images.

The most likely meaning is a reference to the incarnation. The one who has ascended to take a place above all other things is none other than the Christ who walked among us, and who showed his humility by descending to 'the lower parts of the earth'. 'Lower parts' should probably be taken at least partly as a metaphor, along with 'above the heavens'. It is a statement of the completeness of Christ's humility, just as his ascension is a statement of the greatness of his present status.

The end result of Christ's descent and ascension is that he will fill all things with his heavenly rule (1:22–23).

Gifts for the church

The writer now returns (v. 11) to the subject of gifts. Other lists of spiritual gifts can be found at Romans 12:6–8 and 1 Corinthians 12:8–10. An obvious difference between Paul's lists and that of the author of Ephesians is that Paul lists abilities, while the writer here lists people with abilities.

Thus the first of the gifts is not the gift of apostleship, but of apostles themselves. Some see this as a sign that Ephesians envisages a more rigid church structure than in the earlier Pauline period, with defined offices and those ordained in some sense to fill them. There is no real evidence of this in Ephesians, and all we can say is that the author uses terms that he expects his readers to recognize. (Paul follows a list of charismatic abilities with a list of some of those who exercise them in 1 Corinthians 12:28–30, and this list may lie behind the one in Ephesians.) It is more likely that the author is stressing the fact that gifts are useless unless they are exercised. Those who exercise gifts are themselves a gift to the Church. By recognizing the importance of individuals, the author is providing a necessary balance to his emphasis on the Church as a whole.

A PRAYER

Lord, may I recognize and use the gifts you have given me,
so that I may be a gift of God to others.

EQUIPPING *the* CHURCH

In outlining his list of gifts, the writer gives no indication of what they actually did in a congregation. His readers would have known. We can have a fair guess, on the basis of other occurrences in the New Testament, and especially in Paul's letters.

The first of the gifts, both in importance and in sequence, was apostles. The apostles were the founders of the Church, sent by Jesus himself (*apostolos* means one who is sent, thus 'envoy' or 'missionary'). In Paul's case, that sending was late, but was none the less a personal commission from Christ (1 Corinthians 15:8–10). Apostles gave the link between the Church and Jesus himself, and were witnesses to the resurrection. This latter point makes apostles a gift for one generation only, in which the Church was founded and the story of Jesus handed on to those who would follow.

Later Christians would come to use the term of missionaries, and particularly of missionary bishops, stressing the importance of founding new congregations and handing on the Christian tradition. The term was always used somewhat loosely, though, and the distinction between the original apostles and those of the Church's foundation (2:20) has always been maintained.

The second gift is that of prophets. Like apostles, these are seen by the author as belonging to the founding generation of the Church, ensuring that the tradition handed on by the apostles was always freshly invigorated by the living word of God. At the same time, the tradition acted as a check on the pronouncements of the prophets. 1 Corinthians 14 envisages prophets as making a significant contribution to worship, perhaps including the leading of the service. Prophets would give direction to the church, and address specific issues of immediate importance. There is also a good argument that they had a teaching role, interpreting scripture and tradition under the inspiration of the Spirit. Prophecy as an active ministry faded away quite quickly, as the Church became more organized and gave greater weight to the more predictable ministry of teaching, based more firmly on tradition. There is no evidence that this had happened by the time of Ephesians, and prophets, while they are obviously respected for their role in the past, should be seen as having an active part to play in the writer's vision of the Church.

'Evangelist' is a term that occurs in only two other places in the New Testament. In Acts 21:8 Philip is termed an evangelist, and 2 Timothy 4:5 calls on Timothy to do the work of an evangelist as part of his overall calling. It seems likely that evangelists were people whose particular gift was the proclamation of the gospel to unbelievers. In Ephesians, evangelists are part of the set of gifts that is given to promote the unity and maturity of the Church (vv. 12–13), but this does not necessarily mean that they preached to the converted. A church that is fulfilling its calling to spread the good news is one that is on its way to being mature and complete.

Pastors and teachers form a pair (as is indicated by the Greek). The two are not identical in the sense of 'pastors who are also teachers', but there is a necessary overlap between the two ministries. Those who 'shepherd' (the literal meaning of 'pastor') the people of God need to do so in the context of Christian teaching, while those whose main calling is to expound the faith must do so in a context which looks to the spiritual and physical needs of the congregation. It is possible to find congregations which are caring but have little awareness of the basics of the Christian message. It is equally possible to find very doctrinally educated Christians who seem to regard love and compassion as purely theoretical subjects.

One obvious point about the list of gifts that are ministries is that they are the preserve of very few in any given congregation. At first sight, this is a move away from the assertion in 4:7 that grace/gifts have been given to all. Verse 12 begins to redress the balance. The gifts listed are given in order to enable the ministry of the whole congregation. The whole Church exercises its gifts in the context of a leadership that comes through the gifts of apostolic tradition, speaking the living word of God for today, proclaiming the gospel to the world, and teaching and caring for the congregation.

A PRAYER

Lord, may I use my gifts in the framework of your Church,
to build up your body here on earth.

GIFTS *for* MATURITY

The gifts listed in 4:11 fall into a particular category, which might be termed loosely that of 'leadership'. This is an inadequate term and could just as easily be called 'servanthood'. The main reason for listing the gifts is that they provide the framework of teaching, caring and Christian tradition in which all other gifts are exercised. Those other gifts are not named, for they are too diverse and numerous. There is a tendency in some Christian circles to count the number of gifts specifically mentioned in the New Testament, to attempt to identify them, and to present them as a checklist for modern Christian service. However, each of the 21 or so gifts specifically mentioned in the New Testament is merely an appropriate example. Christ provides the necessary gifts for his Church to fulfil its purpose.

Those with the gifts listed in 4:11 exist to equip the saints (v. 12a), so that they may exercise their own ministry or service (v. 12b). That equipping will be through teaching and encouragement, inspiration and outreach. The end result is the ministry of the whole Church. This also might include prophecy, teaching, pastoral care and evangelism as well as a host of other activities from the leading of prayer and reading of scripture, to offering hospitality, financial support, administration and so on. The fact that some individuals are recognized as teachers or prophets does not necessarily preclude others from performing the same functions.

It is the exercise of the ministry of the whole Church, of all the saints, that builds up the body of Christ (v. 12c), a point which is reiterated in 4:16. This should make it clear that the office/gift of apostle and so on is not a ground for pride. It is a humble role, the aim of which is to furnish the members of the Church with whatever they need to exercise their own gifts and bring the Church to maturity.

Verse 13 states again that final goal of the building of the Church. It is to come to unity in the faith and in knowledge of the Son of God. Faith here is not a reference to the believers' trust in God, but the faith as an objective body of belief and doctrine, the faith as held and practised by the Church. It is close to what is meant by 'knowledge of Christ'. This is something that the Church is counted as having (4:5) but which still has to be attained. Once again, there is a difference between the Church as it exists in the sight of God, and the reality, which still has far to go. Unity, therefore, is something that still lies in the future, as does the full knowledge of Christ.

If Christ is the first of the new humanity, then the Church will fully measure up to him only in the world to come, when the new creation is completed. We must beware, however, of letting that become an excuse, or even a justification, for inaction in the present. Whether or not the final goal is fully achievable in this world, the Church, using the gifts and ministries Christ has given it, is to move on towards its fulfilment. In fact, the goal of being the fullness of Christ is the spur to growth and maturity in the present age.

Individual or corporate?

There is debate among scholars as to whether the writer has individual Christians in view in his vision of a mature and complete Church, or whether it refers only to the Church as a corporate entity. It is most likely that he means both, for a church of immature individuals is unlikely to be the mature body of Christ. Moreover, in verses 13 and 14, the writer speaks in the first person, 'we', taking up the similar 'us' in 4:7. The thought is that the Church is indeed the focus of attention, as the temple of God and Christ's body, but that it attains its full status only as individual members grow, exercising their gifts for the common good.

The Church is not an ant colony, with workers being expendable or interchangeable. It is a community in which each member is to be valued, a body in which each member is vital to the whole. In our individualistic age, we need to learn that the Church is not a resource to fuel individual spiritual experiences or equip individual lives of worship and service. While most Christians spend most of their time apart from the Christian community, it is in the Church that they find their true place as part of the people of God. In their lives at home and at work, they are not lone Christians who look to Sundays for replenishment, but extensions and envoys of the Christian community, which through its separate members reaches out into God's world with his message of love.

A PRAYER

Lord, may I bring the life of your people into the life of the world.

CHANGEABLE CHILDREN

Verse 14 brings in a contrast to highlight the argument so far. If the Church is to be mature, then it is to be no longer childish. Children can be silly, hard to focus on one thing and forever looking for new toys. None of these qualities is bad in children, of course, but mature adults need to keep focused, aware of the job in hand. The Church must put aside childishness and aim for the goal of maturity. Or, in another picture of indecisiveness, it must not be like a boat in a storm, riding each fashionable opinion and being thrown from side to side by every new idea.

This is the safeguard against new and attractive teachings which, under the guise of philosophy or the offer of new spiritual experiences, might threaten to dilute the gospel and lead the Church away from its devotion to Christ. Probably, no particular teaching is in mind here (as opposed, for instance, to Colossians) but that does not mean there was no real danger. The early Church lived in a seething marketplace of religious ideas, and many people were happy to wander round tasting and sampling. The religions and philosophies on offer are described as 'human cunning' (NRSV 'people's trickery'). This is human as opposed to divine—the cults and ideas on offer have their origin in human beings and not in God. As a result, they seek to ensnare by trickery, rather than appealing by a clear statement of what is on offer.

Truth and love

The Church's response must be the very opposite. It must speak the truth (v. 15)—both the truth that embodies the gospel and the truth about what that entails. Christianity is not a religion of secrets and mysteries which can be revealed only to the initiates. It may well be that only those who embrace its message can fully appreciate the extent of the grace of God, but the fact of God's grace is proclaimed openly to all. Moreover, it is proclaimed not out of a desire for more members or more money, but out of love, which seeks the saving grace of God for all.

This speaking in love applies to relations with the world around the Church and also to relationships within it. The process of growing more fully into union with Christ, of attaining maturity and completeness, is one of love and truthfulness. Truth without love is a dangerous tool, and causes a lot of damage. Love with no regard for the truth lacks direction or the ability to offer decisive help. It is in the loving acceptance of each other that Christians are bound together more fully in Christ. In speaking truth, differences and enmities may be faced honestly and find healing, those who are failing may find support and those who are burdened may find help.

Growth and unity

This process of mutual support is empowered by Christ (v. 16). Here the body metaphor is reiterated and embellished. Christ is the head, towards which the rest of the body looks for its goal and purpose (v. 15). He is the source of its strength and its gifts, which are used to bind the whole community together.

The joints and ligaments are probably to be seen here as a reference to the gifts that enable the body to remain in one piece and promote its growth. They include both the gifts of the leadership ministries, and those of the rest of the body, each of which must play its proper part if the body is to grow.

That growth is once again characterized as growth in love. Love is the means of the growth and the test of growth. If there is no love, then the Church has not progressed, no matter what other achievements it may choose to boast. With the reminder of the need for love, the section on the Church's growth draws to a close and comes full circle, for in 4:2 love was seen as a requirement of the life that is worthy of Christ.

A PRAYER

Lord, may we grow in love, learn to speak the truth in love,
and share your love with those about us.

CHRISTIANS *among* PAGANS

The topic changes now from building up the Church to a contrast between pagan and Christian living. The seriousness of the call to a holy and pure life is stressed—the author 'affirms and insists', a double statement which means 'strongly declare'. Faith must be seen to result in action, and that action must show the presence of God in believers' lives.

When they were separated from God (2:1–3), the readers lived as pagans did, but now that has changed, and the contrast must be visible to all. Pagans are described as 'Gentiles', for the Church has been brought into a relationship with God that mirrors (but exceeds) that of the people of Israel. Separated from the wisdom of God, the unbelievers are characterized as unable to perceive the things of God, which includes the proper way of living (v. 18). More than this, they cannot apprehend the ultimate truth or glimpse the reality that gives meaning to the world, for it is found only in God.

Their separation from God is due in part to 'the ignorance that is within them'. This ignorance is a result of sin, having its origins 'within them'. More particularly, the second reason for their alienation from God is their 'hardness of heart'. This is a definite attitude which turns away from the creator, and seeks its own way.

As a result, they have become numb, and seek an increasing intensity of pleasure (v. 19). This lack of sensitivity means on the one hand that they no longer feel the pangs of conscience and are able to indulge in practices which should cause repugnance. On the other, it leads to an eagerness to 'practise every kind of impurity'. This may seem to be a typical preacher's exaggeration, but is in fact a simple description of a life that is lived for sensation. That which is at first exciting and fulfilling palls after a time, and ever more intense thrills must be sought. The terms 'licence' and 'impurity' usually have a sexual connotation, and probably that thought is on the surface here. The ancient world had an attitude to sex that was much more casual than we often imagine. Pagan licentiousness is not limited to sexuality, though. The main idea is of a search for ever greater gratification, a self-destructive excess.

In stark contrast, that is not what the readers have learned in their teaching about Christ (v. 20). The phrase 'how you learned Christ' suggests that the Christian ideal is embodied in Jesus himself. It is he, the living example of a life filled by God, who stands in stark contrast to the way of the pagan world.

Walk the talk

Verse 21, 'if indeed that you have heard about him', is a confident assumption, and means 'of course you have!' It refers back to their first hearing and acceptance of the Christian gospel. They have put their old life behind them and started a new way of living. It is a reminder that Christian teaching must be attended to and put into practice. That teaching is the teaching about Jesus, who embodies God's truth, the message of salvation, and the pattern of life for his people.

The challenge of the gospel came to them and they responded, learning to put off their old self, their old way of life (v. 22). The image is of undressing and casting aside the old garment, and may well be associated with the practice in baptism of stripping off prior to entering the water. At any rate, decisive change is called for, and indeed has taken place, for the readers have put their old life behind them. Or have they? Why, then, remind them of the need for proper living? The answer is the one that has run all through the letter. They now belong to God, the new creation has begun, but in this world it is still incomplete. They must work to become what, by God's grace, they are in his sight and one day will be indeed. The old human nature still exerts its influence, and the world around them still calls enticingly at times of weakness. So effort is required to make concrete in their lives the spiritual reality of their existence in the sight of God.

A PRAYER

Lord, I too am surrounded by temptation and prone to weakness. Help me to put off my old self and be renewed in your image.

111 EPHESIANS 4:22–25

IMAGE *of* GOD

Not only must there be a stripping off of the old, but it must be replaced by the new (vv. 22–23). Their minds must be renewed, giving a new outlook based on God and his vision for the new humanity (Romans 12:2). This is a renewal that pervades the Christian's inner being, and is rooted in the deepest core of their true self, described as the 'spirit of your minds'. (This is the only place in Ephesians where 'spirit' obviously refers to the human, rather than the Holy, spirit.) Perhaps the intensity of the phrase suggests that such a deep-seated transformation must be the work of God as well as the believer. Human decision and divine grace meet in the renewal of a Christian's true self.

The renewal that is called for by the gospel is further explained in terms of putting on, or clothing, oneself with the new person. This, like verse 22, may reflect the process of baptism, as the new convert emerges from the water and is given a new garment. In verse 24 it becomes clear that this process is not simply a human one. The new self has been created in the likeness of God.

In Genesis 1:26–27, God created human beings in his own image. God has made humans in such a way that they reflect something of his nature and character. Yet that image is at the very least damaged or defaced by human sinfulness. Now it is being restored.

The likeness of God is something made by God, but put on by Christians through their response to the gospel. God calls his people to co-operate with him in becoming what he has called them to be. You might say that we are called to grow into a new suit which is too big now, but will one day be a perfect fit. This growing into the new nature or likeness of God is something that applies to individuals but also to the Church as a whole. As the Church is the body of Christ, it must corporately show the likeness of God to the world, as Christ also showed the nature of God. As individuals, each member of the Church must also be transformed, and so take his or her place in the body.

This ultimate likeness of Church and believer to God lies in the future, as the new creation is brought to completeness. It provides a goal to be aspired to in the present life among the temptations of the pagan world.

That likeness is described, literally, as 'created in righteousness and holiness of the truth', which here have an essentially moral meaning. These qualities, which are best described in terms of God—his goodness, his desire for justice, mercy and compassion—spring from the truth found in Jesus (4:21), which opens the eyes of those who respond to the reality of God. With that vision of ultimate reality restored, life can once again find its true meaning, human pleasures find their true setting, and life be lived in the presence of God (see 4:17–19).

Holy hints

The call to be renewed by the creative power of God leads to examples of what this may mean in practice.

The first is truthful speech. Verse 25 takes up the themes of truth from verses 21 and 24 and reintroduces the concept of the body, as the readers are reminded that they are members of one another.

Christians are to speak the truth to each other. 'Neighbours' here means fellow members of the Church, who deserve the sort of respect and integrity implied by truthfulness. To lie is to belittle someone and hold them unworthy of honest relationships.

To deal falsely is to deny the integrity of the body and strike a blow at its very existence. If the Church cannot show in itself the presence of Christ, it has nothing to offer to the outside world. Of course, truth must be spoken to all, Christian and pagan alike, for the gospel is the very essence of truth, and its proclamation must necessarily be in the context of open and honest dealing. But it is in the Church that the new creation can be seen, if its members show the truth and love which are the hallmark of that renewal.

A PRAYER

Lord, give me the love that enables me to speak truly to others.

ANGER & HONESTY

'Be angry' (v. 26; see Psalm 4:4) is an honest recognition that our fellow Christians do indeed anger us, for all sorts of reasons. The writer is not contemplating the possibility of righteous anger, but recognizing that anger does occur. Undoubtedly injustice and cruelty, for instance, should anger us, but that is not the issue here. The point is that our response must not be sin. It must not be violence or cruelty of our own, be it physical or emotional. The author of Ephesians does not spell out what our response should be—at least, not here. He has made that plain enough, with his call for truthful speech and for love, and for humility and meekness (4:2). To confront those who anger us in love, and to seek reconciliation and understanding, is the path to follow.

Sometimes true peace is attained by a respectful acknowledgment of differences, and a hammering out of the issues that concern us. What must not be done is to allow anger to fester, to change into resentment, bitterness and hatred. So when anger arises, it should be dealt with at once, before the sun goes down, and so no room will be left for temptation to wallow in self-righteousness, self-pity or the despite of others (v. 27).

If truth is to be a hallmark of the Church, it follows that dishonesty is not, and falsehood must actively be rejected (4:25). Hence those who once stole should do so no longer (v. 28). This is not simply a negative command. Those who give up doing wrong need to take up doing right. So honest work and a sharing of its results reverses the self-centred preoccupation of the thief, and replaces it with a desire for the good of others and the building up of the community. The author is not interested in pursuing some of the possible objections to this command. We might ask, what about those who cannot work, or whose choice is between theft and starvation? The two answers that the author of Ephesians might give are that those who are working should help those who are not, and that we can worry about the difficult cases when we've got it right in the easy ones!

A third area of concern is 'evil (literally, 'rotten') talk' (v. 29). This is a common concern in Jewish teaching (see Proverbs 10:31–32).

The injunction covers more than just lying; it addresses any kind of speech that is destructive. It could include using terms that degrade or belittle others, jokes that work by robbing another of dignity, spreading gossip or malicious rumours, and so on. It stands in direct contrast to speech that builds up. Encouragement, sympathy, good humour, expressions of concern, offered at the right moment, all raise another's self-esteem and draw the community closer together.

Such language is a vehicle of God's grace. The words translated as 'give grace' in NRSV can mean simply 'bring benefit', but in the light of the stress on God's grace, and the sharing of it with others (3:2), it seems better to see here the possibility that the right words can indeed bring God's blessing to others.

Grieving Spirit

The kinds of behaviour that the writer describes as destructive of the community are also damaging on a deeper level: they strike at the relationship between the believer and God. The presence of God and of Christ in the Church and in the Christian is the presence of the Holy Spirit of God (v. 30). This particularly solemn reference to the Spirit stresses the severity of the effect of sinful behaviour. It actually causes the pain of grief to the Spirit himself. The nature of that grief is not explored, but an analogy with human relationships seems to be in the author's mind. When we behave in a way that betrays the trust or confidence of a friend or lover, we cause pain. When we speak in a manner which denies that friendship or love, we cause grief. So it is with God, who is a part of a Christian's life, but whose presence may be implicitly denied by the actions of the one he indwells.

Although it is traditional to use a personal pronoun when referring to the Spirit, there are relatively few places in the New Testament where he is seen in strictly personal terms. Verse 30 is one of them. Here, the Spirit can feel grief, or pain, and does so in response to the sins of his people. There is a similarity here to the thought of 1 Corinthians 2:11, where the Holy Spirit is compared to the human spirit and is seen as the innermost self of God.

A PRAYER

Lord, may my words and my deeds do justice
to your presence in my life.

113 EPHESIANS 4:30—5:2

SUFFERING GOD?

For the author to write of the Holy Spirit's grief reflects a standard assumption of the biblical writers, that God has feelings. This came to cause problems in later theology, as the influence of Greek philosophy took hold. Emotion, it was argued, must imply a change in God's state of mind; and if God is perfect, any change must be towards imperfection, which is unthinkable. Hence in traditional theology, God was seen as 'impassible', unfeeling in the human sense, with emotional language describing something like fixed attitudes rather than responses to particular events or actions. However, if God is three persons in one, it is possible to see him as a dynamic system, with a continual interplay of love and giving, obedience and sacrifice. In this interplay, there is room for God's response to human acts and attitudes, and his love can be seen as intimate and personal rather than the fixed characteristic of classical theology.

Spirit's seal

The Holy Spirit, as the indwelling presence of Christ, is the mark of God's ownership (1:13) and the down-payment on the new creation which is to come (1:14). To act in a way that grieves the Spirit is therefore to act in a way that denies one's belonging to God and effectively rejects the future inheritance that awaits his saints. The writer does not suggest that sinful acts negate the effect of God's grace, however. The mention of the Spirit as seal and guarantor of salvation is not a threat, but a spur to right living.

Verse 31 gives a list of actions that grieve the Spirit. These can be read as a cumulative process, the one leading to the next. Thus the Christian must put away all bitterness, the seething sense of hurt or resentment which can burst out in wrath, or rage, and settle down into the continuing hostility of an attitude of anger. Out of such hostility grows wrangling (literally, 'shouting'), or angry words, which can culminate in the abuse and insult characterized as slander. All of this comes under the heading of malice, an attitude of ill-intent to others.

Christians are called to show the love of God and to deny any opportunity to ill-feeling and resentment (v. 32). They must show kindness, an attitude of concern for each other's well-being. This reflects the nature of God himself, who has already been described as 'kind' in 2:7. Their attitude must be one of compassion, the ability to feel for others; and above all, it must be one of forgiveness.

Sometimes in the New Testament, being forgiving is seen as necessary for receiving God's forgiveness (see Matthew 6:14–15). At other times, as here, Christian forgiveness is a reflection of the forgiveness that has already been received from God. Perhaps the two go together. Those who know their need of forgiveness are more likely to be forgiving themselves, and so are open to God's forgiveness. Similarly, having received forgiveness, they are more likely to recognize the need to forgive others.

In short, Christians should show in their lives the nature of God himself. Like children mimicking their parents, they should imitate God (5:1), seeking to show the family likeness. Again, the underlying theme is the call to become in practice what they are in fact—and what they will be for all eternity.

This will involve living a life that is characterized by love, for God himself is recognized by his love. That love took concrete form in Christ, whose own divine love led him to die on behalf of his people (5:2). The sudden shift from imitating God to copying Christ is a good indicator of the inseparability of God and Christ for the writer of Ephesians. In 4:32 it is God in Christ who forgives. God's forgiveness cannot be separated from Jesus, nor can Jesus be seen as anything other than the love of God in action. Indeed, God is defined by the sacrificial love of Christ. The fact that Christ's death is a pleasing sacrifice to God does not conflict with this line of thought. Christ does not placate an angry God, offering himself to absorb the wrath that might otherwise fall on sinners. Rather, God in Christ takes the consequences of human sinfulness on himself as an act of loving forgiveness that appears in history in the incarnation. There is a circular motion in the thought of this verse. God reaches out in love which is embodied in Christ, whose love offers it back to God in the form of a sacrifice for the sins of his people.

A PRAYER

Lord, help me to copy your love, so that you may be seen in me.

SEX & SUCH

In stark contrast to the purity of Christ's offering stand the sort of things that the pagan world wallows in through its alienation from God (4:1–19). These things should have no place in the Church. The writer focuses on three particular vices—fornication, impurity and greed. 'Fornication' translates the Greek *porneia*, which can cover a range of sexual sins, but generally means sex outside of marriage and sex with a prostitute (*porne*). 'Impurity' is a term that generally refers to a range of sexual sins, indeed almost anything that may be regarded as essentially dirty! Given the sexual connotation of the first two terms, greed should also be seen as having a sexual meaning. It refers to the quest for ever greater thrills, regardless of the consequences for others.

In an age that prides itself on its sexual liberation, it seems decidedly old-fashioned of Christians to go on about sex. 'Why does the Church have a hang-up about it?' we are often asked. There are two answers. One is that in the course of Christian history, a very unbiblical notion crept into the thinking of the Church's teachers—that sex itself was a bad thing. This is quite simply wrong, and should be dropped. (Sadly, in popular thought, this attitude is laid at Paul's door. This only goes to show that very few people actually read Paul's letters.) The second reason is that the Bible has a quite definite attitude to sex. It is a gift of God, and forms a delightful part of a loving relationship. For that very reason, its misuse is destructive.

In fornication, impurity and the search for deeper excitement, the physical pleasure of sex has become an end in itself, and all sense of intimacy and commitment is lost. At the same time, the sheer physicality of the act speaks of intimacy and relationship—the very things the fornicator wishes to deny.

Indeed, it can become more than this: it can become a false god (v. 5). The search for more and better pleasures can become an end in itself. Once it becomes central to a person's hopes and desires, it usurps the place of God and becomes an idol. Certainly it can act like a drug and become the goal and purpose of life itself—which, let's face it, is pretty sad.

These things, says the writer, should not even be mentioned in the

Church (v. 3). This may be an exaggeration, and probably is, in the sense that such things are bound to come up in conversation. More generally, though, he is probably quite serious. An atmosphere in which coarse, vulgar, generally foolish, sexually orientated language is the norm conveys an impression that such matters are unimportant or acceptable (v. 4). They are not. The reason is that they are not fitting—they do not harmonize with the attitudes of love, compassion, humility and so on which characterize the God-likeness of the saints, the holy people of God.

The idea of 'what is fitting' comes from Stoic philosophy, which encouraged its followers to adopt a life of harmony, putting aside all that was discordant, and, in an attitude of inner peace, to accept what fate put into one's path. For Christians, the harmony is found by living in accordance with God's will, so that the outlook of the believer is in tune with the inner working of the Holy Spirit, and both work together to bring God's new humanity into being.

Dire warning

It is for this reason that the harsh words at the end of verse 5 sound their warning. No one who does such things has any inheritance, any share, in the kingdom of Christ and of God. This follows from the characterization of lust as idolatry. Any covetousness is a form of idolatry (Colossians 3:5) since it raises the object of desire to the status of primary importance. It takes what God has given and, instead of giving thanks to him for the gift (v. 4), attempts to seize it and take it for its own. As a result, the idolater worships what is created instead of the creator, and thus turns away from God.

'The kingdom of Christ and of God' is a phrase that occurs only here, but a similar thought is found in Revelation 11:15. It is not intended to differentiate between the kingdom of Christ and the kingdom of God, which in Paul are respectively present and future (1 Corinthians 15:24; Colossians 1:13). Here the rule is seen as jointly that of Christ and God, for it is in Christ that God's kingdom will find fulfilment (1:10).

A PRAYER

Lord, may I always put you first, and give thanks
for all you have given me.

BEING DIFFERENT

It is not easy to be different from the world in which one lives. Why stand out in the crowd? If everyone thinks in a certain way, and acts that way, can it really be all that bad? These are empty words, which spring from a lack of awareness of God. Therefore, the readers of Ephesians are not to be swayed by the arguments of the society in which they live. The standards of behaviour which are so acceptable to the world at large are the very reason for God's coming judgment. 'Coming' is actually in the present tense (as NRSV) but has a future force. The writer is not thinking of the outworking of judgment here and now (for that idea, see Romans 1:18–32), but of the judgment that will mark the end of the present age.

For this reason, Christians must have nothing to do with the practices that mark out the Gentiles. Verse 7 does not make entirely clear who or what it is that Christians must shun. Some interpret it as a call for complete separation from the unbelieving world. This is unlikely, since it goes against the thrust of seeing God as creator of all things and therefore at work in the world at large. For that matter, Paul seems to oppose just such a misunderstanding of the call to separation in 1 Corinthians 5:9–11.

A more positive reason is given in verse 8. Once, the readers had been a part of the blinded world that cannot see God (2:1; 4:18); so much so that they could be said to embody darkness itself. Now they embody the light of Christ, and must become in practice what in fact they are—children of light.

Light and darkness

The main thrust of this light-and-darkness imagery is about how to live—as children of light or of darkness; that is, by showing the characteristics of the realm to which one belongs, the kingdom of God, or of the ruler of the realm of the air (2:2). Light enables things to grow and be fruitful, and so the fruit that the light of Christ brings forth is everything that is good and right and true (v. 9; compare Galatians 5:22–25; Philippians 1:11). These three adjectives are extremely broad, and cover just about every virtue of behaviour and of faith and spirituality—the whole of the Christian life, in fact. Since

God is also the creator of the world, it is possible to say that what is good in the world at large is also a sign of the presence of God in his creation. In looking for God's work in the world, there are two opposite dangers to be avoided. One is to assume that everything outside the Church is bad (which is to deny creation) and the other is to assume that whatever is considered good by non-Christians automatically is so (which is to deny human sinfulness). On the whole, the Bible walks that tightrope carefully. The fact that writers such as Paul and the author of Ephesians can use ethical teaching which was present in the world around them points to their recognition of a common view of the good that reflects God's will in creation. The fact that they can warn strongly against the ways of the world shows that discernment must be exercised in the light of God's will as it is revealed in Christ.

Discernment is the key thought in verse 10: 'Try to discover what is pleasing to the Lord'. 'Try to discover' translates a Greek participle which could as easily be rendered 'discovering', and which would then follow on from verse 9. One walks as a child of the light by discerning what pleases Christ. There is often no simple and obvious right choice in a given situation. It requires the ability to discover God's will and the best way to put into practice the love that underlies all Christian ethics. For Paul, that process of discernment was possible, springing from a mind that had been renewed and refocused on God by being part of a life offered to him (Romans 12:1–2). The writer of Ephesians agrees (1:18). The mind, the outlook, of Christians is being transformed, and that transformation enables the discernment of God's will.

A PRAYER

Lord, may I know you well enough to know your will,
and have strength enough to act on that knowledge.

SHINING *into* DARKNESS

In contrast to light, darkness is a sterile environment, and its products are unhealthy. While light produces fruit, an image of growth and wholesomeness, darkness produces only 'works', with their sense of effort and, in this case, futility. Such works are too shameful to name openly (v. 12). Rather than joining in such practices, Christians should expose them (v. 11). The idea here is not a phone call to the *News of the World* or the *National Enquirer*, but that by living upright and moral lives, believers will show up the degradation of the surrounding society for what it is. The secrecy in which these works take place is a reference to the pervading darkness. They are not visible, and so are not seen as bad.

The contrasting light of Christian behaviour has a positive effect. It does not merely expose the works of darkness so that the Church can glory in self-righteousness. Bringing the light of Christ to bear makes visible human sinfulness (v. 13). This is not an end in itself but has the effect of making that which was darkness (5:8) become light (v. 14). The chain of thought here is condensed, but its meaning is fairly clear. The Christians who are addressed by the writer used to be darkness but are now light (5:8). In the same way, by shining that light into darkness, what was dark will also become light—that is, become Christian. It is by shining as a light in the world, by demonstrating the kingdom of God, that the Church brings others to faith.

The primary thought here is of the converting nature of Christian behaviour. The existence of a better way of life will draw others to seek that life, and so find Christ, in whom new life is possible. There is therefore a partnership between the gift of evangelism, the overt preaching of the gospel, and the church's lifestyle. A church that demonstrates no discernible difference of life from its surrounding culture has nothing to back up its words. A church that manifestly is in the process of transformation into God's new creation has something visible to offer. It is saying that the gospel is not just empty speech, but is life-changing experience.

New life in the light

Several scholars suggest that the language of light and darkness in 5:8 onwards reflects baptismal teaching. That seems to be the likely source of the quotation in verse 14b, introduced by the words, 'Therefore it says…'. This is probably a fragment of a hymn, and its imagery of waking into the light would certainly sit well in the context of a baptismal liturgy. The 'you' in verse 14b is singular rather than plural, and is best envisaged as addressed to the baptismal candidate. Notably, in the hymn, it is Christ who is the light, rather than Christians, unlike the rest of these verses. This suggests that the hymn is about the moment of approach to the light. Once they have come to Christ, the new converts also share his light, and become light themselves.

The change from darkness to light has happened to the readers, and was given outward expression in their baptism, of which the hymn fragment is a reminder. Once, they were asleep, dead to God (2:1), but in response to the call of God, echoed liturgically by the congregation at baptism, new life came to them and they entered into Christ's light.

The reminder of baptism is a summons to live in accordance with that new life. Baptism issues a continual call to Christian living, not simply a once-for-all initiation into a static state. Conversion is a day-by-day process, as the Christian grows in knowledge and understanding, in Christ-likeness.

The words that the writer uses to introduce the hymn are interesting. The same formula, 'It says', is used in 4:8 to introduce a quotation from scripture. This suggests that the hymn would have been recognized as carrying authority. It would seem that liturgical texts were seen as means of transmitting Christian tradition, and used in teaching. The same holds true today. A good liturgy bears within it a wealth of instruction, and by its repetition drives home basic teaching to its users.

A PRAYER

Lord, may I be a beacon to light the way to you.

117 EPHESIANS 5:15–20

WISDOM & FOLLY

The Christian life, to which baptism is the gateway and the call, is no game. Attend to it carefully, says the writer; live wisely. In the Bible, wisdom is based on knowing God and carrying out his will in the world. It is the meeting of spiritual and worldly concerns, where the knowledge of God takes form in actual behaviour. Indeed, the admonition not to be foolish (v. 17) conjures up the image of the fool of Psalm 14:1 who 'says in his heart, "There is no God"'. The essence of folly is to leave God out of consideration, as the pagan world has done, and found itself in darkness. Christians are to follow the way of wisdom, which is the way of God. As we have seen (5:10), this requires the ability to recognize the will of God (v. 17) and put it into practice.

There is a sense of urgency about the call to Christian living. It is something to be done here and now. 'Make the most of the time,' says the writer (v. 16), using a term from the marketplace which means 'Buy eagerly'. Snap up every moment! The time given to us is a gift to be used, and the Greek word *kairos* means time as moments of opportunity, rather than time as it simply flows past. The reason for such an approach is that the days are evil. Christians live in the midst of a pagan world, which ignores God and goes its own way. As a result, it is a world under judgment (5:6) and in urgent need of redemption. Who knows when the end will come? So work now, and be prepared to be found at your proper task when God demands an account for how your life has been lived. If Christians seize every opportunity to make the life of Christ apparent, then there is a greater chance of the world's darkness being illumined and of others finding their way into the light of God.

Intoxicating spirits

Unlike the pagans, Christians are not to find their solace or entertainment in drunkenness, the sign of a life of debauchery (v. 18). The introduction of excessive drinking at this point seems a bit sudden, but it was also used by Paul as an example of godless living, in a similar context of light and darkness (Romans 13:12–13). The writer may have that passage in mind, as it also contains a reference to the armour of light, an image which will be expanded later in Ephesians.

In contrast to the life of drunken debauchery, a life out of control, is the life which is controlled by the Spirit of God. (The pun on the meaning of 'spirit' in our subtitle only works in English, and not in Greek, but it seemed too good to ignore!) The readers are commanded to be filled with the Spirit. Christians are to be open to the Spirit's work, co-operating with him in being Christ-like, and expectant that he will work in them. They are not to keep him out by wrong behaviour, but must enable him to control their lives, make clear the will of God, and supply the wisdom that he conveys from God himself.

On the surface, there may even be a degree of similarity between the manifestation of the Spirit and drunkenness (Acts 2:13), not least in the production of singing. The songs of worship that flow from a Spirit-filled life are different, though, in that they spring from a heart filled with joy and thankfulness (vv. 19–20) to God. Some commentators suggest that these are what give rise to the fullness of the Spirit who is encountered in worship, and NRSV seems to suggest this as well. It is more likely that the worship is seen as an expression of the Spirit-filled life, although of course participation in worship will undoubtedly encourage openness to the Spirit.

The different words for 'songs' (probably borrowed from Colossians 3:16) may stress the possible variety of hymnody; all are to be pressed into service for the praise of God. A modern list might include plainsong, Anglican chant, anthems, hymns and worship songs or choruses. All are ways of expressing thanks and praise, and perhaps it is fair to say that the abundance of God calls forth an abundance of celebration. Notably, the songs are addressed 'to each other' (NRSV, 'among yourselves'). The sharing of hymnody, and presumably other acts of worship, is addressed primarily to the Lord, but is also an opportunity to recognize the corporate nature of worship and to share mutual encouragement and fellowship.

A PRAYER

Lord, may I sing your praises and share my cause for celebration with those around me.

RIGHT WORSHIP, RIGHT LIVING

The phrase 'singing and making melody in your hearts' (v. 19) does not mean that the singing is silent! Rather it stresses that the worship that is offered springs from lives centred on God, and from an inner awareness of all that God has done. Similarly, the injunction to give thanks for everything (v. 20) refers to everything out of the whole stock of spiritual blessings that God has conferred on his people (1:3).

The fact that Christ is entitled 'Lord' at this point makes it very likely that, as elsewhere in Ephesians, 'Lord' in the nearby verses 17 and 19 also refers to Christ. If so, then he is portrayed as the object of worship and one whose will is the same as the will of God. Since it is the essence of idolatry to offer worship to anyone other than God, we have here another indication that the writer happily thinks of Christ in divine terms.

The Christian household

The writer now ties together his teaching on the behaviour of the church with a simple command: 'Submit to one another in fear of Christ' (v. 21). The command to submit takes us back to 4:2: Christians are to be humble, gentle and patient, and to bear with one another. All this has been expounded at length through chapters 4 and 5. Now the writer focuses on one particular example of what that will mean in practice.

Much of the material in his section on Christian behaviour has been based on Colossians 2:5–17, though he has expanded and re-worked it to meet his own concerns. Now he does the same with the household advice of Colossians 3:18—4:1. By doing so, he transforms it into a deep and powerful reflection on Christian marriage and household life. The parallel passage in Colossians, we have argued, is an example of how to serve Christ in a pagan environment. In Ephesians it becomes a guide for ordering a Christian household. This is evident from verse 21, which is about the behaviour of Christians towards each other as fellow members of Christ's Church. The theme of mutual submission is taken up and applied to the household, where submission is found to have different meanings depending on the status and responsibilities of each member. The writer sees no contradiction between an overarching command to mutual submission and a hierarchical structure in which each member plays their own allotted role in an attitude of humility.

We argued in the section on Colossians that it was unrealistic to assume that Christians would live in uniformly Christian households. That may have changed by the time of Ephesians, as the Church expanded and households grew up with a tradition of Christian faith. The focus of Ephesians is on the Church, and how to reflect the kingdom of God. Even if a fully Christian household was the exception rather than the norm, it makes sense for the writer to continue his theme, looking at how relations between Christians should work out in daily life.

Since the household was seen as the backbone of society, on which all else rested, he retains Paul's earlier example, but reworks it to his own ends. In this he, like Paul, stands in a long tradition of written advice on household management. What has changed is the reason for, and manner of, ordering the household. It is now to be done in the fear of Christ (v. 21).

It is hard to capture the force of the word 'fear'. At one level it does mean fear as we normally use the word. Christ is the one who rules over the cosmos, and is the Lord of the Church. As such, he is not the cause of terror or panic, but he certainly commands more than the mere 'respect' of many modern translations. The very awesomeness of the extent of his love is enough to demand more than respect: those who begin to grasp it are as likely to tremble as to shout with joy. To live out a life under the shadow of a love that is cosmic in scope is a responsibility to be worked out in fear and trembling (Philippians 2:12).

None the less, there is still a distinct contrast with the mutuality of relations envisaged in 1 Corinthians 7, and the affirmation of equality in Galatians 3:28; 1 Corinthians 12:13 and Colossians 3:11 (a passage that the writer of Ephesians does not borrow). We will return to this issue later, but first we need to examine the relationship of husband and wife that the writer presents.

A PRAYER

Lord, may my worship and service spring from a vision
of the majesty of your love.

Husband & Wife, Christ & Church

The attitude of wives to husbands is closely tied to the preceding verse. In fact, there is no verb in verse 22, so that a more accurate translation would be 'Be subject to one another… wives to your own husbands as to the Lord.' The attitude of wives is to be part of their general submission to fellow Christians. However, there is a distinct imbalance in the relation of husbands and wives. This reflects the normal position in society at that time and place. Women were expected to be submissive, and in law had much less status than men, being generally under the umbrella of their husbands or other responsible menfolk. In fact, the situation was much more complicated than that, but the general expectation was none the less of patriarchal authority.

The writer does not challenge this expectation. It could be that he was concerned with establishing the Church as respectable in the public sight, so that its witness would not be clouded by side-issues. Certainly, any group or individual that was accused of undermining the social order, and especially that of the family, got short shrift in those days, much as there is political mileage to be gained today by defending 'family values'.

None the less, the rationale of his teaching is radically different from the traditional pagan household rules. Women are treated as responsible moral people, whose role in the household, and relationship with their husbands, is entered into freely, as an act of worship to Christ. The phrase 'as to the Lord' should not be taken as suggesting that the husband stands in place of Christ to his wife. It means that the submission offered to her husband is part of her Christian service to Christ and is therefore an offering to the Church's Lord.

It is noteworthy that those who are least powerful in the household are mentioned first in the list, wives before husbands, children before fathers, slaves before masters. They are granted the dignity of being treated as morally free individuals.

Christ-like husbands

Husbands do, though, have a Christ-like role in some respects. As Christ is the head of the Church, so the husband is the head of the wife (v. 23). The image of headship here is undoubtedly one of authority, but the nature of that authority needs to be seen in the light of what the writer has said about the headship of Christ. It therefore includes power and rule (1:22) but also a role of promoting unity, growth and well-being in the household, as Christ binds together the Church (4:15–16). Christ is the Church's saviour, a thought which refers to his saving death, and which will come to the fore in the next few verses. It is unlikely that the writer means at this stage to apply the analogy to husbands: the main idea is of headship as authority and binding force in the household.

Therefore, just as the Church is subject to its Lord, so wives ought to be subject to their husbands in everything (v. 24). 'In everything' does not, of course, mean in things that are immoral or conflict with the duty of obedience to Christ. The wife's submission is an act of worship to Christ, and on the analogy of the Church's submission to the Lord.

On the same analogy, the husband to whom such complete submission is offered is one who will love his wife without stint, will seek only what is best for her, will be willing to sacrifice his very life for her. If the wife is to deny herself and submit, it is to a love that will encompass her without asking for any reward.

Husbands are to love their wives with the sort of love that led Jesus to the cross (v. 25). This marks a radical alteration to the normal expectations of the writer's society. Pagan readers (and probably a good few Christian ones!) would have expected the call for wifely submission to be followed by a call for wise rulership on the part of the husband. Instead comes this call for the husband's love (fairly rare outside of Christian teaching)—the selflessly giving love of *agape*, which is a word never applied in non-Christian household teaching. As Christ's sacrifice calls for the response of worship, so the wife's submission is not to dictatorial authority but to sacrificial love.

A PRAYER

Lord, may my life at home be ruled by your love.

RADICAL LOVE

The call to self-sacrificing love does not do away with the patriarchal hierarchy of the first-century household. It does, however, change its basis, and by so doing opens the way to its questioning. If the rule of the husband is based on a total commitment to the good of his wife, even to the extent of a willingness to die for her, it becomes possible to question whether a husband is worthy of such submission, for a husband who does not show such love cannot demand the willing submission that Christ demands of his Church.

Spotless bride

The submission of the Church is to the one who 'gave himself up for her' by dying on the cross. The love of God has gained concrete expression at a particular place and time, and the cross stands for ever as a measure of God's self-giving, to which the Church is called to respond. The husband's love for his wife is a specific example of the sacrificial love that should be the hallmark of the Church (5:1–2).

The purpose of Christ's sacrifice is to create a new humanity that finds its present embodiment in the Church (v. 26). It is to be holy, reflecting God's own moral qualities, separated from the pagan world by its transfer into the light of God's kingdom. Just as the Church became possible through Christ's death, so its holiness comes into being as it is washed by him in the water of baptism. The cleansing of the Church is not by water only, but by the word of the gospel, which brings the message of reconciliation and forgiveness, and by response to which the Church is called into being.

There is also a secondary meaning to the washing in water, which becomes apparent in verse 27. In Jewish wedding ceremonies, the bride was formally bathed, before dressing to be presented to the bridegroom. So Christ desires to present the Church to himself as a bride, perfect in beauty and youth—without spot or wrinkle (2 Corinthians 11:2). Of course, the images of washing and being without physical blemish do not quite go together (lots of people would pay handsomely for a technique that washed away wrinkles!), but the next part of the verse goes on to explain that the blemishes in question are moral ones. The aim is that the Church will be holy, which is both a state of belonging to God and one of moral purity. It is to be without blemish in its life and behaviour.

In Paul's use of the marriage image in 2 Corinthians, the wedding lies in the future (compare Revelation 21:2, 9). In Ephesians, the Church is already the bride, prepared by the death of Christ and made his through baptism, though it still must strive to become what in essence it already is.

We must not forget that the comparison with the Church is secondary to the description of a Christian husband's role. He is to show the same love, the same desire for all that is best for his wife, as Christ showed for the Church.

Nurturing the body

The writer now turns to another image, suggested by one of his favoured terms for the Church, the body. A husband should love his wife as he loves his own body (v. 28). Lying behind this apparently simple statement is all the richness of the relationship of Christ to the Church. As Christ nurtures the body, provides its direction and encourages its growth, so should the husband love his wife. This line of thought also looks forward to the author's quotation of Genesis 2:24 in 5:31. Since man and woman become one flesh, it is fair to say that a man who loves his wife loves himself, for the two have become one unit. The unspoken corollary is that a man who harms his wife damages himself.

The next statement (v. 29) is strictly not true: there are people who hate their own bodies and there are those who do themselves considerable harm. Yet the author's point still stands. There is felt to be something unnatural about those who show such an attitude. The proper approach is to care for oneself, one's body, and respect it (v. 28). In the same way, a husband should care for his wife.

A PRAYER

*Lord, as you care for me, may I bring care
into all my relationships.*

ONE FLESH

So close should be the relationship of husband and wife that it becomes possible to say that when a husband loves his wife, he loves himself. This statement springs from Genesis 2:24, which the author quotes in verse 31. First, though, he continues his interweaving of the two themes of marriage and the Church's relation to its Lord. The care and nourishment of one's own body finds its parallel in Christ's care for the Church (vv. 29–30), which he also builds up, since it is his body (4:16). If it is unthinkable that someone should not care for his body, it is equally unthinkable that Christ should not care for his Church.

The writer does not go quite so far as to say that in loving the Church, Christ loves himself, and it would be wrong to push the analogy that far. The Church is not a continuation of the incarnation, and does not embody the being of God in the same way as Jesus did. If the author wished to say that, he had plenty of opportunities to do so in the exploration of the body-of-Christ image. The Church exists by being in Christ, not vice versa. When the author wants to speak of Christ's indwelling of the Church through the Spirit, he prefers the image of the Church as a temple (2:21–22). This is probably quite conscious, since it was recognized that God dwelt in his temple voluntarily (2 Chronicles 6:18), and could depart at will. He was not bound to it in the indivisible way that prevents a person from being separated from her body.

The two themes of marriage and the body of Christ come together in verse 31, a quotation of Genesis 2:24. This verse was considered fundamental for the early Christian view of marriage, and remains a major text in any theological thinking on the subject today. Paul quoted it (1 Corinthians 6:16) and so did Jesus (Mark 10:7–8) in widely different contexts. The author uses it without flagging it as a quotation (compare 4:8; 5:14), presumably because he could expect his readers to recognize it.

The writer introduces the verse for two reasons. The first is that it is the proof text for the union of husband and wife. The two have become 'one flesh', a single entity. Hence, the argument from verse 28 onwards that a husband should love his wife as his own body is firmly grounded in scripture. Interestingly, the verse contains a statement that runs counter to the writer's assumption that a wife should be submissive to her husband. According to Genesis 2:24, a man leaves his parental home to be joined to his wife. In the society that produced Genesis, as in New Testament times, exactly the opposite happened: a woman left her parents to join the family of her husband. The writer of Genesis is therefore being rather subversive in his (or her?) view of marriage!

Mystery

The second reason is that the writer of Ephesians is able to introduce another level of interpretation into the verse. It is a mystery (v. 32) which he is able to reveal to his readers. Elsewhere in Ephesians, 'mystery' refers to something made known to Paul and the other apostles and prophets. It is likely that here, 'mystery' means that the writer has been given a fresh insight. He sees the verse from Genesis as describing the relationship of Christ to the Church. Just as a man is united with his wife, so Christ is united with the Church. Even so, we need to bear in mind the caution we noted earlier. The verse provides an analogy, not an allegory. The general sense can be applied, but not the details. Otherwise, we would have to ask how Christ left his father and mother (what mother?) to be joined to the Church, when in fact the Church is to be presented to Christ (5:27). The author is keen to stress the care and nurture that a husband must show his wife, and that Christ exhibits towards the Church. Both unions are as close as possible, but he does not define what the limits of that closeness may be.

That last point also defines one limitation of this passage. It says nothing about whether the union between husband and wife is a permanent one, involving an indissoluble bond. That is a question (pertinent to debates about the permissibility or otherwise of divorce) that must seek its answer elsewhere.

A PRAYER

Lord, make me aware of your closeness to me.

REFLECTIONS *on* MARRIAGE

Finally, the author sums up the relationship between a Christian husband and wife in a first-century household. A husband is to love his wife as himself, and a wife should fear her husband. Many modern translations balk at 'fear' and render it as 'respect'. However, it is the same word as was applied to Christ in 5:21. A wife should have the same awed awareness of her husband's love and authority as she and her husband have of Christ's love and majesty.

A modern reader is likely to emerge from an encounter with Ephesians 5:21–33 with mixed feelings. There is a wonderful picture of Christ's care for his Church, and its challenging demand for love in marriage. On the other hand, there is likely to be a sense of frustration that the demands made on husband and wife are so unbalanced. Why does the husband have no gift of submission to offer to his wife? Why does the wife have no call to love her husband?

In approaching the passage in Ephesians, we need to remember a few points. Firstly, the household envisaged is the traditional Greco-Roman first-century household, which existed within a set of social expectations that no longer apply. Secondly, the writer affirms the moral responsibility of women: their role is one that is freely accepted as a service to Christ. Thirdly, the authority of husbands is secondary to the love and care they are to show to their wives, and indeed is the basis of it. If wives are to fear their husbands (v. 33), it is on an basis analogous to their fear of Christ (5:21)—the depth of love that is shown. Fourthly, the whole list of household rules comes under the heading of mutual submission among members of the Church. Finally, and most importantly, this passage does not give the biblical view of marriage.

Any view of marriage that claims to be biblical must take into account many passages throughout the scriptures. We have noted one contradictory element in Genesis 2:24. We can imagine the writer of Ephesians being quite happy with Paul's statement that a wife's body belongs to her husband (1 Corinthians 7:4), but was he fully in agreement with the statement in the same verse that a husband's body belongs to his wife?

Mutual submission

In formulating a view of marriage for the present day, we need to take all these points into account. We need to realize that parts of the Bible reflect cultural expectations which no longer apply. We can look at the present passage, see its call for mutual submission, and apply that equally to husband and wife. We can look at the call for sacrificial love and apply it to wives as well as husbands, and see the call to nurture as going both ways. In other words, the pattern of the first-century household dictates the direction in which duties flow. Once that pattern is removed by the passing of time, there is no reason to see specific duties as applying to either sex exclusively. Verse 21 will be given the weight it logically has, as the heading to the set of household rules, and provide a basis for interpreting the passage as applying equally to husband and wife.

Does this undermine the authority of the Bible? Surely not. The writer of Ephesians has himself taken Paul's vision, but has developed and reapplied it. In each generation, the Church has returned to the scriptures and found means of applying them to its own time.

Moreover, such an approach to the marriage teaching of Ephesians gives weight to other passages of scripture. In 1 Corinthians 7:1–16 Paul goes out of his way to apply every statement equally to husbands and wives. Such a measured equality surely demands to be taken seriously in formulating our own approach to marriage.

In short, a Christian and biblical view of marriage will give equal weight to both partners, demanding mutual submission, mutual love, mutual caring and nourishing; yes, and even mutual fear—of the awesome responsibility of the love to which we are called in Christ, in whom there is neither Jew nor Greek, slave nor free, male nor female (Galatians 3:28).

A PRAYER

Lord, may I find in your love a love to share
with those closest to me.

CHILDREN

In 6:1, the writer continues his teaching on the Christian household, and turns to the roles of children and fathers. Children are to obey their parents. The word used for 'obey' is a different one from that for 'submit' in 5:21–22, but the meanings are more or less interchangeable, so there is no significant difference. As with wives, children are told to offer their obedience as responsible Christians. They are taken seriously, as real people, with a service to offer 'in the Lord'. The command is further reinforced by the comment that such obedience is 'right'. It was commonly accepted in the ancient world that the primary duty of children was to honour their parents, with the emphasis being on obedience. The author accepts that this is the proper order of things, and reminds children of the fact.

At the same time, he stresses that this is also a command of God, and quotes the Septuagint version of Exodus 20:12, which had the additional words 'that it may go well with you…' from Deuteronomy 5:16. Thus, by conforming to social expectations, children both offer a service to Christ and obey God's will. This is a significant addition to the sort of teaching offered to children in the first century. By treating them as responsible followers of Christ, their worth in the Christian community and in the sight of God is affirmed, and their value stressed.

It is worth noting that children are regarded as full members of the Church, with their own responsibilities. They are not a future congregation in waiting, nor are they an embarrassment in worship, to be put out of sight and mind. They are addressed in their own right, and not only have obligations but also have rights, as do their mothers, to be treated well and lovingly.

Loving parents

As in the Colossian household rules, parental obligations are focused on the father. This is not because mothers had no role in bringing up children, but because the legal power and authority was vested in the father as head of the household. In Roman law, a father had the right of life and death over his children, and examples of harsh treatment of children were far from unknown. The legal rights of children differed little from those of slaves. By the time of Ephesians, it is likely that very few, if any, fathers actually executed their children (though there is some evidence that infanticide, especially of girls, was regularly practised). Indeed, most fathers had the same love and delight in their children as we would expect today (and we too have plenty of tragic exceptions).

The writer of Ephesians assumes that fathers have authority, and sets out to show its limits. Fathers are not to make their children angry. This is the same sort of anger as in 4:26, the kind that is provoked and can give the devil an opportunity. Fathers are therefore not to be unfair, harsh, niggling, discouraging, or anything else that will cause resentment. They are to treat their children fairly and bring them up to follow Christ. The words that NRSV translates as 'discipline and instruction' (v. 4) both have wider meanings, and are virtually synonyms, meaning 'upbringing'. The thrust of this teaching is that children are to be brought up in the knowledge of Christ, and in an atmosphere that reflects his love.

Sadly, in modern churches, many parents seem to have accepted the popular judgment of secular society that it is somehow wrong to teach their children Christianity in any disciplined way: 'We don't want to put them off by ramming religion down their throats.' If we believe our faith to be true, the best we can possibly do for our children is to teach it to them.

A PRAYER

*Lord, let me value the children who are part of my
church community.*

Slaves

Slaves are encouraged to serve their masters wholeheartedly, and not just when being watched (vv. 5–6). The reason is that their service to their masters should be offered to Christ, as service to him. The 'fear and trembling' in which they are to serve their earthly masters is not fear of the master, but of the Lord, who has given them the responsibility of living out their Christian lives as an act of worship and of witness (Philippians 2:12; Ephesians 4:1).

Once again, we have to remember that slavery was such a part of the first-century environment that it was taken for granted by almost everyone. Discussions on the proper treatment of slaves were fairly common. Questioning of the institution itself was unheard of. Even the slave rebellions of past times (the most famous was led by Spartacus) did not seek to do away with slavery as such. It should therefore come as no great surprise that the author of Ephesians, like Paul, does not question the practice of slavery.

Slavery

Another reason for this is that slavery was very different in the ancient world from what it was in the 19th century, which tends to colour our modern perceptions. It was not based on race (racism as we know it is a fairly recent invention) and slaves were on the whole treated moderately, if only because that was the obvious way to get good work from them. Some slaves were, in fact, much better off than free people. They had housing, food, clothing and the possibility of social advancement. Imperial slaves effectively formed the empire's civil service, and could wield considerable power and influence. Most slaves could look forward to eventual freedom, though as freedmen their lot might not be much better than their present state. Greek slaves could own money and even other slaves, and Roman slaves often were allowed to keep money they acquired, even though it technically belonged to their master. At least, this was true of slaves in the towns and cities and the country villas of the wealthy. Slaves in the mines and fields, or chained to the oars of galleys, were treated very differently. Their life was brutal and short. Their lot was rarely considered, just as modern Western citizens rarely consider the plight of those in poorer nations—and for the same reason. They were out of sight and out of mind. For that matter, they were often condemned criminals or rebels, effectively sentenced to death. The slaves addressed by Ephesians are the domestic and urban slaves with whom most people would have been most familiar.

Slaves are therefore to carry out their tasks wholeheartedly, as an offering to God, knowing that their service, reinterpreted as service of God, enables them to do his will. The will of God here is not that they be slaves, which is simply the state they are in, but that they should live out the new life they have in Christ, by showing the presence of Christ in their lives. Thus, even in slavery, they are able to shine the light of Christ into the world's darkness (5:10–11). Such enthusiastic service (v. 7) is not for the sake of their owners, nor indeed to gain praise from human beings, but to do good (v. 8). The 'good' here refers back to the good works that God has prepared for his people to do (2:10) and are the hallmark of the indwelling Spirit, the signs of God's new creation.

Such good works bring their own reward from God, whether the one who does them is free or in slavery. There are two important thoughts here. The first is that how we behave in some way affects the coming judgment of God. Christians are saved by God's grace, accepted by faith (2:8), but will still have to answer for how they have used that grace—for the deeds they have done. The second is that God's judgment applies impartially to slaves and free alike. Although in the present world, and in the Christian household, the social distinctions are maintained, in Christ there is no distinction, and in the light of the coming judgment they fade into insignificance.

A PRAYER

Lord, may I make no distinction at all between myself
and other Christians.

MASTER & LORD

Just as slaves are to serve their masters as an act of service to God, so masters are to use their slaves in a way that honours God. 'Do the same to them' refers back to the whole attitude that slaves should have. Masters should know that they too are slaves of Christ, called to serve him as much as are their Christian slaves. There is a play on words here, since the Greek for 'master' and 'lord' is the same word, *kyrios*. Both slave and master serve the Lord Jesus, and both should see him as their master.

This attitude on the part of masters will lead to fair treatment of their slaves. They will stop threatening them and, indeed, cease any form of abuse, since those who are their slaves are at the same time their brothers and sisters in Christ. Both will equally have to answer to Christ for their attitudes and acts. The masters are therefore reminded that God does not show favouritism. The same warning was addressed to slaves in Colossians 3:25, to warn them that their low status will not earn them God's approval. Now it is addressed to masters, to assure them that God is not impressed by high social status either.

From our point of view, there remains an obvious tension between the equality recognized by the Church and the inequality manifested in the Christian household. In Paul's view, the new creation that the Church is meant to express shows no distinction between slave and free (Galatians 3:28; 1 Corinthians 12:13; Colossians 3:11). The writer of Ephesians belongs to a later time, when the Church was becoming more settled and making more compromises with the surrounding culture. It is probably no accident that he does not quote the formula of equality, much as it would fit with his view of the Church.

Paul could encourage slaves to seek freedom when it was offered (1 Corinthians 7:21) and write to Philemon in terms which would make it hard to treat Onesimus as a slave. Here the writer takes up Paul's advice to slaves in pagan households in Colossians 3:22–25 and reworks it for a Christian relationship, but, for all the reasons we have already mentioned, stops short of demanding freedom and social equality for slaves. To do so would no doubt have been politi-

cally disastrous, certain to brand the relatively new Christian movement with charges of corrupting society, and would perhaps spell
serious persecution. This raises an important question.

Then and now

It is sometimes necessary for the Church to conform to a culture and
society that acts in a less-than-Christian way. This may be either
because the Church does not recognize the conflict, as may have
been the case with slavery, or because it lacks opportunity to act effectively, which would also be the case with slavery. Where does it draw
the line, and how? There are no easy answers, and to reach them demands continual discernment of God's will.

Such discernment led eventually to the abolition of slavery in
Western countries, but not until nearly 2,000 years had passed. In
fact, defenders of slavery in the 18th and 19th centuries quoted
Ephesians and Colossians in support of their position. Biblical texts
are often conditioned by the assumptions of the society in which they
were written, and the use of the Bible demands a recognition of what
is purely the product of a particular time and place, and what is the
underlying principle that must be put into practice in new situations.

Today we do not face the issue of slavery very often. There are still
many slaves, but in parts of the world that few readers of this book
are likely to visit. However, many social differences are acceptable
to modern Western Christians—differences between rich and poor
nations, between social classes within the same nation, between different members of the same church. If the Church is called to show
equality as a part of the pattern of the new creation, how does that
translate into practice? Such questions raise hugely complicated
issues, of economics, the nature of society and sin, the role of the
Church in the world. To attempt to answer them is difficult in the
extreme, but to fail to face them reduces the Bible to a document of
purely historical interest.

A PRAYER

*Lord, I live in a complex and difficult world. Guide me through it,
and let me contribute to it as your servant.*

The PANOPLY of GOD

The author has now reached the end of his presentation of Paul's message for the Church of his time. He sums up the main thrust of his message in an image that has become one of the most well-known passages of the New Testament. Christians are called to serve God in a world which has turned its back on its creator. They are to be light in the midst of darkness, and they can expect the darkness to press hard upon them. Their task is therefore to stand fast against its assaults, and continue to shine the light of Christ into the darkest places. Like a Roman legion behind its wall of shields, it must throw back all that the world and the powers of darkness can muster, and at the end of the day be left standing on the field of victory—a victory which is assured by the work of Christ.

It is Christ who supplies the necessary strength for the task that he has given. Three words for 'strength' and 'strengthening' pile up in verse 10, stressing the power that is available for those who serve God, the power that raised Jesus from the dead (1:20). Now the new life is characterized as armour (v. 11). Paul had used the image himself (Romans 13:12), but here it is expanded into a catalogue of virtues and gifts necessary for Christian life.

Protection is necessary because the devil stands ready to trick Christians into sin, seizing any opportunity for evil (4:27). Once again, the trick is to stand firm, resisting the onslaught. The writer makes it clear that this is not a conflict of physical violence—at least, not on the part of Christians. The battle is against those spiritual powers that rule the world (v. 12) under the devil's control, and seek to keep it in darkness. In a real sense, they have already been defeated, and are under the rule of Christ (1:21; 3:10), whose heavenly rule is shared by the church (2:6). In this world, though, the new creation has not fully dawned, and the powers can still pose a threat by luring believers away from Christ and by keeping those outside the Church under their sway. The battle is therefore real, even though its final outcome is assured.

So, the Christian must be equipped with the armour of God (v. 13). This means the armour that God supplies, but may also mean God's own armour. In Isaiah 59:17, God is depicted as an armoured warrior. Now God lends his own protection to his people. The armour is the full equipment (*panoplia*) of a Roman legionary, and while it is not described in full, enough is listed to give the picture.

Standing firm

Once equipped, the Christian warrior is able to stand firm on the evil day. This means firstly any time of temptation or spiritual conflict. When troubles come, the armour of God provides defence. Secondly, it is the time of tribulation and turmoil that was believed to precede the final end of the present age. By not specifically defining the day in question, the author allows both ideas to run together. The Church is already in the end times, for the new creation has begun. There will yet be further tribulations as the final coming of the kingdom draws near. Whatever the specific conflict, God's help is available for those who have put on the armour of the new life.

The specific meaning of each item is not always certain, for the writer is more concerned to stress the availability of God's protection than to limit it to particular virtues. The first item to be put on is truth. This is like the legionary's belt, a broad leather apron which went under the metal armour and prevented it from chafing its wearer. Truth, the foundation garment of God's armour, is probably in the first place a reference to the gospel, the true word of God that brings the call to new life (1:13). Its acceptance prepares the way for all the rest of God's blessings and also issues a call for truthfulness and integrity of life, which are vital to growth in the knowledge and love of God (4:15, 25).

Next comes the breastplate, the body's main protection, which covers the vital organs. It is the righteousness that marks God's people as his own (4:24) and is that quality of uprightness and moral wholeness which comes from doing God's will. It is a sharing in the moral qualities of God himself.

A PRAYER

Lord, may my life reflect your presence and be a
protection against evil.

The CUTTING EDGE

A literal translation of verse 15 would be 'Shoe your feet with the readiness (or firmness) of the gospel of peace', which is pretty bad English but makes it clear that the feet and their readiness, rather than the actual footwear, are the main items in view. This in turn points to Isaiah 52:7 (see Romans 10:15): 'How beautiful upon the mountains are the feet of the messenger who announces… good news.' Readiness to proclaim the gospel is itself a firm foundation for the fight, like the studded legionary boots. There has been little mention in Ephesians of the need to proclaim the gospel, since the letter is concerned with building up the existing Church, but the mention of evangelists at 4:11, and the shining of light into darkness at 5:14, makes it clear that this is part of the task of the Church. Here it is seen as a vital part of the battle against the forces that seek to keep the world in darkness.

A vital piece of equipment is the shield (v. 16). Roman infantry were equipped with large rectangular shields of leather-covered wood. Before battle the shield was soaked in water, so that flaming arrows could not set it alight. This, says the writer, is faith—the resolve to trust God at all times—which will effectively extinguish anything the devil can throw at the Church. It is tempting to note that the Roman shield was not just an individual weapon, but was designed to be used by companies of soldiers working together. By overlapping the edges of their shields, legionaries could present an unbroken wall (and even roof) of fireproof protection. Did the writer have this formation use in mind? Certainly the letter is addressed to the Church as a whole, and he has stressed the importance of mutual love and care for the Church's growth and well-being.

So far, the armour has been composed of virtues or attitudes that Christians can adopt for themselves. Faith, truth, the gospel, peace, can be taken up at will or put into practice by a personal decision. The two remaining items are purely gifts of God. The first is the helmet of salvation (v. 17). Even today, a helmet is a vital part of the soldier's equipment. Salvation provides the spiritual equivalent, the certainty of protection against attack. It is to be received from God as his gift: it has been bought by Christ's death. The final item is the sword, the short stabbing weapon of the Roman legions. The fight is not purely defensive, for the sword enables the Christian to strike back against the foe. It is the word of God, the gospel. The power of the Spirit gives it an edge that cuts through the world's tangle of deception and illusion, and challenges the powers that rule it. By its proclamation, the gospel draws people into the light and diminishes the rule of darkness. Note, too, that the gospel is part of the armour of every Christian. It is not the preserve of those gifted to be evangelists, nor of those ordained to pastor and teach. All Christians have good news to share, for all have received good news.

The powers

How do we take the talk of such spiritual warfare today? There are those who are happy to speak of actual hostile spiritual powers. Others, as we saw on 1:21, would prefer to speak in terms of ideas and institutions that embody sin, be they political, economic or personal. On the most important level, it does not really matter, provided the rule of the powers is challenged. Even for the writer of Ephesians, this was not simply something that happened on a purely 'spiritual' level. It consisted of speaking the truth in love, and thereby challenging the power of falsehood; and of proclaiming the gospel, so as to challenge the power of the ignorance of God that keeps so many estranged from him. It meant living lives of personal integrity and holiness, to challenge the power of sinfulness. In fact, the conflict of spiritual warfare takes place in the arena of the physical world, whatever spiritual entities may or may not lie behind it.

This is not to say that the spiritual dimension of the conflict is purely a figure of speech. It can only be won with God's help, for without him the opposition is too great even to contemplate. With him, the victory is assured. The gospel can only be preached by human beings, but only the Spirit of God can drive its paradoxically healing blade into the human heart.

A PRAYER

Lord, dress me in your armour, that I may stand firm and deliver your good news to the world in which I live.

KEEP ON PRAYING

Reinforcing the spiritual nature of the Christian's warfare against the cosmic powers, the writer ends his account of the armour of God with a call to prayer. Prayer is not a part of the armour but the force that undergirds all Christian endeavour. Prayer is empowered by the Holy Spirit, who takes the feeble human effort at prayer and transforms it into true communication with God (Romans 8:26). The writer calls for every possible kind of prayer, and in every kind of situation. Such prayer demands alertness—an awareness of God, of the needs for which prayer is offered, and of the need for prayer itself. Anything that arises is to become the subject of prayer.

In keeping with the main thrust of the letter, prayer is to be offered for fellow Christians, wherever they are. Prayer is the means of including God in the process of building up the body of Christ, and of strengthening the Church in its struggle. To that end, the readers must persevere in prayer. It is not a matter of a one-off intercession, but rather a constant and unceasing offering to God of the needs of the Church. It is probably not too much to say that the writer envisages all of life becoming a prayer.

Prayer too is to be offered for the writer. In verse 19, he once again explicitly dons the guise of Paul, envisaging the apostle in prison but still forging ahead in the task of spreading the gospel (v. 20). This is more than a mere literary technique, a part of the process of writing a pseudonymous letter, though it is that as well. The writer reminds his readers that they are part of the continuing work of spreading the word of God. Through Paul's ministry, they are now Christians, but the work goes on. Paul was an ambassador for God (see 2 Corinthians 5:20), speaking words on his behalf and delivering his message to the Gentiles. Through that message, the mystery of the unification of Jew and Gentile in Christ has been made known (v. 19), and Paul proclaimed it boldly. So too the writer, as a follower of Paul, must also be an ambassador and speak out even in adversity.

The picture presented is of the spread of the message of Jesus, even in circumstances which would be expected to curtail it, such as Paul's imprisonment. The readers are encouraged to realize that the message they too have to proclaim is one that can overcome all obstacles.

There is also another note of encouragement in the writer's request that he be given a message to speak (v. 19). The proclamation is not dependent on the messenger, but on God, who gives the right words for each situation. Anyone can speak on God's behalf, for he will speak through them.

Final greetings

Paul's letters normally end with greetings to and from his co-workers, and news of his plans. Here there is only the commendation of Tychicus (vv. 21–22), which is taken from Colossians 4:7–8. This has led to the suggestion that Tychicus is the author of the letter, and is reminding the readers of the trust Paul had in him. This is impossible to know. For that matter, Tychicus might still be alive, and be the actual bearer of the letter, or it may just be a reminder that Paul had previously written to the same area of Asia Minor and had sent Tychicus with the letters. Again, all is speculation. The author is very restrained in that he does not include greetings and travel plans. This may suggest that he did not intend the letter to be passed off as a genuinely Pauline epistle. Enough colour is added to give the flavour of Paul's letters, but beyond that he does not go.

In typically Pauline style, he ends with a benediction. Peace is wished for the whole Church, with love and faith. These qualities are from God, as his gift, the result of accepting the gospel and the new relationship with God that it opens up. In fact, they are from God and Christ, for the gift of the one is the gift of the other. It is in Christ that God pours out his blessing on his Church. Those blessings include the all-inclusive grace that comes to those who love Christ, and the immortality that grace confers. The last two words of the letter are 'in immortality'. NRSV takes this as referring back to love, hence those who have an undying love for Christ. It could also refer back to grace: 'grace to those who love… and immortality'. Either way, the letter ends with a note that looks to eternity, and both interpretations point to the single truth that those who love Christ will do so with an undying love, for in him they have found eternal life, and so will know him for ever.

A PRAYER

Lord, may I know and love you now, and keep on getting to know you for all eternity.